the Liberty Watch

the Liberty Watch

✦

Our Country's Most Priceless Possession

Charles E. Miller, Ph.D.

iUniverse, Inc.
New York Lincoln Shanghai

the Liberty Watch
Our Country's Most Priceless Possession

iUniverse books may be ordered through booksellers or by contacting:

iUniverse
2021 Pine Lake Road, Suite 100
Lincoln, NE 68512
www.iuniverse.com
1-800-Authors (1-800-288-4677)

Because of the dynamic nature of the Internet, any Web addresses or links contained in this book may have changed since publication and may no longer be valid.

ISBN: 978-0-595-46470-8 (pbk)
ISBN: 978-0-595-48735-6 (cloth)
ISBN: 978-0-595-90768-7 (ebk)

Printed in the United States of America

Contents

FOREWORD

In these commentaries I have discriminated between freedom and liberty for an exact reason: Freedom; is all too often today rearded as an amorphic collection of rights without authority or discipline or accountability being inseparable from them.

"We have the freedom to do anything we want to do!" Or, "I make up my own rules! You can't stop me!" These are the frequent cries. But it is not freedom to say, "This is a free country. I can do what I want!" That is anarchy. I needed to neutralize the present-day use of the freedom cry when it is perverted to suggest that it is an anarchistic license supposedly granted under the Constitution. License of this sort if anathema to the law.

The freedom exercised in public disturbances and blatant outrages against the people by demagogues, regardless of their age or activist cause, is not liberty in any sense of the word, nor is it even the freedom mentioned by our Founders.

One must understand that when freedom, as a semantic problem of cultural references, is used by other peoples in other parts of the world, their meaning may be similar in usage and pragmatic action by their leaders, but ethnic differences called "blind spots" preclude freedom from meaning all that it means in America.

Allowing for differences in interpretation, tolerance can become our vice if we permit cultural diversity and special interest groups to destroy America's unity. *Traditionalism* is the lodestone that attracts foreigners to come to this country where all else in the world is in a state of chaotic flux, terror and uncertainty.

Liberty and divisiveness are incompatables, not because debate and disagreement are inconsistent with democracy but because divisive—and divisive—agents wish to use the clamor or free speech to destroy liberty under moral laws. Such anarchy self-destructs and does no good for the people's sense of equal justice or for the promotion of social harmony. To use the shrill cry of "free speech" as a means to gain either acceptance for a cause or the attention of the majority is senseless and absurd. If a clause panders to violent conduct and prohibits its counter claims, it begs the right to an audlience in a free country and deserves to be shunned.

I wanted my analysis to reflect this distinction between freedom in the contemporary irresponsible usage and liberty with its significant differencs of rules for conscionable moral conduct derived from absolue values of religious faith, values which account for the inner strength of this nation. Can one honestly say that laws guraranteeing rights with no responsibilities are the best laws whatever the situation? That is madness. I personally would not want lhe advocate of this view to lead me to safely through the mountains by a compass with no fixed reference points.

Do not assume that Amerlica can continue to debase the values she was built upon without bringing irreparable harm to her vision, her people and her spiritual stamina. Liberty is our most precious possession. Always take care to separate true liberty from irresponsible anarchy, both personal and societal, taking account of where we are coming from in order to know where we are headed.

PREFACE

Truth is always in the position of editorializing when it confronts falsehood. Liberty is truth in action, tyranny is falsehood institutionalized. The plain statement of the conflict gives rise to this impression. However, that cannot be helped; they are bitter and implacable adversaries. If segments in this small volume appear to be to heavy in editorial content and commentary, I simply state the facts and the observations from my perspective as an American citizen.

I do not pretend to total objectivity, although I have intended to discourse chiefly on the meaning of liberty Morality will always be dogmatic or else conviction is meaningless and Nihilisms will become, as it has today, a prevailing social philosophy. That, too, is dogma. Secular Humanism, Man's worship of Man, is its underlying creed. Even the belief that nothing matters is dogma; and evident as tolerance is what used to be called "social conscience".

Indeed, tolerance in our society has taken on the coloration and implications of dogma. If one has a conviction, he is frequently labeled as intolerant, though his conscience tells him what is the right thing to say or do. If his decisions are fashionable by consensus, though he may condemn them within himself as wrong, he is said to be politically correct. Indeed, *political correctness* is a major curse to free speech and intellectual honesty in America today. It is a form of thought control that I will deal later with.

Our society inevitably has these inner tensions within which true liberty governs the actions of most circumscribed, law-respecting persons. I have tried to set down in these pages my own observations and understanding of our marvelous liberty in America to make our own choices according to information, conscience and moral-ethical discernment. May that always be so.

Tujunga, CA

THE LIBERTY WATCH

A Commentary on Liberty
Conscience and Honor

Liberty is an individual concern, freedom a shared response.

Liberty without implementation is an empty promise.

Liberty with integrity is righteousness.

Conscience and the liberty to exercise it are not produced by government—although that is a common assumption nowadays.

A leadership without integrity will abdicate that responsibility.

1. MAN'S NATURAL REBELLIOUSNESS WITHOUT MORAL DISCIPLINE—A VALUELSS SOCIETY

The yearnings for liberty among men oppressed by an evil sovereign or a tyrannical government—unless they bear the impress of a religious doctrine or pagan philosophy—most often spring from man's rebellious nature, a spirit he attempts to glorify as the desire for civil liberty.

To be free is natural to man, as it is to the animals that roam the plains and forests. Yet when this impulse is disciplined and directed and supplied with ideological content that preserves that freedom while guaranteeing security, comfort and wealth, the rebellion will then appear to claim liberty for the people.

Liberty issues not from jungle survival but from civil discontent. What seemed like rebellion clothed in ingratitude, as it did to the King in Colonial America, becomes in actions and content the clamor to be free under the banner of liberty. In this manner the desire for freedom that springs from natural rebelliousness is tamed, directed, supported by law and endorsed by the authority of a benevolent government or of a sovereign God. For man without a value system cannot long

1

support his self-sovereignty without his returning to his more primitive state of rebellion. The scenario of wars, international crises, intercene hatreds and familial feuds have in the past dramatically demonstrated the truth of this axiom. Rebellion is Man's natural state, a governing authority with tenable values is his artificial one. Without the second, the first leads to chaos, but with the exclusivity of the second, absent the first, man becomes an automaton and slips into abject slavery under a despot. A certain degree of rebellious dissatisfaction is necessary for man's improvement of his civil self-government

> **Liberty of action is the right to chose, liberty of thought is the freedom to judge, liberty of conscience is the right to be wrong.**

> **Liberty is a consuming passion to the patriot.**

> **Why ought the common people to put up any longer with self-appointed representatives of what is not theirs to control—liberty of thought and action righteous before God?**

> **Keep liberty and defy anarchy, discard liberty and accept chaos.**

2. ENLIGHTENED REASON UNDERMINES PRAGMATIC RESOLUTIONS, WHICH UNDERMINE REASON

With the absolute stress put upon reason during the 18th Century Enlightenment, pragmatic reason being the salvic methodology for societal failures and human unhappiness, the sovereignty of reason in time was no longer sovereign but, contending with other methodologies in the marketplace, became a commodity to be tested by pragmatic justice. And so it is to this day, that justice increasingly issues from pragmatic experiment, and the general unhappiness that results from that trial-and-error living has brought men even greater unhappiness. When neither King, God, Government nor society is sovereign, as mankind have reasoned away troublesome controls, they have lost their way and their principles for life's directions. That last sovereignty—man's reason—is ironically no longer sovereign but has become a commodity to be tested by pragmatic justice and electronic confirmation. Empirical results more often than not govern men's affairs in today's Western society.

The unhappiness that stems from their totally pragmatic lifestyle has brought, for the millions of individuals participating in it, disaster to the family. For if none of the other entities is today sovereign in America, all having been rejected by sovereign men with their sovereign reasoning, we face social chaos and irreparable ideological schisms. Quota enlistments, gender biases, lifestyle clamor for separate political treatment, ethnic purification, cultural isolation by choice in schools and community and fragmentation of time-honored institutions like marriage and parenting—these are evidence of America's divisive protests for separate group recognition based less on utilitarian reason than on reasonable pragmatism. The one involves thesis and antithesis, the other applauds results—the deteriorating force in today's schools. What was once a reasonable way to rear children has now become the object of mathematical scorn through polls, test scores and percentage results.

The last sovereignty—man's reason—is no longer ruler over his conduct, since his rebellious narcissistic practices belie the name of reason. The *situation* increasingly controls the "principles" and the result directs the premise, in brief, the end justifies the means. The outcome of this parochial selfish aggrandizement against "them" represents the absence of absolute laws for principles. Man has attained to a state of irrational depravity and in his technological culture, a material smugness and contentment.

Reason has in this manner undermined the proposition of a rational value system which has become in effect no longer a structure of principles for living but variable guidelines for a multitude of separate "causes." Masked as liberty, we have achieved a virtually valueless society that supports the control of man's rebellious nature, his freedom without principles, and his conduct by self-gratifying hedonist sensitivities only. He finds liberty to mean the government of his life by his feelings, his course directed by his impatience and his obsession with convenience. For millions of Americans, their vulnerable feelings are the repository of their wisdom when they chose a Representative to Congress. Stereotypical feelings have made conformity a *sine qua non* to wisdom, political correctness, and right and wrong. The image of righteousness, not its controlling values, is everything.

He who uses his liberty to vandalize his neighbor will, in the end, face annihilation himself.

Try Liberty as "criminal Grace" and the jury will defeat the Prosecutor's case.

Mankind, being fallible and fundamentally corrupt, his liberty resides in release through Christ from Hell's chains—for evil is a closed value system.

3. LIBERTY SELDOM DEFINED, OFTEN INTERPRETED

Samuel Adams was a radical of the American Revolution and founder of the secret society *Sons of Liberty*. He fought for total separation from the oppressive British monarch. Tea merchants ought not to have to subsidize the East India Company's tea surplus; by invitation he held the Boston Tea Party. The Colonists could not put up with British military domination. He inspired the Boston Massacre on The Green. Adams understood liberty as *moral activism*.

Liberty as comprehended by Jefferson with his Enlightenment ideas eschewed the "absolute arbitrary power" of despotism when he transcribed the Declaration of Independence from the pens of Franklin, Jay and Madison within the venue of the Constitutional Convention of 1788. The influence of Englishman John Locke is evident in the Declaration's assumption that men are "by nature free, equal and independent", and that the law of reason ought to govern their society. Constitutional law in America had, in part by its inception with Locke's thinking, transmitted to Jefferson the ideology of Natural Rights-life, liberty and the pursuit of happiness (at first "property"), rights given to Man by "their Creator" and therefore of divine origin—a stunning idea at the time.

Washington saw an America that was free, yet in isolation from the old-world entanglements, an invisible geo-political Rubicon that ought not to be crossed. His faith was strongly Christian Deist, similar in deference to that which Locke paid to Old Testament law as Deistic government for men. God created the universe, wound it up and let it run on its own without His interference, a concept that was compatible with Revolutionary disengagement from England.

Liberty for Madison was a mutual concurrence of a federal government with citizen-ratification concessions by the former. They were to be reposted in his sponsored Bill of Rights and the division of powers between Federal and State governments explicitly set forth. For John Adams, his concept of liberty demanded total independence from Great Britain. Samual Chase of Maryland gave stirring speeches against British tyranny. Charles Carroll urged the Colonials not to trade in British goods. George Clymer from Pennsylvania spoke out for total independence from England. John Dickinson of Delaware supported a plan in the Continental Congress for two legislative bodies. Franklin defended the Colonists against British arrogance, and he negotiated a recession of the Stamp Tax. Richard Henry Lee of Virginia pressed for a Bill of Rights and for America as an asylum for religious and political refugees. Hamilton initiated the two-party system. Benjamin Harrison from Virginia committed his enormous wealth to the

Revolution. John Jay instituted American diplomacy and arbitration between Britain and America. John Marshall ruled as Constitutional the power of judicial Review by the Supreme Court and emboldened the court to sit as co-equal with the other two branches of government. John Hancock was a political activist who, like Harrison, committed his wealth to the cause of liberty. There were others, the Minutemen, the Regulars, the Spies and the Volunteers.

Thus is that down through America's history liberty has seldom been defined in a strict rote sense. It has often been interpreted by men who believed in it to the extent of pledging their lives, their wealth and their "sacred honor" to obtain it. This phenomenon demonstrates how elusive a definition can be yet how encompassing was the early understanding of the American people. They understood tyranny by personal experience.

Liberty ought never, therefore, to be miscast as empty freedom or license or unfettered image-making, simply because to do so impairs the peopled clear vision into the power of the values operating within the ideological context of *natural rights.*

If we say that Americans love liberty, we say next to nothing about the nature of that attachment or the measures for achieving it. We might as well weave together wanton violence and legislative anarchy as to call the results of a value-less social experiment by the name *of diversity.* The ends sought are today's embedded in agency welfare and the colossal granatoid bigness of non-elected official-dom. Petty hirelings and aides are deluded into believing that liberty is theirs to dispense, indeed, that today's Federal Government is the source of our rights and our inheritance of liberty.

The overweighed bureaucracy of American government represents not just a profligate mismanagement unequaled in our history; it represents the simple concept that power defines its own extra-constitutional parameters of liberty. The mere existence of the plethora of controlling officers and regulatory powers is not proof of their constitutionality. Instead, that top-heavy structure of hordes of bureaucrats and a million regulations attest to a growing insidious dependence upon government for both our rights and life's amenities. That dependence was never intended by our Founders.

There must in consequence of these excesses be other contending parameters, firmly placed around liberty that will insure its permanence, such as (1) that there ought to be a mutuality of obedience under the laws that protects and benefits all; (2) that the citizens acknowledge that human error is an inherent component of liberty; (3) that its fundamental justice must affirm the existence of the human conscience by which right can, indeed, be sorted out from wrong; (4) that liberty must include legal deterrence that both avenge and indemnify for the preservation of the citizen as well as the state, not the latter at the expense of the former, and (5) that all elected officials are subject to the same power of Constitutional oversight and discipline as is the common citizenry.

The state is a creation in perpetuity of that citizenry with its explicitly delegated powers to supervene in the lives of all its citizens, and to temper, alter, adjudicate and guard their choices and decisions. These powers are represented in structures and compromises granted by the people themselves and have their source in the both the Constitutional and the case laws of common men, either by default or by election.

Extra-legal bureaucratic control has, however, become so overwhelming and intrusive that the people must, paradoxically, find recourse in the state for their unhappiness. In this circular, tautological way, Americans have substituted the sovereign state of the new world for the sovereign king of the old, the modern secret bureaucracy for the open laws of a visible and established government.

Out of their desire for maximum autonomy in today's America, free men have created an instrument for the annihilation of their liberty. If God is dead in America, then her people need only to consult their personal feelings for social redress, by which action they have appointed bendable ethics and godless passions to be their judge advocate. Crimes of all kinds are the result of this modern man-centered interpretation of liberty. The *inalienable* natural rights have become objects for lip service to the extent that conscience is seared, discarded and ignored and thus made mutable by individual whim.

Curse liberty and you applaud the dark devices of thought-control.

The "free press" will ultimately destroy the knowledge of the understanding and the use of liberty in America by silencing all convictions but theirs.

The concern of the politician is for his own immoral welfare, of the statesman for the people's moral Betterment. The two cannot Be sustained By the one Congressman.

Liberty of action is snot the same as outer freedom to roam but, instead, is the inner capability to act morally.

4. LIBERTY'S RELIGIOUS IMPLICATIONS

Civil liberty, which is often called a *faith* by those who cherish freedom of conscience and ethical public conduct, can never be separated from its religious beginning without defaulting to wrong-doing. Although morality in government does not consist of the opinion of the High Court put into action, nonetheless the statesmanship of men of integrity anticipates and sets its own precedent for moral leadership under the law.

Likewise, the Courts makes no attempt to rule for or against tolerance as a public attitude, their domain being justice within the law. Tolerance, therefore, is a republican morality and must arise from the good conduct example of law-aiding citizens regardless of whether or not specific religious sanctions are openly brought to bear upon civil conduct.

Tolerance is, therefore, the exacting of a price for the presence of differences of kind, opinion and appearance. Tolerance is not to be mistaken for license, as in a mindless obliviousness toward the several arenas of a state's existence, its politics, commerce, military establishment and the like-the which are vulnerable to corruption whether that society is free or slave. Tolerance is, in fact, the yielding by its possessors of a certain weight and rule of power into the hands of a stranger, mindful that the grant can be rescinded if the alien proves to be a spoiler or a defector from the public will and providing that that will is lawful. The law is the agent of power.

The power of liberty is the power to grant that tolerant acceptance, that power which in a Republic reposes in the people and their Representatives. The liberty to do so is consequently never a shared right until its source is identified by the obvious yielding of limited power to whosoever granted. A free people show their tolerance by their acceptance of what is alien to their ways. This pre-condition of power-ownership keeps wrong practices in the name of liberty from becoming the tyranny of a majority by their oppressive seizure of other men's liberties. In order to yield the power of liberty to one who differs in culture, religion, or mores, as to an adversary or an alien, the people must first possess it. A primitive culture cannot empower an alien to that culture with anything but life, which is not theirs to give in the first place.

Early American history is permeated with a people's acknowledged concessions to an Almighty God, rendered with their awareness of His providential hand upon the history of our nation. Many strident voices in these times have sought to disenfranchise the people of America from their historical-religious past. Indeed the conduct of her people has often betrayed an ignorance of or an indifference to that past. But it is there, in place and in time and as real as the words of her greatest leaders. Reason quantifies that ancient faith, yet faith, in her turn, affirms reason by which tolerance finds its rationale under God's laws. They represent His grant of tolerance—or grace—which is ours to keep and to share with each other and with the rest of the world. Christ answered the lawyer as to the second greatest command, it being—to love one's neighbor as one's self. That is tolerance.

Whether or not our Founders' faith deserves recognition today ought not to be a question for debate but, instead, an historical fact. Whether or not that faith ought to operate in the affairs of men today is their decision yet, even so, the choice of the living cannot effect the choice of the deal lest we endeavor to convert America into a nation without spiritual taproots. In this sad state of weakness, she will die because, believing themselves to be infinitely capacious and self-sufficient cynics and atheists, Americans can—and will-ultimately fall amid the ashes of intelligent cynicism.

By altering liberty's markings so as to make it acceptable as license and a heresy on our heritage, we Americans in no way change its content into embittered fatalism and diminished moral stature that bear the name of *mediocrity*. Our forefathers would that we preserve the old standard of liberty with honor. Should we instead heed these detractors, we shall simply pitch out our moral strength into the rubble of stones and dead timbers that once belonged to civilizations in existence before ours.

The eclipse of tolerance by divisive feuds and factions of parochial isolationism, when extrapolated into politics, signals the failing of America's greatness. By their denying God, Americans know not the true meaning of *grace*, which accepts error and weakness as mortal.

> **He who transgresses liberty by defying its divine source and power commits an immoral act, since liberty cannot be defied except in the commission of a wicked i.e. immoral deed.**

> **By proclamation to say of personal liberty "It's mine" is to say of freedom "It's ours."**

> **Foster dishonest judgments of others and you put a blight upon liberty, since dishonor and liberty are alien to each other.**

5. INNOVATIONS MASKED AS LIBERTY

Liberty is seldom championed by the adversaries of freedom. Lacking that fine judgment to discriminate freedom of conduct from the license of mayhem and riot, rabble-rousers for radical change will crawl to the feet of a tyrant rather than endure the tribulations attendant upon conscionable change by law. They there-fore undertake-all radicals warped to the task—to reduce men's proudest achieve-ments and noblest aims to the groveling of scoundrels in the streets. A Frenchman who knows little about liberty and much about democratic license has written that our Republican system of checks and balances are the work of Colonial aristocrats to checkmate the village rabble.

The projection is clear. The adversaries of liberty will proclaim their radical accomplishments *as just* and enshrine them as enlightened justice. A people so subjugated by radical deviations from proven tradition cannot rise to greatness. The resultant majority so double-minded, torn between the radically new and the traditional must ultimately sink into mediocrity for the plain reason that when an adversarial government imposes its standards of licensed diversity and mediocre performance, it obscures those finer judgments that are fostered in freedom's atmosphere to risk and achieve. In brief, conformity produces mediocre accep-tance of what is expedient and easy, a dangerous tribute of today's highly techno-logical culture in which struggle is minimized by the computer machine and achievement made common by the focus upon results. That shift makes pole-fig-ures popular, statistics controlling, and risk automated by the microchip instead of by character.

What perverted forms of justice then, without notice, masquerade as innova-tions and change, long sustaining society's malcontents while thwarting other men's finest yearnings for enterprise without the destruction of government interference. The hue and cry is out. In this "masque" of the invisible bureau-cracy for conformity, there exists a self-serving empty integrity that, like a fatal disease, can be transmitted from the government to the people. The disease of failing integrity affronts those selfless leaders, sacrificial if imperfect and not always right, who championed liberty over two hundred years ago. Scandals pre-vails. The words and vision of our Founders is momentarily shrouded by the stri-dent noise of the attention-getters, particularly via television, and the empty cannonade of civil strife by those eager to reform centuries-old tradition and institutions, like the family and the conventional marriage of a man and a woman and the security of private property and an open religious faith.

Chance is not the offspring of liberty but only concedes random gains to the astonished observer.

Quest for liberty and you may discover wisdom but search for wisdom and you will certainly find liberty.

You may keep the practices of moral freedom in abeyance for a while, but you cannot suppress its open dissatisfaction with the state's bureaucratic edicts.

To educate a child does not mean to elicit a politically correct ethical choice-pattern by the simple change of situation. To educate a child is to teach him to discern right from wrong regardless of self-salvation. The choice is not elite-patterned but is based upon a system of absolute values that are a curse to the proud.

Religious liberty is not an anachronism for the tolerance of religion in secret. Tolerance has deposed liberty in lie name of "correctness." Yet who is the judge except the self-appointed elite?

Accommodation unmasks the spurious tolerance of "allowance" for religious practice in private

6. CHARADES OF MORALITY

There are arrogant politicians, "the people's Representatives," who sustain a loss of conscience when they see open possibilities to raise their already fabulous pay in the face of on-gong national bankruptcy. Such men of dishonor suffer from *squanderlust,* a fatal disease that remains with them until they leave office. They bilk secret pay increases from the taxpaying public-a form of "bait and switch," a fraud in the marketplace. They are abusers of Congressional privilege, taking advantage of their power and like bats seeking the entrance to a cave they fly into its dark maw to commence their terms of cozy residency, kiting check, tripping abroad for their squalorous den of oil barons of the Middle East. Who do they think they are, these spoilers who, with flair, with class, parade before our watering eyes as the sensitive self-exiles from American life—the strategists, Political Action Committee members, the professional scriveners and special-interest coattails—they who, in time, leave behind them their uncouth corruptions on liberty.

These corruptions—government contract partiality, "burning the books." as government-corporate price-gouging—they will attempt to conceal just so long as they get what they want when they want it until they are caught. Meantime, this common parasitic practice of corporate dishonesty sucked away the life-savings of thousands of employees.

There are, of course, others who abuse the public purse—the Party sycophants of both genders-the lobbyists, staff scriveners, not to mention the grandiloquent media who hypothesize the administration's agenda in order to obtain a scoop, utilizing a dinasaurian strategy that is as certain as price-fixing and controlled betting. In doing so, this army of monied supporters for higher-taxes and self-serving investments also emit their conjectures on public benefits-jobs, security, education—from behind their protected lobbyist status and the journalist's shield laws, where they can be found editing out the opposition as censorship.

None of us is persuaded that visual press conferences are legitimate but the press corps enjoy their subtle charade on free enquiry and, if liberals, their playing god. None of us dares to refute their findings. Their low opinion of the American intelligence, the perceptive intellectual, is a farce in innuendo and censorship. Naturally there is nothing wrong with competition—unless it is that power begets power, spending begets spending, unaccounted for public money begets theft and corruption begets corruption.

Charades! Most often the party in power that suspends good judgment to meet the approximations of the press, snipping here, weaseling there-as on campaign promises—becomes by these maneuvers a menace to the very survival of these maneuvers and to the very survival of the Republic. New laws which adorn the Party's name-like cutting taxes, phasing out "sunset" agencies-do not hoodwink the people into thinking that their dollars are well spent. Not at all. The "Invisible Government" of the bureaucracy and the office-holding manipulators of foreign policy, vis-à-vis the international Monetary Fund and world bankers, trot out the American middle-class to show the world how backward this great nation is and how desperately they need government help. These charades are done in the name of freedom—and yet there is a subtle evil, an immoral and flamatory ruse hidden in these machinations, domestic and international, and that is the intrigue of high-finance politics to which the media are honored guests. Little do the American people realize how they are being used and manipulated by the power mongers of the media fourth Estate. They, however, are growing wiser.

These are the charades on liberty, on the morality of right and wrong that seems almost sensescent and so alien to these sycophants and social planners.

Who in all of Congress has to the courage to refuse to pay the dishonest manufacturing and service charges against us, the tax payers? Taxpayers find to be outrageous the overcharges, the run-on estimates of costs by industry against the government, and those line-vote pork barrel inserts. A pork charge is nothing but a politician's bribe for the votes in his district. They are the well-heeled liberals who often affect pleas of compassion for the helpless, the homeless, the school children, the aged. The truth, also, is that most millionaire Congressmen do not read the budget. There is a price to pay for their neglect and ignorance.

> **The print media in general and by majority do not speak from a platform of liberty. They speak through the bars of insular opinion they call fairness, in essence their parochial i.e liberal agenda.**

> **Thought-control by public censure is tolerance in reverse. It is propagandists Congressional investigating committees enjoy this swashbuckling display of power. Liberty of conscience is enmity to evil.**

> **Do not abuse liberty by calling it illusion lest it return to mock your ridicule as <u>natural rights</u> beyond your reach.**

> **Counsel a man to be faithful to his covenants and he will honor liberty.**

> **To destroy liberty is to imprison a people's capacity for joy.**

7. LIBERTY'S RISKS COMPARED

One cannot discuss liberty without reference to the Reign of Terror of France's "democratic" 1789 Revolution, a bloody exorcism to exterminate an entire class who were the privileged minority, the Aristocracy and their sympathizers. This sort of "cleansing" has happened often in history: in Russia in 1917, the class was the Kulak peasant farmers; in Germany line 1933, it was the Jews; in China in the 1960's it was the intellectuals, in Kosovo in the 1980's, it was the Serbs; in Iraq in the 1980's, it was the Shiites. Karl Marx trumpeted the classless society; in America today, those who voice politically incorrect ideas must be silenced or discarded.

France's Revolution pivoted upon the Jacobin purse of justice to traitors, the exercise of sovereignty undergirded by moral "virtue," and the enlightenment's proclamation of the natural rights of Man. *Liberty, Equality, Fraternity* was the battle cry against crown sympathizers and France's rulers, Queen Marie Antoinette and King Louis XIV. Liberty-as the street mobs knew it—neither envisioned the flowering of natural rights nor the stabilization of a cohesive democratic state. The rabble's surge against the Bastille prison July 14th—to chop off the heads of its Aristocratic prisoners—represented a rebellion, not to exact a new state and install a Republican government of triumvirate justice but to raise the voice of protest against food shortages and capricious taxes for war and luxury levied by an immoral sovereign. They would temporize a government later, when the Aristocracy was out of the way.

By comparison, the American Revolution was fought to claim, not to dethrone. Its method was to institute, not to butcher; its vision was to build, not to vacuumize. Its result was a nation, not a chaotic dream with mandates only to justify the agony of birth with the blood spilled by the Innocents. Of course, this is a perspective and in either case the Revolution had to be fought to a resolution.

America's earlier Revolution of thirteen years (1777-1788) could not have been the inspiration for the French massacre for the reason that the Americans fought not to democratize an ancient regime but to separate totally from it. King George III was a despot who had abused the Colonies by his unwarranted and illegal acts of politico-military invasion—among the numerous offenses contained in the Declaration of Independence. "Liberty" to the Colonials had reasoned causes whose basis of homage was not to Great Britain any longer but to their leadership, the purpose of "forming a more perfect union," and to an omnipotent God. Numerous documents attest to this fact of the American Revolution—that the patriots believed in God's laws rather than a fallible human morality, and they embraced the risk of His Providence based upon His will and His design for them. In the speeches of Rebespierre there, of course, were tangents. He inveighed against arbitrary justice and absolute power, while he appealed not to a providential God but solely to Man's reason.

The American religious background was both Deistic and strongly Calvinistic, bringing to our shores a pious people to establish a "New Jerusalem" at the feet of an unrighteous king they deemed no longer fit to rule over them. They came to confront, to endure, and to thrive-and that reality endured with small provisions and few practical skills. There was hunger that first year in Jamestown; half of the settlement died of starvation, dysentery and the bitter cold. Yet the individualism in the American character of and its vision of her independence had begun to assert themselves from the outset.

Frenchmen on the other hand spoke out against deprivation through "mobocracy," as some critics have called the appeal through violence. Lives were important in the aggregate, civil liberty amounting to what the angry mob considered instantaneously to be patriotic and moral and good for the nation. Theirs was vigilante justice. In the Colonies, civil liberty dwelt upon their disfigurement by Indian attacks and British exploitation. The British troops were more oppressive than protective. The bourgeois class from which the Colonists sprang, among whom were wealthy London merchants, was already in place, sailing to the settlement to make a new start. A weak comparison might juxtapose the French Nobility alongside the lobesterback troops of His Majesty and the British-appointed Governors and Custom House supervisors, as the Crown Colonies sprang up. They were bad enough to justify house-razing, tar a feathering and rail-riding out of town. Violence by Colonel "commoner" mobs probably constitute the one valid comparison with the French Revolution of rebellious peasants. Yet the differences are too deep to go further. Immigrants to the New World took risks unknown to the French comrades in arms and the Proletarian mobs.

After these British offenses there followed the war, which the French did not have to face. From the American experience, there arose a nation not revitalized by political infighting and endless Cabinet changes that would wrack a Republican France. Instead, fifty-two Colonials created a structure designed to survive under laws acknowledging and protecting the personal liberties and common bonds that had all but eluded the French. Robespierre went to the guillotine for his democratic ideas, flailed as he was by his accusers for being a demagogue and a dictator. Washington, against whom was leveled the charge of aspiring to be another king, finished his life with great honor nd popular acolades. Reason in no small way illuminated not the soul of a man but the course of his journey. A faith such as General Washington possessed most often bares the soul to show that it is empty of guile that scorns conspiratorial deceit, is guided by reason informed by experience and a belief in God. The risks of the American Revolution were taken for the future of a new country and the liberties it would grant to its citizens; the risks of the French Revolution were endured for the realities of the present, unfettered by an oppressive Plutocracy and class hatred.

> **Liberty is the tyrant's to dispense, since he asszumes that it is already his by default—and this may be true.**

> **The moral good in a man does not improve his welfare so much as it con-dems his vile practices**

> **To discern right from wrong is not an easy matter if the adversary is personal power.**

> **Honor liberty as the keystone of all laws. The liberated conscience will Govern one's choice of means.**

Floating downcurrent is always easier than struggling upcurrent, just as it is easier to lose liberty than to preserve it through vigilance.

8. LIBERTY AND REASON

The acceptance of the belief in liberty has always possessed an element of individual anarchy in its defense., yet modern day Hedoninsm with its fascinating descriptions clings to the pain-pleasure principle, the cognition of which gives validity to that anarchy as a release, whilest liberty engenders the discipline of application. For example, it is better i.e. more fun, to gamble with the voters' money than to risk one's own venture capital, or, "I need to gather some information on the Eiffel Tower for my constituents, consequently I plan a trip to Paris." Such is the character of thought owned by the average political liberal in America.

Reason then validates the immoral choice of ends. It follows that reason is used to justify rebellion as well as the immorality, the rebellion of political integrity. It is in such a role that reason has become condescending and consenting alike, the icon to which liberals appeal for answers to their paintul and their pleasurable dilemmas for self-promotion.

The rebel's capacity to reason cannot, however, be relative and absolute at the same time, cannot bond with the situation yet remain indifferent to and absolute before the "big questions" e.g. is perjury under oath ever admissivle in the courts of law? Or, ought liberty always to be censured, it alwlays veing vulnerableto censure? For us in the Western world the liberating power of reason is investigative and constructive, as compared to the unquestioning and dogmatic applicaion of reason in Graeco-Roman cultures. Reason has become a two-headed Janus, at once benevolent and fitting for one's analysis of liberty of conscience and for honor, although reason can be treacherous and undependable when confronting things that give men pleasure and release.

But how can this be so—that liberty armored as reason in action has a double purpose—is disciplinary and yet anarchistic, finds moral conduct both good and evil, or acceptable and the unethical as desireable? It does so by its concealment of its true meaning, by the specious rationalization of awareness which is neither action nor substance but is ideological symbol, the dogma of "my way" that is consistent with faith not in its God-oriented righteousness but in its man-focused *Tightness.*

When reason has become the suitable replacement for God, it allows cognition to supply all answers to faith in our "inalienable rights." In this context, then, analysis comprises the framework for testing social answers with little or no recourse to divine interpretation. Indeed, the computations of computer analysis are beginning to replace logical deduction in police work and scientific laboratory analysis. The laboratory panel of a patient's blood supplies data that far outweigh former deductive analysis by symptoms. Enter into a computer the factual details of a crime and the computer will derive the solution, or possible solutions, to that crime!

If reason is the logical god, the icon of advocacy, liberty can best be understood through reason, a tautological resolution without any premise of dogma, secular or religious. The moral strength of America is, therefore, presumably shaped by mind—and what better superimposition of mind is there than an elite corps of minds? So it is today that the recrudescence of the Enlightenment is found in the "think tank" and in the molds of the "social planners." The wisdom for human conduct in Western man is set aside or made obsolete by Man's pride in his technology.

The capacity to think, to reflect, to weigh the ends and to resolve dilemmas always brings liberty to heel lest it result in anarchy. Yet the agency of cogntion is mere process; it is not content. It is simple evaluation, not conclusion. The scientific method is inductive, not deductive. Does cognition icon-ocize emptiness or methodology? Reason answers this query with utilitarian solutions. The solution to a crime is empirical in its diagnosis. To put more food on the table, the Government must materialize jobs like some immense pagan miracle-worker in Washington. To improve the economy, the Congress must strip the money to do so from the providers of money, the taxpayers. To stay in office lawfully, the Representative must pander to his creditors out of earshot of the people, in a word, his contributors. One can think about welfare as commendable and moral, but if larceny or extortion are the means, then their immoral value extinguishes all of the moral goodness of the intention. The doctor who deliberately murders a patient at the request of that patient so as to end the pain destroys the goodness of the intention. Doctor-assisgted suicide thusvecomes moral in the context of deliberate death.

Liberty as an element in merchantile philosophy, is inseparable from business and financial risk. It is incontestable, therefore, that in socialist countries where liberty is quenched by social schemers and despots, investors take fewer risks, as a conequence of which, despite the inept moves and decisions of social pinning, the power-hungry controllers presume a susperiority in the conduct of daily trade and social intercourse. That bureaucratic control is anathema to the liberty to invest at personal risk.

On the basis' of the same irrational, illogical understanding of what liberty means, Americans today, with taxes, sustain a monolithic government that competes with the private sector to the latter's detriment. Big goverment is antipathetic toward small business, to cite one example, because entrepreneurs practice an efficiency that is alien to the mental makeup of bureaucratic rulemakers. Only nominally is safety involved. Instead it is their desire to control what they do, not to possess, that makes most of their small-business regulations insidious and immoral, in a word, *evil.* For example, this extreme view is embodied in those regulatios that prohibit environmental cleanup to benefit a corporation. There had to be laws that reversed this cause-and-effect of circumstances. A small farmer, who is a businessman, is prohibited from further work on his land when a Federal agency declares his farm to be wetlands or the niche for an endangered species. To ruin him and his farm for these reasons is immnoral.

The invisible bureaucracy costs the common silent people great sums of money for its inefficient and callous spendthrift ventures. What government "risk" lacks is the interpreneurship of the 18th century and the drive for wealth that began in such early industries as whaling, cotton milling, timber, tobacco and smuggling activities in which the risks were taken by individuals intead of by agencies riding "free" on the backs of the people. There indeed, is no accounting for the corruption and the blunders in government agencies that can be described as *good.*

Liberty meant to those pioneers pure and simple risk-taking. A miller could not build a mill, a timber baron construct twenty miles of creek-water sluce to float his logs to the river, or a hardpan miner purchase a burro and grubstake himself without his hopes facing risk. Each was a risk adventure. Government risk largely consumes wealth and capital investments held by private owners. His risk chances only the Congressman's re-election to political office. It is obvious, therefore, that the liberty of Americans to engage in merchantile enterprise is utiliitarian and pragmatic, not elgalitarian and socialistic, possessing as it does in the beginning individual choices prioritized above group biases. Here one has the Colonists understanding of liberty. Should the Colonial farmer risk planting crops of rice and indigo before tobacco. Should the Bostonian Colonial merchants absorb the exhorbitant tax on British tea?

To the degree that risk is quenched and tlurned aside and crippled, the government destroys the venture of capital and the willingness of the people to take risks. There occurs in the slow, almost invisible shrinking of the economy, the surrender of risk-liberty. By defrees thus do a free people come under the heel of petty tyrants and a despsotic bureaucracy. Liberty becomes an operational mode of the past, and class envy sets in out of sheer frustration and the impediments, champioined by n'er-do-wells, the hapless and the improvident, battle against the *excellent* and against rising above *mediocrity*. Out of fear the State insures its survival by the control and suppression of excellence, perverting what is good, beneficial and instructive for the people, often, as in the case of the arts, substituting a corruption for the genuine—as the salacious, weird excretions for non-utilitarian expressions of beauty. The Natioal Endowment for theArts, a Feeral bureaucratic venture into the graphic arts, all too often spews its corruptions for public display in a scandalous manner that is distasteful, ugly and offensive to most Americans.

The people tend then to become cynical when they presume they must look to the Federal Government to receive their grant of liverty, a fallacious hope which by its very nature is morally wrong. The people are offended by an immoral leadership, a leadership without integrity or consistency of time-tested values. They sluffer thereby lfrom the substitution of a changeable statute of ethics for a permament, constitutionlly fixed system of laws prioritized by ideals. Whereas it was unethical for a politician to squander his left-over war chest his last year before he left office, this year it is "ethical" for him to do so. He breeches a social contract that pivots on the trust of his constituents. In either case his seizure amounts to an inequitable theft, the violation of an absolute value that one must not steal, the eighth Commandment of God, which is the fixed epicenter of social laws of mutual trust. It would have been better had he pro-rated the leftover moneys and issued a check to each consituent in his district, than that he pocket or squander the balance.

The long and the short of lthe matter of risk is that it is not the Federal Government that liberates the people, but, when left to their own self-sufficiency, they will liberate themseles. The oppressive nature of America's bureaucracy, that silent python of total social control, has today all but choked out the meanin of liberty in commerce, in business and, increasingly, in personal relationships and in home life. 1

Why, or example, have motion picture companies gone abroad to film? Why are industries, retail outlets and factories being out-sourced to countries abroad where labor is cheap—profit and market prices, if not quality. Why must a child obtain a social security number that qualifies him to whitewash a neighbor's fence? As if to exalt their power, the bureaucratic agency heads have claimed as their own those who, confronted by bankrupcy and bureaucratic retaliation, have surrendered their liberty of fabrication-choice to other nations, a moral declision which destroys American labor. Small manufacturing companies that have filed a Chapter 11 are legion. It is almost as if agency chiefs, such as the quota-conscious bounty hunters in the IRS like to see heads roll. Nowadays, health insurance regulations had put down many a small business.

At this juncture the Government prides itseslf on taking the initiative to find myriads of enterprises that were formerly private ventures—a methodology suggestive of one's breaking the will of a police dog before retraining it. Despite these discouragements to entrepreneur merchantile liberty, warped to laws and tethered by excessive State regulation, business generally still carries the ensign of daring risk. Entrepreneurs risk their money, time, lives, families and property. That is their most admirable characrteristic and moral suasion ... For economic, merchantile, entrepreneur risk has always been a matter of persoal choice, whether or not the risk-taker choses to call it *moral*

> **Happiness is the right to make the optional choice, not the liberty to aggrandize against the right of choice.**

> **The pursuit of happiness always involves a conflict of interest, while the inalienable liberty to do so cannot be contested.**

> **Keep liberty strong and cheat the oppressor. Let liberty falter and admit the spoiler.**

> **Liberty comes rarely without a cost. Most often it must be fought for.**

9. LIBERTY AND CRIME

For the judge to sentence a man to prison for a crime when the law specifically states the penalty for the criminal offense, affirms the liberty of socety to protect itself from harmful acts. This has long been the case in Wesern societies, except when a dictator, king or militarist has commanded otherwise. Certain violations of the people's safety, whether or not they bring harm to their perpetrator, have occasioned cases based on statutes of reform that eliminated injustices of past days such as the early child-labor laws governing conditions in the work environment, particularly the in the coal mines, mills and sweatshops.

Nonetheless, the liberty of the courts to mete out sentences, voice rulings and issue injunctions has often, in the past, anticipated retaliation or has interdicted vengeance. The power of the courts either to fine or imprison violators of the law exacts a retribution that is moral and has the result of preserving the moral fabric of the people. Opponents deny this. However, expefience has proved that severe crimes require severe penalties or else all crime reduces to mere meloncholy misdemeanor.

Alibis blaming others or the environment or society in general, or the mental aberrations that motivated the crime—all are efforts to flee accountability which, after the commission of a crime, or a misdemeanor, do not affirm a person's innocence. Instead, light sentences often elicit perjury of the truth by the miscreant. On these occasions, the penalty is seen by society as not so much a moral retribution as a sentimental corrective. The more often this sort of meretricious sentencing takes place in our courts, the weaker the moral strength of Amnerica becomes. A corrosive vulnerability begins to show itself in the form of scaling down penalties, the courts perceiving the crminal as a disadvantaged *victim*. This is the stance, more olten than not, of political liberals. These alerations to the basic morality of conscionable justice—a moral retribution by which the penalty fits the crime—are attempts to paint out the spots on the leopard in order to make him appear to be more acceptable company and to mitigate the pain of his "victimization."

What are we to say about those crimes in a society that increasigly tolerates them, indeed that pleads to legalize criminal behavior—e.g. mental aberration, rage as "self-protection," third party cupaility as in, "he made me do it," the leglaliation of marijuana, and outright denial with "defensible lies." Indeed, a witness's lie under oath is gradually diminishsing in impact and consequencesl, being the result of the accused's "helplessness." Do-or should?-criminal acts, such child-abuse and corporate cheating, eventually become moral, acceptable, practiced and eventually customary because a judge says they are nominally acceptable, the penalties incurred unfair Such crimes, therefore, are not punishable to the full extent of the law. If this twisting of justice becomes endemic, then perhaps there is honor among thieves.

Morality ought to be inflexible and adamantine while compassionate. A Nation's survival depends upon her people's discrimination of right from wrong. Today, howdver, honesty is a condition of the situation, loyalty is a mater of feelings, character is a product of self-esteem, trust is subjective, tempeance is sociological, greed is cultural and poverty is the "other guy's fault." Right and wrong are matters of opinion only, not sprinciple, which is inflexible. All are mixed messages; all are double-standards, all are vainly designed to make of liberty a monstrous calumny of wisdom, a denial of the common-sense validity of right and wrong. Personal opinon has already become, in many situations, the governor of moral choice, not a choice by any law in and of itself. With this thesis, the criminal court becomes an adjudicator of opinion, not of the law.

These semantlic dodges are subterfuges for a law-breaker who seeks a logical, rationl excuse for his offense. In a word, they are fraudulent and, being fraudulent, initiate the liberty that tolerated and gave license to the criminal for his criminal act in the first place. The projected logic of this rationalization is that the retribution is, itself, unlawful, being the wrongful application of a reasonable penalty to a "reasonless" *i.e.forgiveable,* crime and therefore a misjudged use of the judicial process, or in the words of the caring, compassionate Egalitaians with the tenderized consciences—a "miscarriage" of justice. By redefining the terms of *justice* and *mercy* and *morality,* the Egalitarians would purge the moral concept of evil from liberty and leave it an empty cell. In this manner the crime which society has neither tolerated nor is willing to endure, critiques liberty as having brought about the licence to kill, to plunder, to steal from the people. Liberty is, therefore, in the docket. The judicial process—which has issued from conscionable liberty—is condemned as needing reform, and judges are thus set free to legislate from the bench.

These changes result from society's discard of moral law, which is a product not of blind acceptance but of open-minded credence given to certain human truths long proved workeable in civilized societies. This acceptance of certain kinds of lawlessness in the name ofl freedom is, in fact, a reaching back into barbarism, to ancient times of neo-law, pre-Magna Carta, when offenses in Western cultures were almost always resolved on the battlefield. Liberty to debate, affirm, compromise and accept slowly replaced combat as a means to resolving disputes and defeat with the sword. Yet the ideal is still unaccomplished, as is evidenced largely by criminal recidivism rates, the failures of the United Nations., wars of the 20th century and the Cold War.

When free choice that leads to an immoral act, that is a crime or even an intention by the criminal to act immorally, his crime expunges his liberty at the instant that the knife plunges into his vicim or the gun fires killing his enemy. Insfead of being at liberty any longer, he has entered the way of anarchy that all criminals experience when they kill or they plunder or they defraud in high places, e.g. presidential obstructions of justice. Mere transitory rebellion found in political resistance of marches and street demonstrations is not identical with the violent anarchy of riots and pathology of anti-social violence against authority.

The self-will which produces such latter anarchy of action has instantaneously desroyed he criminars liberty of action. As a consequence, it is an irrational judgement and an immoral disgrace to betow upon the criminal act the vapid censure of liberty "abused," to call a crime a "mistake of judgement," a murder a" human folly," the victim of a crime a *tragic* character. For the crime is rarely retroactive to the conscious moment of conception in the criminal mind. The naked violence of a television murder is hardly ever implicated in the real crime of hatred awaiting its chance to be acted out. The act begins with the idea and is inspaable fom it. The retroaction occurs in the eyes of a sovereign God, whilest the intention walks the dark path toward anarchy where no restraining law existed in the criminal's mind. In brief, liberty to chose and criminal violence are antithetical before the crime; the latter expunges the former.

The corrolary to the criminal act is the harm to society that occurs when the deed is glamorized or made to seem desireable and worthy of emulation. Television has glamorized the ugliness of raw murder, especially in the eyes of the young. Every heinous crime bears within its schemata certain options, or alternatives, of action that are moral choices, *everruled,* that are therefore the poison of anarchy. For this reason it is an irrationall irony to refer to the *law of the gun* or the *code of violent victory* or the *statutes of a criminal's rights.* These contradictions betray man's inability to cope with evil, with sin, with barbarous wrong-doing on his own without the intervention of a higher Power than the threat of law-enforcement and penalty for the crime. True prison reform must forever remain humanistic without God.

Peronal liberty is a "bargining chip" in the sense that its enligtened possessor can—if he choses to do so—and his is a moral choice—trade it for bondage of a prison, for harm to self or to society, or for suicide. Surely, however, once extinguished by a major crime, liberty to chose one's lifestyle it is gone forever and can never be recovered but can only be petitioned for anew by the cleansing power of repentance and forgiveness and the serving of sentence. Unless tlhe former takes place, the latter is of nominal effect on the criminal, therefore we have recidivism by the crimianl. That personal liberty with its accountability is, therefore, the citizen's most priceless possession because from it flow all the good things in a man's life, or his pain and his death. Amderica ill fall prey to demagogues ie fwe do not discriminate liberty from anarchy. Indeed, that His more important to our survival as a free ntion than are curicula in the sciences, math and technology.

Immorality is the way of the lost since they have abandoned the self-reproofs of a conscionable liberty.

To insist upon what is "correct" in politics, in society, in education is to make fashionable lhe predelections of those in seats of power and their followers. When enforced, that "correctness" constitutes tyranny.

Consider conscience the access to liberty and you honor God, its source. Consider it free of obligation and commitment and you honor the merciless one. Grace is mercy.

The will to survive is a compact with God, the supreme provider of liberty while, without Him, one remains in chains. The dictates of conscience presuppose absolutes of right and wrong which expunge the relativisms of moral choices.

10. THE MORALITY OF CIVIC AUTHORITY: PROTECTIVE ARMS

In a free socliety civil authority contrasts with military authority. It is vulnerable and incomplete without a regulated police and militia that employ not only guns but political power—with the availability of the first and the presence of the second—to protect the people; and to protect the peopled liberties under the law of statutes, case precedents and common laws, in brief, *stare decisis.* They are, among others,s the freedom of peaceable assembly, the liberty to speak one's convictions in a public forum, and the sacred protection for synagogues, churches and mosques, and their faithful who rightfully worlhsip a higher authority, fearing neither vandals, terrorists nor soldiers.

In the supporting ranks of these protective cordons are the uniformed forces bearing arms—the militia. Before them in the front lines of defense are the police, the sheriffs and other law-enforcement officers. The elected judges as a third cadre sit under the parabola of a benign moral authority, the laws and ordinances that govern a people.

In these times a strong police presence signifies an anarchistic mindset in American society, flaunted by those who are continuallhy agitated into anger and rebellion by special interest cliques against the "status quo," by an elitist media and strident barkers for special causes. Neighborhood malls, schools and streets are places for the violent-prone malcontents to ravage the law-abiding citizens, claiming to symbolize by violence their objectives with the "puniest of motives." For examples: there is the boobytrap placed in tree bark to discourage a timber harvest; there is the deliberate freeing of dozens of Rhesus moneys used in experiments in the name of animal "rights." there is the shutdown of a farmer and threatened confiscation of his land because he killed a kangaroo rat by accident; there is the closure of homestead lands to the generational owners because a cureaucrat declares them to be *wetlands;* indeed,s there is the seizure of property by *eminent domain* because the land's lnew owners promise a higher local income as his reward. Our Marxist Supreme Cour has just recently made his sort of illegal seizure possible with bad law. There are many more of these covert gestures of environmental protectionism and economic gain in the name of freedom.

Following the above entities of authority, the environmentalists, the save the forest advocates, the local officials, mayor and and his in-the-pocket Council, then come the courts of justice. They can be decapitated by the subversion, the intimidation and bald-faced lies if ever the military regime takes control. Soviet courts were pupppets of the Commintern. Colonial justice in America was meted out secretly by England by the king's Star Chamber, a secret court, one of the causes of the American Revolution. Under the despotic control of evil author-ity—that is to say, a-moral if not immoral, which has nothing to do with God's ordinance of obedience to His government, source of Dieism, and since the State is therefore is God-less, the people willingly transfer their police powers and pro-tective agencies, including the military, to the new godhead of power, a charis-matic dicatorial leader. A coalition of politico-military forces often follows that erect a facade of benevolence to appease public fear and suspicion. This is being done today in the cause of anti-terrosism protection.

The "common defense" provided by the Constitution, Article I, Section 9, whould not act to extinguish dd laws of civil liberty, found in the Madison's Bill of Rights-the very reason for thier addition to the Laws of the Three Branches, the government of the people's freedom. Article II, Section 2, gives the Executive authority over the military'the law is explicit in this regard of limitation. Execu-tive Military authority is an incipient power, which war calls forth in the form of conscription, and that controls the executive decisions, war policy and anti-sub-versive restaints and threats of terrorism. The tension between civil and mitlitary authority is most unnoticeable in peace time. America's aversion to war and her people's fear of a mililitary dictatorship have given the elected President chief command and control of her uniform defenders under Article II, Secction 2. "The President shall be Commander in Chief of the Army and the Navcy of thellnited States, and of the Militia of tlhe several States, when called intos the actual Service of the United States …" This authority limits his military actions while in office. He cannot order the forces of the rest of the world…. not does he possess the power, lawfully, to suspend civil liberties explicit in the Bill of Rights. That suspension is not _inherent_ in his Executive authority.

Until the 1980's the Congress had to issue a formal declartion of war, as a domstic strategy as well as an historical and Constitutional dictum. Thereafter, war became a peace-keeping and police action, pusuant to which no declartion needed to follow hostilities … or so some strict constructionist minds assumed. Congress was simply the provider, extemnporaneously, of money to fund troop occupation and any intervention conflicts. The second branch of American government became a mere sentry in the defense of the American people but a sentry extenbded world-wide.

It followed that in troubled times there arose, with few objections from the "silent majority," those zealots who tried to undermine our confidence in our leaders and to expose the voice of moral conscience as an expression of religious right-wing coercion, moarlity, and of a fanatical fundamentalist conspiracy. Indeed, there was and is a strength in the moral conviction of a people, howeever, their sinecure is by tradition and *natural law,* both equitable and God given—Americans' "inalienable rights" are vested in the Fundamental Law of the country.

The "common defense," a moral and good prescription, contains two serious weaknesses that reverberate among the ranks of the police nation-wide: (1) the people are the source of police power; God supervenes, therefore justice and force have their basis not in man's schemes but in God's sovereignty. At least that was so in 1789. When the process reverses, society becomes immoral and justice breaks down. (2) A nation cannot sustainl a system of justice that is irrelevant to its values, therefore, today the rootless one-worlders are rewriting American hstory in which history becomes increasingly meaningless to contemporary Americans and less and less acceptable and true before our new-world role of glo-bal oneness. We are taking on the aura and appearances of a subitutionary world Messiah, for whom **liberty,** as a construct of citizen choices under law is turning into mere cant. Expediency and legalese will replace it before the fear of terror by night and world economic collapse by day.

The justice of military force directs the results it produces, which are peace and civic harmony—providing that that force is constituted under law. Under the protectionism of liberty, the pacifist assumes the role of self-exile and ought to be so treated in time of war. Ordinailry, the military forces and the people shield a nation from physical harm and protect the survival of liberty, irrespective of religious beliefs. It is one of war's anomalies that a people look then to God more often than they do to Him during peace times. Here in America the law accommodates war's conscioutious objector who in his integrity clings to his moral conviction that "thoul shalt not kill." The law dos not accommodate trea-son for the cogent reason that although the Nation may be wrong, citizenship demands loyalty and that, if for no other purpose, than to protect its innocents. Sedition is the defiance against the constituted government of all Americans.

The protectionist responsibility by a people of their own members cannot be transferred by political-moral fiat of one man against another nation. He does not become by any situation of circumstances or dictate of our laws the protector of foreign nationals. Rights given to illegal aliens are therefore unconstitutional, since they imply a consangunity with those enjoyed by our citizens. Nor can that duty to his own countlry, whatever the cause, be expunged by charlatans, liberals, or timorous conservatives or amblitionus foreign leaders; nor can that same duty be masked by political expediency. An undeclarered war for these exra-national purposes as transfigurations of Americas global interests, is a fraud against the people of this country that cannot be amended or rectfied by a Presidential dictatorial Execuve Order.

The President has the power to negotiate treaties but **only** with "the advice and consent of the Senate. (Article II, Section 2—paragraph ii). The President does not have the power to write an executive order placing the American people at risk, militarily or a supra-treaty under his authority; for his action then becomes "misconduct" while in office. Nor is he empowered by any *inherrent* war-power to silence debate and declare hiself the repository of the trust of 280 million people, outside Article II provisions which restrict his powers. Hitler applied a similar device in 1933, by appealing to the German people's dissatisfaction with the Versailles Treaty reparations.

In war force becomes the law of the jungle to protect den and lair. The presence of a strong defense ought to be a warning to the Nation's enemies and nothing more. A warning does not occupy the status of a threat. Protecion is moral and no man is at liberty to set the law aside for himself or for any of his countrymen through blockades and disuptive riots of dissent, or through wicked civil conflicts designed either to prolong or to end hostilities. It is incumbent, morever, upon our nation's leaders that they be morally circumspect in their conduct and honest in their words to the people, parltisanship notwithstanding. No mask of sobriety, charisma, ostensible performance of mandated duties can conceal the taint of moral turptitude. A President is not the designer of fashionable morals to promote correct worship; he is the image to be emulated. The power of his office compounds any act or thesis of revelation of moral corruption. If a people are unrighteous, how can they forgive one of their own kind? They but amplify and consecrate his wrongful acts. He puts a curse upon the nation and his high office. So, too, is it with the traitor, his negotiations with the enemy put a curse upon liberty and jeopardize the lives of millions of Amerlican citizens. A leader's oaths of office is the mandate of the law and not of the man, himself, nor of the words of the Chief Justice who administers it.

A nation's weaponry obviously is intended either to protect the people or to attack their enemiels. The parade of naked power is most often the weapoinry of a hostile and dangerous adversary. To brandish the sword for the purpose of bringing about or insuring liberties is a risky undertaking—as the Civil War proved—because it implied that liberty did not exist for all men as a sacred trust after our Revolution, and that the results of bloodshed would exact wanted, though missing, liberties. On the other hand, force at botton is evil where it envisions no moral replacement, no liberty other than what already exists, no future yearning for the perpetuity of freedom. Visible evil proves the lawlessness of coercive conformity which nowadays is called "political correctness."

We have with us copious proofs of the truth of that proposition. The rule of the gun has taken over neighhoods and housing developments, the poisonous fruit of a contagious cynicism, the entrapments of poverty, the alienation with kin the family that stunts child rearing. The rule of the gun has threatened learning and education. "Politiclal correctness" is a substitution for the gun. The rule of the gun vandalizes houses of worlship. The rule of the gun terrorizes citizens and obstructs freedom of movement. The rule of the gun glamorizes the behavior of hoodlums and graffitti signing young punks. The rule of the gun speaks falsely for race hatred. The rule of the un denies that liberty is the best course for civil respect and commuity peace.

In the breech of its duty to defend the people, the State invents slogans as propaganda to blind the people to the truth and exculpate their consciences for the "cause" of their evil plundering, not the least of which is the corrupt plundering by policicians of the peoples' ethical and moral integrity by bad laws. The most recent of these pernicious invocations of injustice is the High Court's supoort for the seizure of private property for another's use by eminent domain. Abortion, atheism enforced in schools, socialist enforcement of health care against corporations, the abuse of traditional parenting by a mother and father, and replacement of judeo-Christian faith by "correct"silence—are others of the same ilk.

Race riots were and are bad; we must understand why. The hue and cry of "racism" is a cop-out of reason. Riots by ordinary peoiple tend to convert pleas of injustice into instruments of evil. Propaganda will thereupon proclaim wicked half-truths of the vicious ones and declare as "righteous" the flamatory actions of the "innoent" prostors against the genocide of class warfare. Yet, whenever the State refuses to condemn the anarchist as against the "conformist" or slthe"traditionalist," it uses these hostile circumstances to oppress the non-participant protestors into the abject conformity of ideological slaves., Radical Islam fundamentalists are of lhis class. The Marxists, to name another, would compel uniformity of belief to achieve their ends, thus we have with us today the pernicious mind-set of a **conformity** that fosters only mediocrity of action, thought and accomplishment.

If he, the protestor, does not conform in a politically correct manner, the State mandate for education, for environment protection, for choice of life style, compels social ostracism. For he has rejected those presumptions of infallible truth which lthe State deems best for the people. His derelictions will destroy him, will bankrupt him socially and perhaps economically and inevitably, morally. That is the state of nations today. By its insistence on political (i.e) Marxist conformity, Statist government will destroy our librties of association, of petition for redress of grievances—they're a matter of opinion—fmoral choices in life, indeed, of intrepreneurship. The baker who does not bake the hoe-muffins of Federal regulation with full coverage insurance fo his apprentice, can be dlriven out of business; and that has been done far too often, as Chapter 11 statustics will reveal. Many new businesses fail because of over-regulation. There protest is driven underground.

The primieval monster of an oppressie central government quenches protest. Thus, the assumption of street rioters, whatever the root cause ... labor grievance, radial tension, etc—is that America is an oppressive if not despotic, and needs therefore to be regulated by a messianic system of government. Political radicals and *religious jihad* fanatics would agree on lthis. A politically correct silence imposed y the State, though deemed unconscionab by the ablest leaders, if we are to survive as free, is rarely ever the people's admission of corruptive guilt. For if the people are a righteous people before God and believe in Him and His truths, they cannot mock the heritage of their liberties, regardless of transitory laws of wicked men, such laws as legitimize homosexuality, abortion, pedophelia, ethanasia, no fault-divorce, doctor-assisted suicide and generational welfare.

When the State attempts to preempt the conscience of 290 million of its speople by such auth oritarian laws, persuading them through a liberal press that they are incapable of living their lives without Federalist help, Statist largesse is, in effect, purchases the souls of the people and makes of them willing recipients of paternal care and carriers of the deadly virus of defeatism. The condition of America has ever been thus for the past fifty to sixty years, during which time war, alone, and Regonomics have given some respite from that malaise. Without a higher authoity, that is to say, the Judeo-Christian God as Soveresign Mind, Americans have lost much of their original moral fire and stamina of resistance to evil. Holllywood before WE II was not the Hollywood of today. It is for the retention of these two qualities that the World War II generation was so outstanding. It is for the absence of these two qualities that an increasingly centralized Statist government n Washington has usurped authority, spiritual, social land practical over men's lives in America. Who alive ever remembers God's divine providence?

Any liberty, as of contract and ownership, that is imposed and enforced by the gun or is, instead, enforced by threat of lawful extermination of one's property ownership by declaring it in the public doman, is an illusory liberty. The rights of contract are now hedged about by Federal regulations. Harsh penalties of dispossession, let us say, in the name of environment protection, of tax yield, of developer's profit are imposed upon citizens who refuse to yield to the corrupt bureaucratic seizure of land and ownership rights of the land-owner. This wicked defilement of the land under the gnoses of "protection", of "revenue" has become popular among environmental groups and development contractors and, of course, greedy, corrupt public officials

There is an irony in the specious liberty of conformity which is that in time those who own not just land but other property as well can be brought around to believe that the rest of the nation lives in hunger, insecurity and a similar threat of loss by seizure through eminent domain. The tireless shibboleth of this transition from a risk-taking capitalist entrepreneur society to a plebian-artisan submissive society is the mantra of "the working family." The liberals in Congress and our Marxist court would subvert the middle class as greedy and exploitive when in reality it is the Federal Government that fits that description.

The working-class family has become an mantra-class, as compared to the owning-class capitalist family. That is the evil's cunning. For it tends to create self-pity and dependence upon government instead of upon a spirit of optimism and ingenuous planning that are consistent with Yankee America's history. By this devious route the fashionable New State projected y power-seekers produces, with the help of the liberal media, a manufactured popular will that would criminalize whole industries. The pharmaceutical industruy, for one, has undergone those crimlinalizing charges. The tobacco industry and fast-foods industries are two others. By this devious route the fashionable new "correct" State thrives in America. The conservative reluctance to buy into the popular will only outrages the liberals, those defenders of popular lies of their eternal caring for the masses, read "working families," socialist "working masses." Truly it is a Socialist distraction and an intellectual fallalcy that our system of great enterprise, beneficial to the entire world, must be corrupted, that is, destroyed, in order to achieve social progess. But first, criminal politicians must subvert the family through controlled education and emasculate the Constituion by a careful excision of its threatening (to them) parts.

Rebels bent upon forcing their views to prevail in Congress and in the public consciousness have at their disposal sophisticated ecrtonic gear andd crude devices of surveillance not the least of which are epunitive tax audits and yellow journalism defamation—candidate background checks for public sonsumption. Until recently the wire tap _with_ a warrant was directed toward the known ciminal, today it is often warrantless and directed toward the known terrorist under the banner of war 1 good man needs only to run for a high profile public office to incur the ever-popular wrath of the liberal media pillory. By such signular means can a nation be reduced to mediocrity of achievement and of vision. If ever this should occur, and it is happensing nowadays, the power shifts fom moral and ethical standards, traditional values of a once great nation, to the zealotrty and demagogic persuasion of corrupt politcians whose will is to remain in office and for whom the media, as their mouthpiece, give voice to liberous statements and subrle ridicule. Every clandidate for an office brings with him a past; it is the duty of the liberal media to smear the candidate with that past, as if they themselvlves were pristine pure and clean of all fault. When the media speak with one voice, we have lost the "free spress" that Jefferson envisoned as protector of a "free country."

There are certain rights in a free society the denial of which brings about justifiable rebellion. They are rights writlten into the Constitution, protective of the people against a sovereignty of power. The liberty to express one's self freely is just such a right, though anarchistic formulations occur when leaders resort to symbols of violence, i.e. dispersal of American troops around the world—and to imoral displays of willful defiance of the law, i.e. Executive perjury before a Federal judge,

Powrful lobbies in Washington resort to semantic manipulation and ideological obfuscation to put their messages across to the skillful doubter and to the illiterate. These prospagandistic instruments of mind manipulation tend to polarize resistance to Big Goviernment no matter how justifiable the ends sought. There is in the American psyche an inherent distrust of Big Government; we as Americans can never escape our unconscious history. And so long as the citizen of this great nation lives in a society with other men and his conscience and his exercise of common rights as he choses, he can never be crushed under a plethora of trivial bureaucratic excuses in the name of the "comlmon good." Good is not made common by Government fiat or by Executive order and bureaucratic permission.

God is made good by common consent of the citizenry which the bureaucracy cannot manufacture. That is the real rubicon of change in America.

Trust only honorable men with your lives when free. Any others may dishonor your integrity.

A liberated conscience ie. liberty to make a moral choice, is not the glft of the Government any more than is the gift of life, but America's plutocracy has appropriated both and claims their genesis. Funda= mentalism is under fire, *ad hoc.*

Leaders who squander a people's money are apostles of Mammon and followers of Molech. Their liberty is without conscience and is, therefore, evil. Some will call it "wrong" to in-tellectualize the immorality of evil.

It is an endangerment to the moral healths of a people when they allow perverse passisons to control the offices of authsority and law. The expanison of laws of privacy opens the door lto all kinds of perverse acts. Conscience is travestied by legalized wrong.

11. FREEDOM AND LIBERTY COMPARED

Anarchy and liberty cannot be compared as political likenesses. We have already discused the law of the gun under a code of violence, buried within statues on "criminal rights," as, citizenship rights revoked, torture or any forms of cruelty to the prisoner, visitation rights, right to legal counsel. "Criminal rights" appears to be an oxymoron that conceals from naive eyes the nature of a man's willful anarchy against society, So, too, are freedom and liberty disparate concepts; the first does not foster either moral conduct or rational thought, or, indeed, social responsibility. Freedom *to, by, for, because of* unfettered mobility are adverbs that are attributable to anarchy, whlich imposes no adverbial condition and therefore no causality except irrational rebellion. Thus, a man who commits murder, commutation notwithstanding, does not "repay his debt to society" with his punihment, as is commonly thought, for his freedom is to think and to act cannot be absoluterly ordered by any Court of law. They can only be confined and directed by force. Only a religious conversion can affect a genuine change of heart for belief in God invades the criminal mind and soul to alter them permanently. The end of Dostoievsky's great novel supposes that change in Raskolnikov, the hatchet muderer of the old pawnbroker.

Only liberty as conscionable conduct is ordered by law and, therefore, the prisoner murderer, for example, owed pennance not to society in general but to the source of all equity in law, that is, to God. Freedom must, therefore, be defined so as to insure that it is understood by men as not the absence of imprisonment or detention by chains, as for the beast. Instead, freedom consists in an historical separation of an entire society from a despotic government. Our prisoner-murderer's abuse of freedom being irreconcileable with Constitutional liberty, proves our point. His freedom to kill was not an act of First Amendment freedom, read *liberty*, of expression, though the Supreme court has adopted that view in the matter of privacy in Roe v Wade. The Courts's protection of a woman's private right to chose is, in effect, the protection of conscience. Therefore, the Court in the 1973 case was at liberty to decide whether Roe's conscionable *choice* was right or wrong, not whether she should be denied the right. The decision as to whether her choice was morally right or wrong then rests on the determination as to the value of the aborted child, if not to its mother, then to society in general. The Court det4ermined that the value of the choice superceded the value of the unborn human being.

Liberty is, therefore, not simply unlawfully used, in the above instance of murder. Liberty is expunged within the parameters of the criminal act, forever. The voice of society, represented by the Govenor or the President or the Court can never properly forgive the criminal for his act, amnesty or commutation notwithstanding. A society offended so grievously is forever changed and can never return to its former state of "innocence" before the crime was committed, just as a tree will always show wind-damage to its trunk. The corruption within a sate and the gradual weakening of a people's moral strength, their wisdom and capacity to resist evil, reflect their tolerance on a case by case basis, person by person as a test of the moral purity or moral corruption of its citizens. In other words, crime levels indicate the moral level of civil law as practiced by that society, and its congeniality with moral behavior and attitudes. What crimes, conditions, practices a people will tolerate, in the name of *fairness,* identify its moral health or sickness. "Fair and balanced" identify the state of that moral health, an exercilse in accommodation and tolerance, yet that tolerance eschews absolutes that infringe upon personal choice. That doctrine of *balanced and fair* accounts for the position's popular appeal.

There is, further, an evil mandate that irreparably attaches the affinity of needs to society—first to death as against life; then to hatred and fear as against compassion and the common civility that accompany liberty, e.g. the emerence of "hate crlimes." As for the last, a *hate crime* is an illusion. Hate cannot be charged as a crime until the act occurs, which then, whether out of love or hatred, the murder is a murder, the attitude an unchargeable state of mind, a command for political correctness. The crime of murder per *se* is thus mimimized and hatred is rised to the status of a politically *incorrect* curse.

A pervasive dishonesty of the intellect has pretty much destroyed the earlier sealing of a contract with a handshake, lawyers proliferate in America because of the immoral conduct of her people. A free society, having greater liberty for acts of moral depravity, has a greater opportunity to destroy itself by the distrust and greed of its citizens. With each outrage against society's innocents, that society, ignorant of its liberties under law, moves in the direction of bondage to evil and its demand for oppressive government controls. A free people cannot escape the bondage to evil, its many disguises, when they permit themselves to be protected beyond the law and their native daring. With each outrage against society's "innocence"—today is it pedophelia and child pornography—that society, ignorant of its liberties under the law, moves toward the apathy of dependency on Federal power to resolve matters of conscience, thereby depricating by their innaction their police power to control the evil incursion. They appear often to be oblivious to the power that rests in their hanfds.

The right to life is fundametal to the survival of a nation, the which right includes the life of the unborn. Shared by all, this right empowers a people, within their liberty of moral choice, most often a first Amendment option, to take the life of the criminal if the penitence is not expressed by the condemned man or woman,. A moral society is not obligated to prove its righnteousness before God—or indeed its righteousness before men—by undertaking to cure or to improve upon or to "restore" the criminal to society by reforming him. It is the punishment for the crme and not the mitigation of the sentence that insures the survival of a free society. Young law student Raskolnikov in Dostoievsky's *Crime and Punishment* was brought to face this truth: that the greatness of his idol Napoleon neither raises the murderer above the law nor imputes to him a rightoeusness society can never possess. The punishment can neither restore him to innocence nor society to its former moral strength. The more crimes that go unredressed before God and the public, the weaker, morally, that that society becomes.

A free people have not convenanted with the courts to ignore or to forgive or to overlook a crime. Should this happen often enough, a society will, over time, collapse of its own politco-judicial corruption and its shared depraviy. The just have a duty to rebuke the unjust and to attack evil whateer brand sociey may put on him.

Internal covenants with evil—ambition, greed, power, not their symptoms of bankrupcy and troop disperson for greedy land-control, brought down the ancient Roman Empire.

The poisons of idolatry and the love of luxury destroyed the Medo-Persian Empire.

The corruption of the family through sexual immorality in ancient Greece resulted in the fall of the Grecian States. Slavery, a corrupt institution, was also involved in its fall.

The Babylonian Empire and Nebuchadnezzar's worship of idols of luxury, his boastful mind and pride, and blatant rejection of God and enslavement of the Jews led to his empire's collapse.

Alexander the Great's Realm fell prey to his military ambition and Emperorship pride. Also, I believe, the Huns defeated him in battle

Hitler's Thousand Year Reich was destoyed by his evil murder of six million Jews, the cruelty bred into his Nazi hordes and his insane battle strategy that ignited the vengeance of the free world. The Brutal reparations after WWI were only the politically-correct alibi. He mustered Aryan pride to his cause and failed—as kingdoms, empires and realms have failed theretofore for the same reason: ambition to conquer and enslave.

Rational justice … is there any other kind? Is the justice of retribution reversable? Justice, the truths of justice are not to be found in Mankind's omnibus laws, although the United Nations would have America think otherwise. Our own Constitution is thought to mirror the laws of God, that His grand design for mankind and the true equity in His laws that can be found in His commands and ordinances. Our Founders, many of them Deists and Protestants, carefully considered God's Providential power when they argued and wrote America's fundamental law of the land. Every word counts. There is nothing capricious in the Constitution. Its Founders knew their own weaknesses. Theys relied heavily upon 18th centsury Enlightenment reason. These considerations are for another time.

It is enough to say here that in America the feedom to worship, by God-given conscience, was founded on natural laws that were, and are, productive of the "inalientlable rights" of our Declartion of Independence. It was not intended to be thought of as worlship to pray or mention God's name in a public forums. Yet if faith is confined in its visible manifestations to churches and synagogus, then the edifice only is honored and the faith practiced therein is dead faith and we deny our ancestry and heritage. Freedom of worlhsip: that is the exercise of liberty of conscience and of other freedoms, such as liberty of speech, movement and association, can, however, become a snare and an absurdity if the public, *viz a viz* the liberal court, mandates that the particular right, given order, voice and expression, must be practiced in the privacy of isolation from the larger society. Here again we encounter the right to privacy, but the right has been enforced. Private religious practices are not the issue, oral expressions of faith in public are. A State that enforces exclusivity of its pagan faith is a closed system and is anathema to liberty.

As soon as freedom becomes rigidly structured and circumscribed by social opinion, it becomes despotic and requires a necessary enforcement by a depotic power fuctioning allegedly for majorlity opinion—in our time by the *gerus* of ethnic diversity, usually embedded in the liberal media and on college campuses, professors who have delegated unto themselves the power of Enforcers, the thought police of Orwell's 1984. Clearly, our freedom of religion as a people, articulated in our *Declaration of Independence* and in our Constitutional liberties, must represent neither bondage to the saints nor redemption for the law-breaking criminal. Prayer in a public forum is not intended to be offensive or inoffensive. Yet if it represents the consensual will—as opoosed to a quasi-governmental agency like the ACLU—it should be tolerated.

Liberty must always carry with it the expectation that where it governs conduct, the word has content-meaning and is without specificity of application or imposed conditions. For their part, the beast, the parolee, the anarchist all have "freedom." This reasoning is not specious if one considers that liberty infers purpose while freedom does not; and that purpose is either moral or immoral. Should we make the distinction between freedom and liberty irrelevant to contemporary America, the idea is nonetheless defensible that although the two concepts are similar in laying prior conditions, freedom is a cutting of the controlling social bonds, as in anarchy; whilest liberty, on the other hand, is the apt and imminent installation of informed knowledge and law that were *held in check* or prohibited to it—an action, a voice, an expression, a design, that is not tendered by freedom and is spurious, if you will, in most forms of social anarchy.

One may have the liberty to disobey the law, yet that liberty is charged with responsibility toward others, hence the punishment for its violation. To assert that one has the freedom to break lthe law is not only is flamatory; the assertion lacks all sense of accountability and therein does it reflect its true likeness to anarchy.

Had he spoken as a self-exile or as an irresponsible member of the Richmond township, or, indeed, as a dying man or a lame duck in the office of Burgess, Patrick Henry's famous words "I know not what course others may take but as for me give me liberty or give me death!"—would have rung out as sedition or malfeasance or ill-will agains his own people. Why did they not? The time was 1775, the place was St. John's church, the largest room in Richmond, Virginia for a town meeting. The people could have assumed that his words conveyed not the wisdom, power and purpose of the Revolutionary word _Liberty_, when he would thereupon summon the militia to oppose George III, reminding the delegates of the morality of their noble cause. But they did not presuppose evil in tlhe heart of the speaker and, being well-informed by the Letters of Correspondence between the Colonies and by word-of-mouth and by pesonal afflliction and pain of loss, they responded to the speech with great hope and determination. Had today's liberal, obfuscating press-corps been there at the church, they would in all likelihood have condemned Henry's words as the persiflage of a selfish diatribe against the Crown. Henry's speech was deliberately none of these. They would have challenged Henry's use of the word "liberty" to show—a self-serving political ambition and then examined the cases he lost at bar, most particularly, why he lost them. Was he a slaver with an agenda …?

> **Thought control is never far distant from liberty of thought and conscience. They run concurrently for the office of a people's government and of a man's behavior in good times and bad.**

> **Let nobody rob you of your personal liberty to decide between right and wrong, whether or not you can put the decision into action. For all are born with this capacity of mind, the conscience. Even when removed it leaves scar tissue.**

> **Let no man stand trial for doing a good deed for another hapless human being. A jealous society will mask the Samaritan act in its own eyes as a litigious happening.**

> **Even wicked men acknowledge the conscience in their attempts to eradicate the good in others and to deny the moral imperatives of right and wrong.**

12. INTEGRITY LAND LIBERTY

The deliberate violation of secular laws that protect one person from harm by another is not an exercise in liberty. A crilminal usually tries to justify his crime, and he almost always rebels at his punishment, Prison riots erupt from time to time as symbols of the anarchy brewing inside the walls by which the prisoners would destroy the entire justice system in effigy, burning mattresses, making hostages of jailors and issuing political demands in order to destroy the truth of just retribution and relieve their frustration by violence.

Lenient judges, moreover, have reduced the seriousness of crime to the status of a correctable attitude, this in the face of the fact that the abuse of liberty shown by certain convicts under prison circumstances replicates the criminality of their actions against society outside. Such judges honor the trivial or the fraudulent plea by assigning to it the status of "fair play," "plaintiffs opinion" and the like, forms of intellectual dishonesty on the part of lthe judges, who are *liberal* when theyl do so. Ironically, convicts rebel against the very laws that insure the continuation of the liberty they will enjoy when freed, or when they hope to be freed Liberty of association is one such "pass." Their symbolic destruction almost always fails in its purpose. There exists in th prison society the element of wiltchcraft by which an inmate symbolically recreates in another inmate the countenance of his real victim for the crime against whom he is tried and sentenced—like sticking pins into a symolic doll.

The guilt of a felon is servant to the violation of his liberty, which ought never to be presumed severable but only suspended as the locus of "inalienable" rights while he serves his sentence. The subversion of liberty is a part of contemporary American philosophy, a consensual abdication of moral absolutes, the alternative to which is political correctness, or morality by feelings, by political approval and acceptance socially. Situation ethics, for example, depends not on free choice but on social acceptance as right. Where is the liberty in that paradgm? Also, Liberty is viewed as utilitarian—useful in some situations, but not in others—as in prison. This sutilitarian perspective on morality is simply the old "situation elthocs" warmed over again. Felons sare serving time because society prompted them to break the law. This attitude carries over into the young generation in our schools, kids blaming the teacher for inciting them to misbehave, one of the causes of which is the malfunction of Principal responsibility to confront both the kid and his or her parents. But, woefully, such is never—or only rarely—the case, the teacher herself having to perform this onerous duty.

With the rse in crime and the lassitude of society toward crliminal sentencing and parole leniency, we as a people have begun to question the "utility" of liberty itself. Do we need more police surveillance? Lierty is not, however, utilitarian; it does not fuanction to perform moral acts, such as to set the felon free on the argumentl that he used his liberty unwisely and *deserves* another chance; or that he was *unfairly*—a favorite word—condemned by the jurors or the court because of race, gender, enculturation (ethnicity) or plain bad publicity. Liberty does ot seeks its justification in situations or circumstances that require moral judgement. Conscience under the aegis of liberty performs that service whilest duty as it is evinced by jurors and judge alike, reflect an limperfect judicial system.

The crlminal does not say of liberty that it caused him to chose vadly. Often, however, this is the nature of the indictment that the very liberty under which the criminal, and we ourselves, make choices of right and wrong is nowadays held in disrepute, with the result that average peoplr are constantly and in ever greater numbers running to lthe State for moral direction and official justification of their private and social behavior. The CODA statute, intended for mobsters but directed toward abortion protestors, is one such law. Law suits against companies and corporations for the follies and bad choices of customer-buyers proves this point. There is a *jihad* today against the makers of fattening foods! Such folk solicit State guidelines on how to avoid diseases of promiscuity, how to structure intimate and family relationships for tax purpoes; what methodology children ouhtt to be taught to enable them to make useful (amoral) decisions; or how to mend the shambles of a bad marriage by tax considerations or impossivle apologies. Poll statistics are used to reinforce this amoral advice. In doing these things—looking to the State for moral guidance—the people have appointed the State, a political engine, to be their amoral guide, their alter-conscience, because they have forgotten—or never learned in childhood—that their heritage of liberty is a protector and effectualizer of conscionable human conduct. From a risk-taking society driven by the liverty to exploit opportnity, we have become agenda-driven, motivated by social approval or rebuff or derision for choices that are our responsibility. Political correctness is replacing responsible-moral—risk-taking.

Where men most often discard as and absolute standard of conduclt, that is, a principle of right over wrong, they will often expect to be justified by the secular humanist's creed, which states that all men are naturlly good and it is *society's fault* that they turned out badly. The substitution of *correction* for *retribution* tends to turn justice into a kind of sentimental program of social forgiveness and disapproval that needs but wiping the hands to resolve the wrong, thereby making justice a farce to the "criminal mind." The substitution of personal opinion for absolute values is the attempt to convert a bad conscience into the slave of egoism. A blurrisng of the line between a felony and a misdemelanor has taken hold in American jurisprudence. Already *intent* has become irrelevant to the reality of the crime in liberal courts that trivialiae moral choice and therefore the onerus of guilt. Crlminals are thus freed on a technicality, or the jurors render a politically correnct verdict to avoid the charge of racism. For the sake of beilng poliically correct by according high seriousness to trivial cases, judges more and more are reflxsisng to throw out cases that are trivial for fear of offending the ethnic appellant by their doing so. Afcter all, absolute values belong to the past whose anachronisms somehow get in the way of the happiness cult.

There is an inconsistency that thrives among us in these times. We find certain Congressmen resorting not to alibis that affirm their accountability to the American people as the people's Representatives, alibis such as: "I was dishonest," or "I did some inappropriate things," or "I broke my promise to the Amerilcan people and I am sorry." Miscreant Congressmen, for the sake of their careers, surely do not wish to incrimiante themelves by their mistakes in judgement and their moral lapses. Instead they appeal to the standard of "fair play for fair gains." Yet in due course, the resort to fairness-appeal discharges the sovereignty of liberty, of constitutional-correctness imputed to integrlity, as mere gainsay. Gainsaying liberty of conduct while an incumbent pleads innocence plays upon lthe ignorance of the electorate even while the offender places himself above the law. He then makes himelf vulnerable to bribes.

Congressional cheating by words and theft by deeds is more than a plain scandal: it is blatantly unethical for the people to have to endure this pretense to restiution. Moreover, implict in this rejection of punishment is an invitation to abet lawlessness by silence. To describe such conduct simplistically as *unethical* destroys by suspicion many of the legal attachments and human resolves of a Representative body working in concert for the good of the people. Congressional dishonesty thereupon weakens the moral fibre of the "goodness," if you will, of America. She beomes increasingly wicked by virtue of the multiple dishonesties of her Representatives, initiated by the Congress and condoned by the people's silence. Secret Executive deals tend to avoid that embrrasment.

Honesty as a consistent absolute value, which should be taught by parents, gives a moral and connotative value to liberty. Liberty is not a variable, a specious and axiomatic word which the utilitarian argument attempts to justify.

The State and pro-anarchist Educators, would remove from the curriculum any consideration of morality in history, civics and sociology. They achieve this alehemy by dulling the conscience of the student to discern moral conduct evident in historical events of the past and in relationships of the present. Those same intellectuals would attempt to disenfranchise an entire generaion in order to increase their political power.

This is the direction of the secular humanist who would have the children be so totally self-sufficient as juveniles, yet without resonsibilties, that they dont need their parents but they do need the State. Hitler planned that kind of indoctrination of Germany's youlth from the 1930s on, inculcating into young Aryan minds the utilitarian ethic of power, to wit, that power is right and weakness is wrong as the means to the supreme righteousness of the German Third Reich. "Situation ethics" is a silent precursor to that abomination of total imorality fostered in German youth and tody in America—to the utter confusion about the political meaning of the usefulness of power. By power I mean the use of existing laws as the means, perversely, to justify self-serving ends. The liberal is a natural idealogue for this purpose. His problem is that he has only himelf, and therefore the State, to fall back on. He and therefore the State feel compelld to be the managers of lesser men's lives.

> **Do not allow the shouts of the mob to distract you from right choices or the cries of the anarchists to deter you from moral rectitude. For in the noise of Imany there is often only chaos, pain and vengeance.**

> **Liberty never borrows its theosophy from perfidious conduct except to depict the disaster of its time.**

> **Though liberty may not bear the scars of its adversary, despotism, it will forever dsplay the dishonor of its abandonment.**

> **The "liberty" to defraud the people or to cheat on another person is neither a liberty nor a right. It is simply the enslavement of the will without honor or integrity.**

13. BUREAUCRATIC DEPENDENCY VS LIBERTY OF MIND

It is obvious that the Federal Government by its official reiteration through the Conress and their propaganda on "need," and by the custom of usage and the peoplic's acceptance of the welfare State, doll out a measure of comflort and securilty to its welfare recipients and their liberal supporters.

Ought liberty then to be held up to them as desireable, enabling them to adjust their attitudes and expenditures and aims to the future advancement of their economic indulgences? In other words, why ought they, welfare recitients, to even consider free choice when, under the circumstances, the State makes the choices for them in regards to welfare income and other entitlements?

There sets in like gangrene the malaise of a ficitious understanding of personal choices whose illusion is shaped by the givers of welfare, seeking not to better the life of the recipient more than to improve the politicians chances of re-election.

Yet in this wlay, in the course of a year in and year out rendering of financial aid, the welfare beneficiary in time—and many are second and third generation recipients with entrenched attitudes—comes to believe that his liberty of movement, his feedom of thought, his options of choice are, in only in a few ways, related to what he has not directly earned. He arrives at the determination that the Federal Government *owes* him the money he receives. Ask the typical welfare reciient whom he is voting for and whether or not the Government owes him the money he receives every month without effort on his part. He will surely answer in the affirmative.

He becomes the illusory *creditor* of the people—they owe him—and at the same time the benficiary of earned income within the framework of welfare law. The bureaucracy has by ingratiation germinated a dependency that has become the recipitnt's right to his claim. That claim seems to bear no relationship to economic laws of supply and demand that overrun other members of American society. It appears, however, to be singularly relevant in his own special financial empowerment and to his citizen's political influence Welfare thus tends to generate arrogfance and power among the haplelss yet identifiable segment of the American people.

The source of this welfare largesse is the productive American taxpayers. The help results from the abuse of political liberty by weeping politicians, a largesse that is a form of confiscatory tqxation tht amounts at times to the actual disinheritance of the heirs and producelrs from their land. Elimination of the death tax has helped in that regard, but on the other hand the Marxist Ssupreme Court's ruling that gives license to greedy developers and politicians swusngs the issue back again—more revenue for the welfare burden. Such is fraudulent democratization in the guise of liberty. Property and the owner's money to pay property taxes are the result of diligent efforts, sacrifice and investment year after year, which efforts become a form of credit and philanthropic compassion extended to the improvident folks in cities and towns across America. Often they are the squnderous ones who misuse their free money. Observe, however, that the conversion of inherited property by oppressive taxes to preserve State welfare is rank socilaism based on the "politics of pity."

Too confiscate a house through excessive taxes is to shift investment capital from its earner and investor into the hands of the undeserving and the lazy. Taxes of that magnitude are a form of exyortion, meaning that the State controls the means of producion, a man's possessions being the capital from which he works to employ others and to increase his capital flow. His land concurrently becomes the basis for industry against which he borrows for future ventures. Yet, and again, through the machinations of welfare largesse socialistic taxation, his property is extorted from him . Russsia's Kulak peasant farmers, stripped of their land in the November 1917 Rommunist Revolution, were unable to grow wheat. The United States had to selll them hundreds of thousands of metric tons of wheat to feed Russia's starving pasants. Russia, since 1917, has been destitute ever since.

Any seizure of the land or moneys owed to the State prohibits the landed person's the exercise of his liberty of choice, the right to buy and sell, to grow, to innovate, to barter, travel, and communicate. The welfate State of America is Hayek's _Road to Serfdom._ It is the landowner's investment strategies that are guided and protected by his conscience regarding his personal disposal of his own money; His conscionable choices create that wealth.when Bad laws and state greed interdict liberty of choice and thus deprive the individdual of risk, and of opportunity to increase that wealth through investment and a life-style of economic integrity.

Taxation beomes immoral when it confiscates a man's property. The State in so doing ac cords only token respect to the citizen's demonstration of honesty of acquisition, honor, loyalty and hard work to improve that property. If the property then becomes the State's by seizure—read _theft_—a form of bureaucratic contempt, then the destructive tax has stripped the inalienablel right of happiness from the land owner. The recent Kelo v New London case has done just that: by a Marxist decision—looking to foreign laws—the US Supreme Court stripped a private landowner of their property and gave it to another private landowner. For does he not have a natural right to the enjoyment of his land without promiscuous seizure under color of law? The State quiet naturally, quit of honor, finds an excuse, ie. hghrer staxes, more revenue, for its action to perpetuate itself at the expense of its people. That excuse is Egalitarianism, the curse of contemporary politics in Americal—see outcome based education—which mandates absolute political and social equality. Note that men are _not_ all equal in character, intellect or things. This creed and not moral values are the absolutes found broadcast throughout America today, the tyranny of an unspoken political correctness and a fraudulent humanitarianism masked as sensitivity to diversity. When has America ever not been diverse? And why do liberals claim a monopoly on sensitivity, as they assuredly do in all quarters.

Liberty protects the demands of the purse only when the citizen is free to enjoy its benefits of investment.

Liberty will confront tyranny to the extent that it appears attainable. For this reason all denegration of common freedoms ought to be con= fronted.

If you keep a man enslaved for just so long, he will envision freedom's absence as a natural state of things, a vision without a possibile future.

If you think youl can compel society to accept your depravity as good and just, you do compound its nuisances, its evil effects and its self-condemnation.

Few will be those who espouse the submission of liberty to carpicious leadership, unless to share a popular approval; yet they will often mindlessly enjoy the moral degredation thereof.

14. CHILDREN GIVEN THE ADULT RIGHT TO SUE PARENTS FOR NEGLECT, MALTREATMENT, DIVORCE

Are children underage—below 18 years—to be given this right by society, or is it inherent in the parent-child relationship as a natural right, and if natural, therefore denoted to be a "liberrty (freedom) of choice to which society acquiesces? Or do children,eighteen years of age and younger, *learn* the right to sue by virtue of their companionate presence in the household? Do they have *natural* grounds for any protest to the extent of having litigation power which the court mgiht discover as a natural, God-given or court-legislated enablement for a law suit?

It was in past ages, in aMedieval times if not earlier, that children were treated as little adults. Society has almost forgotten that with great social effort, compassionate leadership and leglislative perserverence, there came into existence laws that protect children from arduous labor inl the mines and mills of America, from sexual abuse by adults both inside and outside the home—a classic European abuse—and from illiteracy. These evils were remedied by laws to prohibit society from exploiting children as cheap labor and sex objects and persons without lights.

Nevertheless, the child in American society has been the object of special concern and care, the which have, until technology presented corrupt opportunities, restrained preditors and exploiters from availing themselves and their corporate interests of the use of children as helpless objects without encountering a moral defence of the children by society.

The battle goes on. Pedophelia, pornographic movies, labor-use in the performing arts, IRS exploitation for tax purposes, a plethora *of latchkey* kids of working parents, and toleration of neighborhood gangs: these evidences show that society still believes that children have a political and a commercial value. The concern of the courts in custody cases and in instances of the abuse and child abandonment amounts to the State's interest. But the State's interest is not the same as parental "tough love," control and concern; instead, it is promotional politics, the politcization of childhood. The child is now-adays again a pawn. Our nation pu;shes for a retrogressive childhood-less child that takes us back to the Middle Ages. All the enlightenment of the twentieth centsury is of little avail before the rejection of the truel moral protection of our children. Tthat protection escapes the charge of politicization only and only by encouraging—and sometimes by permitting—the parents again to rear their children without any State interference whatsoever. It is not the State's right to bleed away the authority of the "nuclear" parent-child relationship, ie. the parentally mandated family that is foundational to Western civilization. The State's invasion of ancient tradlitional family rights is a form of child abuse in and of itself.

Upon that prohibition hangs the moral law that one is not to abuse of the child in our society, that our leaders are not to withhold certain benefits that will give the child advantages for adulthood and, ultimately for the good of America—such as an education for competency in our society, and care for the orphans, the abandoned and the lost. The proper function ofl the State is to remedy, not to control. The morally right choice is to demand that the child shalll not work long hours, or in fact work at all in the adult sense of the word, when he or she should be playing and going to school. The present-day politicization of the child by adult corruptions has replaced this time for fantasy, dreams and struggle with responsibilities easily met. In the years of a child's maturation, there should be a reasonable remeldy for delinquency, a compassionate supervision while at school, and by the police and neighbors while the child is on the streets. Rural communities especially have that responsibility. The absence of the last protection has made drive-by shootings commonplace, a phenomenon that violates society's respect for the child.

The lamentable fact is that America has withdrawn from the notion ofl childhood and its benefits and has begun to think of children as grownups with all the legal rights of adults, bypassing **childhood** as a wasteful and unproductive stage of growth in order that the child reach maturity at thirteeen years without the traumas, the painful experiences, of the growing up years. The unrelenting urge is to make children into adults before they are ready, for political gains and social triumphs over disease and inexperience. They are compelled to visualize themselves as little adults who upon threat of expulsion from the team, or of abandonment by their schoolmates, ostracized, they must then indeed make adult choices—like how to put on a condom or how to keep a secret of pregnancy. They are literally forced to accept the corruptions of the adult world as natural for their lives. Let society beware of this shame!

These adult transmutations foisted upon children are shortsighted and diabolicall schemes which, in time, will produce a nation of morally and intellectually stunted youth. You cannot replace maturation with adult knowledge, childhood with instant adulthood, romantic ideals and dreams with biology, innocence with adult adulteration and corrupt attitudes, and not generate a pigmy generation morally andl intellectually. Take heed. I speak from eight decades of experience in life.

Children who are deprived of those years yet are required to behave like adults willl miss the strengthening process of gradual exploration and adaptation. Istead, they will succumb in their time to wicked blandishments and seductions from a lack of moral strength and insight and from the personal acknowledgement of accountability. Their parents will more often than not blame society for the deficit; and so it is nowaday. Yet they, the parents—if they are both in the life of the child—are the very ones who must nurtsure the moral stamina and not parade and foster for appearances' sake this insidious child rearing technique of adult mimicry.

The political activists of the "Year of Child" accused parents of being the enemy. These paragons of a false progress are the real saboteurs of civilized society, not just of the family as an institution, but of the lives of the children of that society. Alas, let it be said, "Year of the Child" is a Chinese cultural borrowing, like "Year of the Dog," and "Year of the Rat." All our years should be for the child, not of the child, as though the childrenl were some sort of prophetic sign and wonder of the heavens, which they are, a gift in the Christian sense of the word. The politicizing of children is pernicious and retrogressive. It is in fact Medieval. It is totally irrelevant to child-rearing that any one year should astrologically be fixed as significant.

Fiendish activist counsellors try to push the 14-year old juvenile into the Courts in order to alienate the child from his parents, on the face of a complaint of "abusel," often one that ignores rationl grounds for an amicable parent-child resoluion, or that encourages the small son or daughter to "divorce" the parents, thereby making the child a permamnent possession of the State, a permanent enemy of the parent(s), and a fit recruit for a fascist politically correct youth corps. Can we not learn from history? It is not a matter of power; it is a matter of moral authority.

Th volatile matter is then to be settled by an inpersonal judge amid the folios of paper work entailed in child adult contests. Thel Juvenile Court, or the Superior Court, should recognize that such lawsuits are to abet the destruction of the family in America, unconsciously or perhaps deliberately, as an impediment to enlighteneed social legislation. Judges who condone such suits should be removed from the bench or put out of office, by petition, as incompetent to rule on what does not exist, the specificity of a tortious action for damages and property in a juvenile divorce decree by the child!

The State's interest in child rearing is not proscriptvie, outlawing some disciplines while condoning others. The interest is concordant—or oght to be—with lthe instituion of the family, seeking ground for a common agreement. Where the child is rebellious and wants out pf the family, the court is not the proper place to settle the matter, for flamily life is most often a bilateral arrangement that begins and has its true genesis in a holy covenant with God. The Court, as an agent of lthe State, is neither fit nor authorized to rescind that covenant. That is the task of a spiritual leader. Yet such juvenile cases tend to encourage, by _stare decesis_ decisions, the expansion of family quarrels into fullblown feuds.

The common belief is, of course, that the child needs to exercise his natural rigfhts sooner, to hasten the maturation process and thereby to bring himl abruptly to face the realities that he must ultimately face anyway, irrespective of his juvenile status. As if the mawkish charades of adulthood have not produced enough juvenile crime already, liberal feminists and tort-reform activists would hasten the child into adulthood, _programmned,_ as it were, for a liberal mindset toward life. There is no absolute right and worng in this view. If maturity is the result of growth, how can there be growth by society's skirting the years when such growth occurs? Tsial and error within the scope of childhood experiences produce not adult indoctrination but, instead, an enlarged understanding of what it means to be a responsible, grown-up person.

The child's liberty, called a "right," to file a complaint against his or her parents is a fairly recent charismatic propositon; yet this right of legalistic free-choice is urged upon the child like a **cause celebre** by which he is encouraged to elbow his way into the adult world lo matter how bloody the encounter. When a child is thus prompted to measure up to adults in a courtroom scene—I'm not speaking of role-modeling—so that he can secure his manhood more rapidly and past hrough that indoctrination, like a rite of passage, he has found a way to gratify his childish envy of the adult lifestyle, its possessions, its facades, its hypocrisies, its grown-up aura. In this manner, via the Courts, are his liberty of choice, conscience, cognition propagandized and politicized to the end that he becomes useful to the State, his surrogate parent(s) and often arrogant toward the rest of society. One will also find that the social attitudes of the parents are oflten communiated to their offspring. In a real sense, members of a street gang have divorced their parents without Court intercession, although they will use them for practical needs, like food, clothing and housing. Thus the child's capacity to make moral choices that could harm himself or others is short-circuited. Discernment of right from wrong will rest upon whatever expedient is made acceptable by the Court, an expedient that always will deliver him from pain and in doing so often lacks mature judgement—like conceeding or accepting his membership in a gang!

This evasion, this unaccountability for actions of a-moral choice prompted by an avoidance of pain or of unconscionable wrong marks the making of a sadist, the murderer or the ne'r-do-well. The court reinforces the process, in effect legalizing a juvenile's bad choices, for he can no longer identify with the pain of another person, ir he ever did. The gang mentality further justifies and stengthens this nascent and all too prevalent sadism in today's society. That society's diffidence toward behavioristic anarchy by juveniles in or out of gangs subtly transmits cruelty to the dominat class of parents and to the public at large. By tearing at the fabric of the family, the Courts along the way have helped in that process of destruction. Yet in their arrogance activist judges call themselves "progressive."

If an inalienable right means that the right cannot be separated from the citizen, liberty must assume the role of rebellion when despotism rises.

The liberty of a soldier portends disaster or death, since it borrows from war's a-morality.

Conscience does not play games; either wrong is wrong and right is right, but never is wrong the right or right the wrong. Confusion of the two purposes, by a deliberate misconstru-al, invites corrupton of the language and the misappropriation of honor.

Moral values exist apart from personal feelings.

Once free, never a slave: the words of freedom wil always returns to haunt the prisoner.

15. RELIGIOUJS LIBERTY AS POLITICAL POWER

Karl Marx called religion the "opiate of the people," a drug that enabled them to escape the realities of their failing bourgeois society.

Any icon-ic loyalty of the people will inevitbly arouse the jealousy of a tyrant, the reason, however, for the Roman legions' hostils attack on Christ land his followers was not only that the God of the Jews and the Christians commanded their loyalty and respect, but that their actions could not be predicted or their thoughts controlled by Caesar. So, too, with all dictators. In a society in which the lives of lthe people are not closely oberved and manipulated by the State, that State's very survival and power held by the leaders are endangered by tlhe potential for rebellion and threatened by thoughts of liberation, providing thereby fallow ground for political intrigue and power grabs. This was the millieu in Russia when Karl Marx observed the coveted and envied success of the Russian Kulak farmers. Strangely, the Politburo could not grow wheat. The inability of the old Soviet Union to folly and officially *track* its citizen-subjects lead to the collapse. Religious faith went underground in Russia, as it did in Germany during the regimes of Hitler and Stalin. Believers worshipped in the woods in Russia, or assumed the mask of Nazi features in Germany.

The significant reason for tyranny's exile of religion, then and now, is that worlshippers of God have no fear of him. They surrender their fear up to the God in consequence of which the tyrant cannot make their day-to-day moral decisions for them. Those choices that are grounded upon conscience cannot be reported, although certain "progressive" schools in this country attempt to bewilder and intimidate childrlen into divulging family secrets. If and when believers chose to worship and to legalize and to sing hymns to God, though compelled to do so clandestinely in the woods or mountains, they do but show the tyrant's impotence in matters of religious faith. He cannot exploit their morality, a power which to him symolizes their strength and is the way to his downfall.

To put a further hedge about the liberty of belief and faith of religion, tlhe tyrant will increase the human elemental fear of carnage or of death by surrounding the saints with the presence of soldiers bearing guns. In this way he continually reminds them ofl their fear and their practical loss of liberty. He knows, furthermore, that by means of certain gratuities of his regime, they willl adjust to the State's omnipresence and consolations and security that accompanys that fear. Guns and tanks bcome protective friends. The dictator's words, reinforced by his troops, become the words of an adoptive father who will protect his children from harm and from racial impurities. The NKGB and the Gestapo, by finding and destroying "undesirables," insured the pristine poltical and racial quality of the common peolple . There needs to be no fear amongst them as political partisans and social communes.

Religious faith, instead of being a narcotic becomes, therefore, a stimulant to promote and to goad the people into submitting to this power transfer from civil liberty to absolute authority, with its attendant loss of those liberties, one by one. In the Third Reich free speech and freedom of association were the first to go. Faith bends before power. Let the State inform those believers that the icon ofl their worship, the Almighty God, is invisible and nugatory, their loss of liberty will need no recompense. Yet will they not point ironically to the invisibility of their personal future, proving them to be the prophets of their own destiny? The wise among them, at the outset of Hitler's rise, foresaw the ultimate "final solution." They assuredly must have after *Krystalnacht.*

Those polish Catholics who opposed him were summarily shot. The holocaust suffered by the Jews resulted not because they did not oppose him in covert ways but because they were helpless to oppose him openly and dared to do so only secretly. It's a well-known fact that the socialist-Fascist Germany of the 1930's made of the Jews the scapegoat for the economiic depression., forcing them to atone for that nation's WWI repartions. The people of Germany survived by making war, by man's evil ingenuity and by God's favor when nflation and starvation assaulted the German people.

One of the contradictions in the authoritarian and totally controlled society is that free moral choice exists at all, that it is possible, for example, to take or to abstain from all opiates, including genocide, a possible escape when religion offers no comfort or hope. When the people are told that the tyrant and this cohorts are the benign and rightlfiil leaders of that country, it is those who have known freedom and struggle who will doubt the utilitlarian uses of power for evil. Between the wars Moral choice survived when it moved under ground yet wore the face of compliance.

Inevitably, it seems, there issues from the entombment of morality, at this juncture, a practiced deceit that is resistant to the cruelties and obscenities of the despotic regime. Patriotism and honor must then take on the appearances of conformity in the desperation of the people to save their souls, their moral goodness and their capacity to endure. The dictator inevitably understands both the courage and the intelligence of a people so subjuated, whether or not they have known all the well-defined personal liberties we we have in this country.

Liberty under the law becomes the right to make free moral choices, which is the conscience not of despair but of hope. Those choices and the capacity for actions guided by conscience are a curse to the tyrant—who may very well have known the free society he exploits. Executive orderrs are one way our President can skirt the law to impose his will upon a public citizenry kept in the dark of ignor-ance. His reasons for destroying any public expression of conscience—for that must ultimately be the outcome—only confirms the irrationality of all dicta-torlships since time began. In ancient and modern times the unreasoning pro-grams, the agencies, displays of pomp and power have selom tasken into consideration the deeper convictions of the people. Austrian-born Hitler did not really understand the German people, except their nationalistic pride. He was oblivious to the catalyist of the Protestant Reformation, for one example, and of the possitive value of German science, for another. Thus subjugated to effectuate his tyrannical-government, the tyrant like Hitler must alwlays caricature the peo-ple, that is to say, he must *simplify* them. Hitler and Stalin both concockted cari-catures of their people in order to manipulate them as puppets without mind or history or danerous personal ambitions outside of State control. That was the delusionl madnss of both dictators.

The peasant mind, for his part, does not fawn upon the State or his own folk community. It finds its strength and its identity through myth, not through power. Those myths are the known, traditional and long-accepted tales of their forebearers who struggled upward out of oppression, tales that are both fictive and actual. Oblivious to their deeper consanguine desires, although pleading the contrary, the dictator proceeds without much worry concerning their rebel-lion—that is not until street battles bring his defeat in power to the State's atten-tion, as at Tinemen Square, the barracades in revolutionary Paris, the street fighting in Colombia, Panama and in Boston Common, and, years later, with the collarpse of the Berlin Wall.

By ignoring a people's grasp of liberty, the dictator writes his own warrant for the death of himself and his regiment, the people's intuition of liberty affixing its folk vision to what was, in ancient heroic days, the mlythial heroic-figure aspect of the Libertys rebellion. In America, the Colonists had not forgotten the *1215 Magna Carta,* the Charter of Enlish liberties by which taxes required the consent of the people and a man could not be imprisoned without a trial—the verity from which dueOprocess arose.

Paradoxically, almost since the beginnings of civilizations, secular laws have moved in the direction of protecting Man's personal *immoral* choices, his right to make a mistake even though that mistake is consensual and becomes destrucive of society's welfare. We in America have today arrived at that *solopsism* of the human psyche, that "the Self can be aware of nothing but its own experiences and mistakes. This is the crux of Roe v Wade, and of the mult-cultlural Balkanization of America, the creeping hedgemony of *political correctness.*

The laws of human rights in the US Constitution's Bill of Rights are con—sonant with all of history's solemn edicts of liberty.

Keep the law, empower liberty, break the law, transgress liberty.

Liberty in America is not a right of the illegal alien. Although his conscionable actions may be protected by God's authority, his participation in American society requires allegilance to our government of laws. He ought to have no voice on the streets or in the Assembly. Let him first disavow his allleg iance to his foreign masters.

To preserve a citizen's freedom, he must be given the liberty to be responsibble for his own actions. This is the sacrifice of true statesmalnship; for the politician coerces and cajoles and bribes, thus marshalls the people's liberty to support his power.

He who takes liberty for granted ignores history.

A people will tolerate chains so long as their daily needs and their desires for wealth are met. In this hapless state they will sell their birthright of their liberty even though justice is corrupted.

16. LIBERTY AND AUTHORITY

The liberty of rebellious and disruptive students may appear courageous to the juvenile mind, and to their peer sympathizers. In fact, their rebelliousness, when unhindered, is a form of intellectual suicide which denies that the authority of the school is not designed to harass them but to provide an arena for their learning.

In many instances of classroom disruption, often in the overcrowded classrooms with thirty-five students, misconduct is ignored or trivialized or, unbelievably, applauded as adolescent maturation by acceptable challenges to authority. That last is absurd nonsnse yet it occurs more often than common society knows about.

If the juvenile choses the option of death to the intellegence, trashing study time and assaulting the teacher, ignoring class work and skipping homework in preferene to television, that student will often go into mental hibernation. He or she will devalue the conscience as worthless, that is, the liberty to make a moral choice of right over wrong instead of obeying the urge to play, to squander time, to make frivolous their lessons and to presusme an importance that is totally self-centered. They will look around them for applause from their classmates.

Not just adolescents but adults, too, have "cut loose" morally and ethically in a death-wish for mind and soul and sometimes to body in an act of gang revenge. Teenage suicides are increasingly common, adult corruptions of what constitutes personal honor are everywhere, euphoric experience has replaced adolescent dreams and visions for their future. The choice to waste one's life with drugs and indolence has destroyed the child's potential, just as much as death in combat destroys the soldier.

Instead of creating a social disharony, most adult citizens conform to the laws as best they can. They accept the realities that the laws are there for their own good, for their survival. Their option is to break the law with the real possibility of incurring fines and punishment. The juvenile generation of this age has created a structure of hyper-feeling through drugs, video games of violence and adult per-missiveness, a high that for them constitutes a rite of passage.

Demands of lthe laws and penalties for their violation make rebellion adverse to happiness, hence the high numbers of suicides. However, an attitude of chal-lenge to the laws exists in a society where the people are taught that they can automously break what they feel are bad laws. The average citizen will often believe that under "the system" he has an inherent right to break the law if he simply disagrees with it, the attitude of the anarchist. He possesses the liberty to do wrong, to deliberately make a "mistake." He attributes little seriouness to the option when he says, "I've got a right to be wrong." Upon that premise, he exer-cises his right to be a lawbreaker, although it is an option and not a right to do so. He will in all likelihood face the consequences of punishment for his defection. If, however, he ignores the consequences, society will act to impose them anyway by bringing him to justice. As in a video game, which neutralizes consequences for violence, the juvenile mindset is to break the law and lower the score.

If a person's harm to another goes beyond fantasy, the injury to society is irre-vocable and often without restitution, as is the cases of such crimes as rape, pedophelia and murder. When reason abets a ciminaFs evil choice, his personal liberty to chose is surrendered to the death wish. The young criminal has willfully destroyed his personal liberty. In order to protect their own sense of guilt, partic-ularly of the parents yet sometimes shown by sociey's indifference, neither malfeasor parents nor an indifferent society will assume responsiility for the child's crime.

If these wrong choices continue and society is harmed as well as the victims, only in the Utopian absence of rules will a criminal enter a plea of injury to himself when none exists, except in instances of capital punishment. His hardened conscience has beens replaced lby a devious, implacable and specious self-justification for his crime. Teen-age arson and homicides against their own classmates or gang retaliation reflect the destruction the conscience, and the liberation of the will to do evil, with an accompanying disregard for concequences and the feeling of invulnerability to punishment, these attitudes and emotions being salted with much contempt for their victims as well as for themselves.

It is the onerous of guilt that prods the conclience to lie and to commit perjury in court. Plea-bargaining is almost always a concession to expediency first,to the conscince and then to the mechanisms of the arrest. If the law remains a deterrent to evil acts, it does not follow that the authority of the law is unwarranted or cruel or weak or even wrong.

Political consensus has led to such laws as abortion on demand, homosexuality that is taught to school hildren as a lifestyle, pemissbile beastiality, necrophilia and incest, but does the permissive consensus make them less harmful? For a man to examine authority constantly then makes these personal choices, protesting the harmful ones protective of himself C. S. Lewis has described a man who has made the "unthinkable" to become the "thinkable." This can happen when men and woman of characer remain silent, refusing or failing by common apathy to project the values they share.

"Challenge all authority" is, therefore, a commonly acceptable attitude, though it can become a dangerous one, as the popular vote in a true democracy is dangerous. Harm to the traditional institutions of a society arises, or can occur, with the elimination of an attitude of benign skepticism and rebuke, in favor of robotic behavior and thinking—one of the scurvies of excessive TV watching—or by an actual injury caused, or engendered by social tumult and demogogic rabble-rousing as when peace marches turn violent or gangs take their activity onto school grounds. It is one of the inalienable rights in America for two hundred and sixteen years that the unfettered consciences of the people hae not only precluded the rise of a dictator, but insured the enjoyment of a maximum happiness in an imperfect world. Whenever juveniles challenge adult authority with good cause and a reasonable attitude of respect, liberty prevails. If the challenge is to destroy what older generations cherish, liberty is perverted to attach a false retributive justice to the evil act. A jury will often decide the outcome of that oxymoron. Can boys, gangster fashion, with absolute cruelty cut down their schoolmates with gunfire and then see justice allow the parents and society to escape culpability? I think not. A democratically constituted authority and true personal liberty are inseparable.

> **Practice making totally ethical choices in your daily conduct and you will earn the respect at least of God, Men will not fully respect what they have no part in or concern with. Rejection of classroom lessons leads to disrespect for the teacher. Its source is disrespect for the parents, or parent.**

> **Liberty rarely transposes itself into messianic power, since it is neither visionary nor salvational but it is es-catalogical and revelational. It marks the end and judgement of despotism and provides the true vehicle for the people's creative ventures.**

> **If a man would dispose of God, he is at liberty to invent the universe. In this mode of thought the universe becomes an illusion without a creator. In the absence of a First and Last Cause—or God—liberty is a mere construct of illusory reason. Mankind's conduct of liberty without God implodes upon itself.**

> **Liberty does not beg for a hearing lest it shame itseslf into silence. In one way or another, it always asserts the reaity of its inherent Truth.**

> **Keep liberty for value and she will shatter; but keep her for justice and she will abound.**

17. LIBERTY AND ARMS

America called for arms in the defense of liberty in 1775 when, at St. John's church in Richmond, Virginia, Patrick Henry and the Burgesses argued for raising a militia to protect Englishmen's rights in the Colonies. The 2nd Amendment of the Constitution reiterates and formalizes that concept of an "well-regulated militia" maintained to secure and to preserve a free State by a show of citizen armed force, the evidence of which should be guns kept by the people, individually, in the event of an invasion or a surprise enemy attack. They and not the State would control the fire-power—an unbearable idea to the modern-day liberal. The meaning of the Amendment is extrapolated into modern times by virtue of its practice in post-colonial America, and by virtue of its purpose, the

which like all the liberty Amendments shall not be abridged by that very power whose threatening gestures and tyannies brought them into existence.

The bearing of arms works also against an oppressive government where force is used to obtain conformity. That force need not be arms but can be oppressive government edicts, such as the formal constraints against the nation's guaranteed personal liberties. For one, freedom of association is under assault today as is freedom of speech, Certain groups, like the Boy Scouts, are being denied the right to control their own membership. Churches will soon fall under the States' *ober dictum* of membership Liberals in Congress are devising a statute that will outlaw opposition to sodomy—in practice and co-equal with traditional marriage and family as a *hate crime*, a type of thought control for the first time in America! A crime is being re-defined as a wrong, or a politicly incorrect, **thought** and the open statement of such that motivates an act of exclusion only! Freedom of association is a corrupted by political efforts to control society in the interests of a special group, whatever that group!

Political correctness, the accursed offspring of muticulturalism, is another silent edict that pervades the campuses of America universities and sits like a vulture in attendance over editorial copy of the major newspapers. To liberal oppressors who assume that these present and incipient forms of oppression are not so, one can say, truthMly, that the destruction of the family will destroy America, and, furthermore, that the United States has always been a nation of diverse cultures—English, Italians, Germans, Swedes, Norwegians, Africans, Asians, Indians, Jews and other cultures out of sight.

Liberals, otherwise identifed as Utopian in ideology, would use *multiculturalism* as a club to gain their own agenda of control. The private ownership of guns, must not be included in the "bargain," therefore, there is today a strong liberal compulsion not simply to destroy the right of Americans to own their owns guns/On the same liberal agenda is the present effort by the Congress to destroy the fundamental teaching-forum for the next generation by the trivializing the traditional family as a "first school," eschewing its training *in* virtue and morality, in favor of Government choices foisted upon the children. Teach them about sex at age eight. Usurp the role of parents with bureaucrats, mock parental guidance by substitutionary a-moral "guidelines", denounce the contribution of religion to morality, convert America into a nation of godless little robotic athiests ready to do the will of a godless government.... and in the reach of these injunctions, deny all Americans the absolute right to associate *freely* with whomever they will. We are on the way.

Hitler tried by his use of the Gestapo terror of the secret police to institute a reign of terror that would bring about Aryan purity of race, conformity in thought and attitude, control of free speech enjoyed in the Weimar Republic, and a propagandists enlightenment of specious falsehood and demagogic lies. To foster these goals, he tried to extinguish an entire group of people expecting by the extermination camps to obtain a pure Germanic identity, a cultural and a "racial" homogeniety ... but not liberty. Private ownership by indiividual Germans of firearms would have threatened the Regime. Crime has risen in England because the British Bobbies do not carry guns! The deterrant to deadly evil is inevitably the gun, the firearm, the weapon of maximum effectiveness.

Arms represent the power of violent retaliation, violent action, violent compulsion all in accordance with the prevailing ideology of the Central Government—the State, or in Hitler's case, the hatreds and bigotries of the reigning despot. Arms are the instruments of preservation or of annihilation. Their discipline of regulation is irrelevant in the morality of their use when political Hedonism and overreaching ambition govern the strategy of the State, as has lately been the rule by example in these United States. An Administration that so grossly exceeds the bounds of the fundamental Constitution is a corrrupt, not a benign government, a boastful and swaggering excursion into a benevolent kind of outlawry that would hypnotically dangle amenities and entitlements before the people's eyes to solidify their acceptance of political wrongdoing ... At the same time America is trying to save the world from itself, outsourcing fundamental jobs in the process of bankrupting the people with a 8-trillion dollar trade deficit—these things to curry the world's favor. So it has been. Meanwhile, of greater importance than personal ownership of arms is the world's arming itself for approaching Armegeddon.

America's 2nd Amendment right to keep and bear arms, with emphasis on the word **keep,** has always been based on a defensive posture for the preservation of the nation yet **not** for the concentration of any unique power in citizen hands. Arms for aggrandizement has always been the stance of those nations and leaders who seek to gratify the will to power of their leaders. Their morality is evil in the indifference with which they deploy their arms against the helpless. Arms can mean either the weapons of tribal combat or the sophisticated armaments of modern armies. Or, indeed, the settler's musket he once used to defend his family and home. Ideological defense of the home and the family has today eclipsed the physical defense of the same home. How parents rear their children is more and more the State's business. Whom citizens accept or reject in their private enclaves is increasisngly Washington's business. Intimiation has set in. That is the cancer to the death of virtue, personal integrity and free-will, which will inexhorably go underground but never be purged by Liberal mainlining ***correctness.***

Since the State has usurped a number of the powers once held by the American citizen—parental authority in matters of preferetial schooling and under-age abortion, to name just two examples—the State has begun to outlaw aspects of that citizen-authority and to place itself in control, establishing by judicial legislationa a legitimate ***stare decisis,*** that contravenes parental discretionary judgements. The tyrannical authority to conrol a child's education is yet another of such oppressions. Thereby can the State shape the child to bow before it and its bureaucratic edicts, and to perform its obligatory functions under bureaucratic authority. The power of the State is represented not just by its oracular power of Representative government but by its lethal protectionist power of military might—meaning guns and fire-power, howsoever delivered.

A lawful government is regulated by laws that are superior, in their power of intention and display, to the actions of the individual citizens of that State. Otherwise, they are not laws but concessions to the people. The precedent-setting common laws of this country control the citizen's use of his firearm, down to hunting license, establishing that a weapon can be used lawfully in defense of home and family and self. ***Stare decises*** includes many intances of this defense right.

To put the matter of obedience another way, Americans are under the law of the United States Constitution, not the Federal Constitution, for the latter desciptioin would rule out States' rights altogether in deference to Washsington absolutist mandates. The fine terms in the 2nd Amendment invite close scrutiny and enquiry as to why guns ought to be kept by indiividual citizens. The "right" to *keep alnd bear* is not defined by the State. To "keep" is to retain possession of, a retention which need not be so stated if the State were certain that the right belonged to it; and to "bear" arms is sheer nonsense when the bearing refers to the militia, for they can do so without consent and in the silence of other regulations, that include the issuance of weapons from a storage armory. Thus, by the 2nd Amendment the people are explicitly reassured it is they and they alone who enjoy this right. For the right to "keep and bear arms" cannot be infringed upon without violating the Constitutiona and invadmg the citizem's right. Of course, it is well if both the State militia and the private citiens both keep arms. There is no Constitutional or pragmatic concflict in that circumstnce. The American citizen is not to be left defenseless in the event of an attack on him or his home, which comes to the same thing. In lieu of a gun, self-defense by butcher knives, baseball bats and hat pins is patent nonsense.

It is true that a people will at times start down paths of immoral conduct before setting forth on new roads of moral change. This happens in Christian conversion to faith in Christ, as literally millions canl testify In our Civil War, Lincoln's administration could not morally retreat in the face of immoral slavery, called so by abolitionists and those citizens who accepted the Constitution's declaration of equality. Many, but far from all, Christians in the South clung to slavery for cotton-income yet brought their house-slaves to brush-arbor revivals, source of the black spiritual—the Mississippi Delta being the legitimate place of origin of the blues amid black pickers of cotton. One can be certalin that many did so with a guilty conscience.

Yet the wanton destruction by the Federals of the Southern landscape showed how abject and bloody can be this plea for moral liberty in the war to obtain justice, if not conformuty by guns. Many a Southern land-owner was shot dead by overrunjning Federals in defense of his property, his action being morally if not lawfully defensible, since the South was no longer under Constitutional protection. Gangs claim as their "turf—by their graffittee on walls, etc.—a territory which they defend with guns, but immorally, since their claims are false, they having no right to posession. The existent reality of gang murders ought not to infringe upon the law-abiding citizen's right to keep a gun in his house to protect himself and his family. Nor ought the deprivation of all the citizens of their guns rest upon the lack of supervision of a few parents who do not teach their sons how to use a firearm, or are slack in keeping their guns lucked up. The home-owner's estimate of his neighborhood ought to factor in vigilance and his claim of gun-possession should be lawful. His possession of a firearm is Constitutional.

Liberty as a battle cry was used during the French Reign of Terror. Arms for liberty in this historical context of the French Revolution—the common citizenry threw pavingstones more often—wreaked their bloody overture to **equality, fraternity and liberty** because arms were weapons of annihilation and not for moral change. The guillotine would have remained the "final solution" *without* a force of arms by the Republicans. The call to arms always requires a specificity of moral purpose in their use, in which neither the preservation of the State nor economic inflation, nor power-hungry leaders supplied a morality or a lasting justice by conquest. That was the conscience that lay beneath Sir Winston ChurchhilFs words of encouragement to the British people when he braced them to stand up to Hitler's Nazi hordes who intended to "work their wicked will" against that stoic, solitary Isle, England. His was the conscience of moral persuasion, the moral value of righteousness he shared with the British people, the which the government had no need to impose. England's moral purpose was to save herself from conquest by a wicked regime and therefcore to preserve British life in all of its profound history.

In America arms for liberty in Colonial times took on a different configuration of justice from that of the French in 1789. Geography was a precondition to civil liberty in our country. With the Atlantic ocean between us and a tired, enfeebled, corrupt and idolatrous Europe, perhaps we should never have aroused our own ancestsory by the cry of liberty. The Minutemen were Englishmen. In a real sense the American Revolution wa a civil war for power and control. The Colonials had the advantage of a certain minority unity—although many of them migrated to Quebec or remained stubbornly Tory or kept silent as in France, where the Nobility and the Republicans rubbed shoulders on the streets of Paris.

In the French revolution, strict unity of the masses was missing. The enemies of the people were identified by their outward symbols of wealth, and the guillotine no doubt cut off many heads that were of the Nobility in appearance but remained in sympathy with the French Commoners. Also, it was not musketry that brought the Crown to face the angry mobs but brute force. On the other hand, the call-to-arms in Colonial America was singularly united, enbued with an assumption of moral right-ness of the cause, and emboldened by a defineable spirit and sense of direction. The common soldier trusted General Washington and his percepion of their cause.

As the eight-year war wore on, participation by the common people did not accelerate so much as it became disgruntled and uncooperative. Farmers refused food and fuel to the troops encamped on their land. Yet the unity of the combattants and their loyalty to the the cause of freedom had the consistency of doggedness. Over in France, with the call to requite the oppressive French Aristocracy for their cruelty in 1789—when we had finalized and signed our Constitution—there roamed, in the Reign of Terror, like a lion seeking its prey through the streets of Paris, the chaos of hatred and the vengeance of death by revolutionary zealots. They did not have a similar "post-war" plan; they had only the violence against a class of Frenchmen. Guns gave them freedom but not liberty as we had won it for our infant Republic.

A just God had apparently annointed the settlers' risky adventure in the New World. The arms of muskets were to be kept not against their own kinsmen but, after the war, against the Indians in the new land. Their religious faith, though denominational, was a powerful motivator in the main—the Puritans and the Pilgrim wanted to distance themselves from England—and from the Netherlands. To them Liberty was "inalienable", a gift that was inseparable from God. The "inlienable rights" Jefferson wrote of in the Declaration of Indpendence inferred that liberty did not need to answer to corrupt men but to God alone. The French Revolution lacked this appeal to divine authority.

Unlike America's revolution, the French rebellion of the lower artesan classes did not enflame the people's sense of righteousness, of being right with God, but of brotherhood, of being right with their compatriots. The French Revoltuon was humanistic, man-oriented. Colonial efforts, on the other hand, were religiously endowed and prompted questions on freedom of conscience—to wit, that faith empowered liberty of the individual to make his own moral decisions. Arms ultimately were to protect that liberty from attack by invasion of the North American continent or from a Government militia against a citizen's protected rights—an inhernt power that was as intensely personal as it was consensual. The fact that the average citizen had never used his gun to protect his rights—to go to the poll, for example, or to worship as he pleased—did not remove that right from his possession.

A recent example comes to mind: The Government's destruction of the of the Koresch religious commune at Waco, Texas, was an example in which the citizens were outraged and destroyed by unlawful FBI action at the behest of Attorney General Janet Reno. Possession of weapons by Koresh and his followers was not an overt attempt by the Comune to occupy Waco by force arms. Their possession, in contravention of the Armory concept, provided Reno with a power-excuse to legitimize her authority as a female Attorney General and to obey a power-hungry President Clinton. The existence of weapons within the Commune was mere hearsay, non-predictive evidence. They posed no threat to society generally. It was mainly the commune's defiance that enflamed Reno and the Department of Defense's FBI "retaliation." There can be tragic mistakes of this sort in a free country, and there will be others for certain in which the interpretation of the 2nd Amendment is twisted for political gain.

Liberty of conscience reinforced by personal kinds of weapons was urging Western society into dangerous, risky enterprises, a new form of government and competition with the Old World's merchantilism and Medieval, jaded authority-systems. The French Revolution was largely for economic justice; the American Revolution was to gather together and preserve civil liberties under a written Constitution and a representative power-base. France eradicated the Nobility; American repulsed them. Conscience to the 18th century Frenchman was a stigma by God that kept him from personal freedom; thus was anarchy born on Paris streets. Conscience to the 18th century Colonial was the very initiator of his purpose in migrating to America.

Singular differnces marked these two revolutions and the meaning of their disparate call to arms. To the Revolutionary Frenchman, a the gun symbolizd the destruction of a whole class of people by another class of people. To the American Revolutionary, the gun represented the means to the eradication of tyrannical pressures and an entire country's, Britian's, long use of quiescent force that lay in gun power. It was the firearm of the Americn patriot that enforced his transition without, strictly so, a class crisis. Geographical separation had everything to do with these differences and that energized Washington's isolationist warning that America should not beome embroiled in foreign "entanglements."

In view of these historical differences in the motivating use of arms, only a capricious, lawless and wicked government—or one bereft of common sense—would attempt to keep arms out of the hands of the indivdual citizens until the State should give permission to use them. The histories of America and France have shown how treacherous and unreliable governments can be. Our founders knew that and therefore accorded to the individual citilzen, subject to ownership, the right to possess for his personal protection weapons of destruction, their secret and immediately available arms, in a word, their personal guns.

Liberty borrows from no custom but to search the unknown, no enchantment but to be free, no wisdom but to try men's souls no God but to One who is the origin of its precepts of virtue land happiness.

To the athiest the conscience is eiher a delusion or an environmentsl oddity; is is useful only as the shibboleth of reason to check human behavior.

You cannot perjure your conscience; you can only appease it or quench or harden it.

Liberty ought never to be claimed by barbarians, since they are ignorant of its origin from God and calloused concerning its uses by men.

Social evolution is a myth. It presupposes in the nature of Western Man, at least, a spontaneous desire for liberty. Laws of resraint only appear to be his invention; they are the resolutions of combat. Our liberties have these *refinements* in them.

True compasss points that lead to good life are the small decisions of ethsical choice and the moments of discernment for loving others.

18. MORAL CHOICE AND LIBERTY

It is said to be a moral choice in human behavior when there occurs a willful breach of a private contract, or of an inlernational agreement, as in trade; or of a governmental pact between lfriendly nations, as a demilitarized zone or, most recently, of the disposition of detainees as prisoners whether of war or for indictment as criminals under the rules of the Geneva Convention. A human predator's decision to kill or to rob, to maim or to cheat or to prey upon the young and the helpless, all these linstances of human failure involve an absolute standard of moral conduct. The conduct in any of these cases can rightly be called *immoral* by the conscience of Justice or *unethical* by the estalished law that is broken. Some violations of the law, murder and robbery for example, are both.

These offenses against conscience and the law arise from a decision by the culpable party that affects the outcome in ways that need not be evidentiary. Such breeches of the common weal and the hedgemony of human conscience predicate a consistent standard of existing and accessable values. That is, the injury, the lhalrm, the damage and wrong done by the perpetrator is consistent with the moral code, the overarching morality controlling the decision, preceent to which the liberlty to exercise moral choice belongs to the offending individual. Th\jat value-possession connnot vle transferred into \the\ hands of a leadership elite or an a-moral person. The moral/ethical values encoded, as it were, into one man's chaaracter are his exclusive possession. Unless he is mad or deluded or amnesiac, there can be no such phenoimenon as a "mindless act." Liability for one's actions of moral and ehical import is not transferable. This precept is true even among soldiers It is more often than not the wrong of immoral conduct that the offender wishes to put upon the back of someone else with a pointed finger. There is in human nature the ingredient of an excapist cowardice.

Decisions, however, of moral choice, when assented to by all who are involved, may comprise a majority of one mind that is consensual. They are called a *majority* in a democratic decision. Such decisions reflect the exercise of each man's concience in a separate act of free will—which are capable of becoming an act metaphorically of *one willl* Whether by a ruler of a junta, the commander of a garrison, the volition of a dictator or the veto of a President, the deciding authority is almost always singular, or appears to be consensual. Although uttering the will of others as one voice—not always reflecting the constraints of the law, the zealot speaks of a crusade, the fanatic of a cause, the leader of his apostles, the Whip of a Majority in Congress; or the Presiding Judge of the Law in a Court:—the plurality in these examples consits in the severable consciences morphed in support of the declaration for all who are involved in that decision. The morphological agreement is consensual,.although the decision must appear to be singular in nature. Fragmented decision is the decision of all bul the in the matter of choice. Mosl alternatives of other choices then remain moot. In the outcome, the naysayers, who have made their moral choice, must comply withsl the majority or consequences of moral/ethical importance will result. If the accused, for example, is not guilty of the alleged crime, then his exoneration has moral/ethical implications according to the nature and circumstances of the crime of which he is accused.

Thus, there can be no such entity as the conscience of the Supreme Court, as an entity in itself rather than a metaphor. There can be no conscience of the State for the same reason. Mass "mind" is an illusion. As a consequence of this truth, a "consistent" value is an "absolute value" while the liberty to adhere to it and to embrace it and to show it in public action is a characteristic of true leader. That is where the ulltimate accountability rests and toward whom the people who are affected by his decision can look for ethical integrity and moral rectitude. Their leader's performance honors their trust.

Integrity is the consistent discernment of right from wrong by a person in leadership, or in the authority he represents, as an Assemblyman in th State leglislature or a signer of a contract. For therein a man can show in his actions the error that is common, which is to equate consistency with regularity, or traditionalism with the "customary way." In each of these situations there is involved a different issue with different meaning politically. For example, a law that governs highway speed is changeable, although for any one time it may be the regulating speed; after twenty years, that speed is inconsistent with changes in trafficand road improvements ...

Although situations change, the consistent person in authority tries neither to falter, nor to lose his moral direction in his discernment, even though his conduct may, as it sometimes does, belie his moral or ethical understandiang. He may, indeed, violate a moral absolute such as honesty or loyalty or honor or his promise to the peoiple. Yet in doing so he has alllowed expediency to shape his decision. For example, he may promise his constituents a cut in their taxes yet surrender to pressures not to do so, a position in which, although he is an honest man who made a promise to the people, he has allowed expediency to shape his decision. If this happens, it beomes clear that moral conduct (right thinking and a considered promise) and conformity to what the leglislator had promised the people are not synonymous actions on his part. He has violated his "social contract "with the people to honor his oath of office, his obligation to obey, which means to affirm statutes of written precedence and obligation, in a word, to follow the law. In this situation, the leader's will countermands public opinion, which is quite frequently, morally wrong.

When another, often an innocent person, cannot rightfully be charged with a particular crime, for example, when the plaintiff will try to conceal his or her guilt from others, he will search out a council or a leglislature or, nowadays, an affluent "deep-pockets" Defendant to sue. It is one of the fractious traits of human nature that men are most oftlen wont to take credit only for a right moral decision, an act that resonates with accord in the minds of others. Human pride would triumph over guilt and human folly in this manner.

In America the liberty act as one pleases in defiance of right conduct, is subject to the enforcement of the law, or to the referendum of the people or, in the next election, to the wisdom or the pressures for social change.

A *right* choice in contradistinction to a wrong choice may include a common law or a statutory law, which law or laws contain moral insight into good and evil. A moral interpretation and decision to act morally and ethically is a Jludeo-Christian choice, informed by wisdom of the good or evil in the decision, is found in both the Talmud and Gospel played . They have played a fundamental role inthe founding and development of this country. Their truths can be found in our Common Laws. Thus can a moral choice, much as the "right to an abortion" or the right to grant "amnesty to illegal immigrlants," embody the right of challenge at the time of the decision by the President or by the Supreme Court, or, indeed, vy the individual citizen. LIn other words, Court Ruling a decision bly the President is not beyond the pale of challenge. That challenge is to the right to deviate from cusltom, tradition and particulary from the realization that history dictates certain proscriptive actions based on the majority value system. In short, the decision by the President or the ruling by the Supreme Court or, indeed, by a referendum, a recall, an impeachment *can be made to appear right* though justiciable e.g. abortion, or *right* though immoral e.g. sodomy, or lawlfixl yet ethically *wrong* e.g. bribery.

The moral conscience which affirms a better and more wholesome side to men's natures appears to be abrogated by riots or "crowd mind" and the tyranny of a majority, in a kind of dismal obeisance, mobs and riotous majorities—as arise in a direct democracy and within the clashes of Capitalism with Collectivism—will approve of their new freedom gotten by violence. Their immorality then consists in the harm, injury, prejudice or destuction done to other men in that free society. Yet they do not nor can they destroy or extinguish or expuge by violence alone those laws,which in a Republic are sacred and secular, laws that insure the continuation of that very liberty and conscience that are abused in the commission of the violent acts. These laws only confirm that such violence, on the rare ocasions when reason, candor, jusltice are not exhausted, is intrinsically imnoral. Right by might, though immoral, is always subject to the challenge of what and whose rights are to be subverted or repealed or defeated. Retributive justice pivots upon the liberated application of moral choices ... and without a code of justice no society can last for long. Thus mob rule tends to destroy, instead of to bring into existence social justice, a kind of justice that used to be positive but has become in reality increasingly corrective, as evidenced by the media's usurpation of formal trial justice; anchor persons have become **extempore** trial prosecutors and deposition-takers. The failure of criminal reform is found in the reality of repeat offenders, a fact that belies the philosophy of evolutionary improvement and secular reform rehabilitation.

Corrective retributive justice is a contradiction in terms, an oxymoron. For justice is by its very nature punitive, or else it is tolerant of crime and therefore corrupt. When forgiving, justice is replaced by the grace of unearned exoneration. To try to correct a criminal's conduct by incareration, rather than by internal change of mind and heart, is absurd and futile. This absurdity and futility occur not because the inmate will learnl new criminal techniques while he is lin prison; but because he bends to the corrective measures with a facade of change. Since that facade is often deceitful, the whole rehabilitative process makes a sham of corrective measures and their results. In the political arena, many a tyrant feigns loyalty, honesty and service in order to conceal his corrupt will. Pretense to a change of heart is surely not new.

Inward change almost never comes about rhough reason alone and mind control alone, but through a religious conversion. When this occurs then liberty regains status as the operative principle in the life of the former criminal. And conscience returns once again to its rightful place as the ruling authority over the individual's moral choices.

A person's liberty is to chose right over wrong must be practiced with caution, respect and understanding of others, for if it is to be effective in governing his actions, it is perhaps the only means whereby a citizen can claim a commonb cause by arms for his own self defense and for the defense of others. Justice is barbaric and inransigent when it is obtained by instant violence or armed oppression such as will promote the so called "conscience" of the State. General Gage's British Regulars quartered in the homes of the Boston people before the Revoluton was one real cause thereof, proved this point—that the State has no concience.

The modern American welfare State suffers from the delusion of its own inherent goodness, ironicaly having severed all but token connections with the historical religious faith that gave rise to the Christian command that man must love his neighbor as himself. Since God is dead for millions of Americans, they have been hard at work, since the theosophy of Darwin and the Marxian optimism, in creating an evolutionary man renovated into their own image, although few knew what the image of the perfect Proletariat man should be. They continue their work to this day with their Hedonism and their borrowed New Age philosophy of the centrist Self. Strangely, concepts of "conscience, of morall right and wrong,of the liberty of personal choice, of "inalianable rights" remains to this day more useful as "relics" of our forgfotten past, a past discarded in the indifference of historical illiteracy. For the most part, the modern generation does not know why it has liberty or by what vision and amazing courage and terrible anguish liberty came about.

America's compassion, for exampe, is a heritage of her past. Yet compassion is today politicized and repackaged by the State to lppear to be genetic. As a result of this transmutation, compassion is much sought after as an instrument of power, to be coveted, purchased and possessed by politicians, and from thence to be handed down to the common folk as some kine of novel gift from the ruling elite in Washington, which must bequest includes the liberal media. This transfer of the charisma of politico-social love has given rise to a kind of "we-are-the-nobility" attitude in the Congress and of the President, one of the "spinoffs" of emtrenched tenure in office. Sentimentalized into the *politics of caring* that belongs to the whosle welfare mystique, by benificien bureaucrats and power-seeking poilitisans, the corruption of biblical loe, as a command of God, turns sour. For that liberal-democrat issue, pruged of righteousness, is attributed to the State as its genesis which, if that is the case, makes of children, the aged and the desperately impoverished the wards of Ithe State In effect, the State has exploited their condition for its own advantage of power. These classes of citzens become the thereby the instruments to power-seeking propagvandists. Centrist Man becomes his own cynical god.

Justice under Liberty is enlightened, benign and protective when it is not inherent in guns but is embedded in laws, insuring its equal and fullest expression in the lives of all the people. The fulcrum of this truth is that freedom nourishes restraints and reason with ever new opportrnities, just as reason causes freedom to thrive by the exercise of intelligent moral choice. Under the canopy of free enquiry, read "liberty," America flourishes. In order to survive, however, she must acknowledge the relevance of moral choices of right and wrong, not in exclusively utlitarian and pragmatic ways, changing with each situation, but as absolute options for human conduct. To cheat, let us say, is not dishonorable one day and honorable the next. To be disloyal to one's own country is not an unacceptable moral choice in one era and an acceptable decision in another. To lie under oath is not forgiveable for one man and yet is so for another. To treat a man honorably when none are watching and yet dishonor and shame his name in public is vile and immoral, in the absence of any evidence to impugn his innocence.

By the foregoing arguments we can see that liberty, conscience and moral choice are indissoluably linked.

Where the State has replaced God in matters of conscience that might harm others, the right or the wrong choice is based not on an absolute principle of conduct but upon submission to a fear of the law.

The law tries intention; repentance for an action is often too late. Morality tests obedience, intention is never too late. Repentence gauges faithfulness, conscience is always on time.

19. THE DECLINE OF DISCIPLINED LIBERTY

Some philosophers will argue that Mankind in the aggregate, all societies, all races, is becoming increasingly perfect, his sciences and the sophisticated applications of his *Zeitgeist* wisdom making it possible. This gradual transiion is what he conceives to be his ethical evolution from out of caveman barbarism, promoted by his narcissistic Self-image, the egocentrism of all his endeavors at cultivating wisdom and perfect self-control. Primitive people must be included in this prognosis. God is no longer a sovereign Being to govern Man's conduct and to exact obedience with his laws and His threats. Rather, the State and its rulership through bureaucratic agencies—the modern equivalent of tribal controls—can readily perform the tasks of human improvement and social stability. The State can proudly accomplish these ends without religion and with much less anxiety to the common masses of people. Western technology introduced in backward countries is a step along the way. With the State—as with tribal Chieftans, the metaphor for bureaucracies—in control, the people will not perish in hell for their failures; they will simply chose others to blame as impediments to perfection to carry on this governmental project of mass betterment. The creation of ever more bureaus to facilitate this inching toward perfection is the modern-day answer to godly improvcement envisioned by prophets of Utopia.

Now that tlhe State and private enterprises have eliminated ancient vehicles of slaugher and rivalry, faith in God instead of an agency of the government being historically purged and condemned by State fiat, usisng the Courts to finalize its claims on human life and property, Man can claim his survival as the fittest by his close adherence to State policies of race and culture purification such as selective abortion, racial homogeniety—not the least of which is sex training for future *Leibensborn* State schools. Americans in particular are perfecting themselves by themselves. In the larger perspective, most of the Western world's govrnments and social skills at peace-making and communalcomity are lamentably behind the evolutionists' paradigm. But stand close. It ought to be projecfed by social evolutionists, that as time goes by Mankind will need fewer laws to control human lehavior. Freudian bio-instinctivism will collapse and the ego-id will implode leaving large scars as marks of former, less elevated wisdom. The rapture of State entitlements will reassure the yearning masses of their *goodness* as deserving recipients of hand-out aid and the State as the benevolent alms-giver. Behavior, like response-conditioning, will be a thing of the past. For the evolutionist's vision will admit of no more speculations about human behavior or preposterous rules for conjectural analysis of virtue's progress. All of those trappings will be swept away by Humanism's theism of Centrist Man—the which cleansing will mean, as is evident nowadays, an inevitable war of religious faiths. The social evolutionists' vision will admit of no more speculations about human behavior or preposterous rules for conjectual analysis, e.g. man will naturally chose right over wrong, good over evil. To think otherwise of man will be, as it is today, "politically incorrect."

Criminal activity unabriged, intercene warfare in Europe and the Middle East, inhuman abuses large and small of man aginst man, as for example, "ethnic cleansing" and fratracide, warrant one in saying of today that Mankind is becoming more intransigent in his conduct and more disobedient of ancient laws that explicitly acknowledge and delineate his depravity—the Ten Commandments, the Code of Hammurabi, the Koran, the Code of Zoraster, the Beautitudes of Christianity, the wisdom of Solomon and Confucius. That the State through its agencies is so presumptuous as to think it can superimpose its wisdom on these ancient testaments to Mankind's inherent inclination to do evil is sheer folly and delusion. The suppositious attitude of the planning Elite in American government speaks to the decline of their faith in our heritage as a free people with Judeo-Christian not Allah roots. For this heritage is the genesis of America's ethical and moral values.

Whatever men do today to modern society is religious. It follows that the rules for living, for parenting, for procreation, for lifestyles, for political thinking and for medical "caring"—again that word—are layed down by the State and forced upon the people, imputing to its agencies the power to punish deviants from its edicts. A "shadow Government" within the traditional government has emerged since the 1930's. Its Constitutional materalism has brought about a split between strict constructionists and liberal innovators, the latter of which is most visible inl rulings of the liberal Supreme Court, most recently in Malrxist Kelo decision relating to the disposal of private property, the seizure of private land for its max-imum tax value. This specific ruling reflets the Court's dependence on foreign law for its *ghestalt*, its philosophy of socio-legal engineering, they having taken a page from Karl Marx's **Das Kapital** in which he refers to the State's re=distribu-tion of land for communal benefit. And the Supreme Court represents the State in America's case.

The bureaucracy in Washington is the Shadow Government, with all of its drones, shudderbrains and clapperclaw offlicials, unelected ly; the people, who concoct myriads of regulations that control the people's lives. They do so on the assumption that the people lack the intelligence to thrive on their own or to solve their own problems without State interference. The bureaucrats convey a demeaning arrogance that belittles conscionable choices as, for example, that of parents who wish to educate their children in ways they think are best for their progeny.

Millions of Americans who are state-obligated conduct themselves as under a privileged Elite, enjoying an athiestic "inalienable" freedom to make moral choices, *viz-a-viz*, education and parenting that conform to State guidelines. That is a key *word—guidelines*, used as if the common people were blind and needed the nefarious, smug, bureaucratic management of functionaries under state control, as in the old Soviet Union, who. willl become even more so in the years to come. As the State attempts to dumb-down children to certain nation wide standards of achievement, mediocre perfomance in school work will be the result. That is shown to be so nowadays and educationists are too dense and muddleheaded to know or to admit the cause to be their own *liberal* controls in concert with activist judges. The insanity of mocking talent to accommodate mediocrity in education will become even more widespread than it is today, a lev-eling process that cannot possibly produce excellence. The reversal to this deliber-ate absurd reduction in excellence will occur when the State realizes that the protection of the child's self-image has led to his mediocre performance, the gull-ing of childish pride by pro-active liberal teachers. Much babble to the contrary,

America's school kids can do well, even better when and if the State gets out of the way.

We in these times see a visible decline in people's forebearance toward one another … in a word, their rudeness and incivility. This barbarity is evident in two venues: on the highways and in the classrooms of America. Such retrogression represents a pervassive alienation between diverse peoples which the athiestic State is impotent to address or to correct though its "agencies for caring." That condition of relationships in a dynamic flux is euphemistically described as "dysfunction," "personality maladjustment," "insanity," "political incorrectness," "variant lifestyles," "quota balance," "bi-polar disorder," "Race and political fratracide," "post traumatis stress syndrome," learning deficit disorler, and on and on that consistently employ State psyciagtrists but rarely the minister, Rabbi or priest. Thesse condtions can be grouped under the cover of *dilemmas* for they often involve guilt due to immoral choices versus the denial of the consequences for an unethical or immoral act of unaccountability. Scandal in the Congress shows this clash between virtue and vice in bribery cases.

These dilemmas are bound to continue so long as politial platforms remain dogmatically athiestic and impervious to the implementation of moral standards, absolutes, for human conduct. Relativistic virtue is an oxymoron and just does not work. We have witnessed, at the same time, a greater personal freedom being transposed into "license" the relsults of which have brought upon us the need for more police, prisons and personal protection. Americans generally have lost their understanding that Liberty demands moral accountability, and that absolute rules of social conduct do matter and that human conscience was never the gift of the Federal Govermentl through its legislation or its Supreme Cout rulings or the policies and Presidential Executive Orders of the outlaw—the above the law—mentality.

Americans are, according to the sociologist's evolutionary prognosis, headed in the direction of the Perfect Man. More recently the Messianic State and better rehailitation for criminals are all that are required. With the assistance of a manipulating Media, all things are possile. That is the evolutionary dogma embodied in Surprenme Court rulings that make freedom of speech consonant with corruption of the mind and soul, as the removal of God from the Pledge and excision of prayer and a child's affirmation of Jesus. State purification of the school curriculum today includes the acceptance of pornography over God's Commandments—the Commandments are a worse evil-gangster rap over a simple prayer and money over ownership of private property, license championed for abortion over parental control. That same Court and with it the 9th Court of

Appeals stationed in San Francisco also favor the killer—the fittest—over the victim—the meek, the lowly and the feeble. Just a technicality, Your Honor. The approach of non-consensual euthanasia, as in Holland, is on the way. Doctor-assisted suicide is already a reality in Oregon. The weakly, the deformed and the useless aged can be gotten rid of by law, not by moral choice! Thus the drift of our society into a letigious a-moral perception and personal choice is at hand.

In the issue of parenting, retribution for the loss of parental authority to the State becomes a-moral and a totally secular concept. Supreme Court rulings, that are socialistic if not Marxst in spirit—as eminent domain rulings—preclude all appeals to the God of Scripture. The Court's endorsement and society's acceptance of that endorsement of the about-to-be born non-right to life places the ugly Nine on the same level as Hitler who envisioned a super-race of the perfect Aryan. They stand courageously behind abortion with the same degree of intense disfavor and corrrupt disregard as the Communist Commintern who endorsed the flawless state-engineered Proletarian Man ... Yert these ultimate images of man never worked literally or figuratively.

While the immoral avarice of religious leaders is punished, the moral desire of conservative parents in to control their children's education is also punished. Thus when avarice and parental conern can adequately be punished, one can safely assert that the State, that is, the Federal Government, lacks an accommodating attitude toward moral conduct while, at the same time, it fosters by concealment and leader denial the moral turptitude of its own members, of the President and of the Congress.

Chiefly, it is the family's wrong parenting that blocks the progress of the State to evolve the Perfect Man. Outcome-based education, the dumbing-down process to avoid offending poor achievers in classrooms, drugs, little minds swathed in television, uninterested parents, busy parents of latchkey kids, the general acceptance of mediocrity (until recently) in school performance—all these factors work against the perfection of man. Through its controls the State attempts to punish "bad" parental conduct with admonitions, fines, deprivation of the child, severe chastening by intimiation, and stern authority management. The outcome of these pressures is that the only acceptable parental control, is that which is defined and tolerated by the Federal agency against child abuse. The absolute right of parents, even one parent, to exercise authority, control, love and influence over the child is made mugatory by State laws and by liberal judges who also liberalize pornographny as free speech and late-terml murder dependent on the mother's convenience an/or a late-term sonogram showing the wrong gender or a physical defect. The infant in the womb has become a ***thing.***

This judicial liberalism marks a decline in the effective potency of Liberty for all Americans in the exercise of those choices of conscience that visibly define right from wrong for the next generation. To stop an epidemic disease, for example, one makes a valiant effort to alter, through the peruasion of law morally grounded, a dangferous conduct that leads to the perpetuation of the disease. Sodomy is that danger. While "do not commit adualtery" cannot be construed as a statute, the foreknoledge of a disease carrier of his infection can be the cause for action in tort by his infected viction, because the AIDS disease is as deadly as a gun.

Today parents are often urged to inculcate feelings of self-indulgence in their childlren. Selflish enjoyment, having its genesis in the parents, is reinforced by an attitude of survivorlship superiority without struggle, a most common occurrence in an affluent age. Indeed, the State itself mandates against the struggle to live by making danger comprehensible as risk—note the requency of that word's empty use—and by elevating welfare to respectability. Bureaucrats feel that they must control your and my conduct, even to the extent—a coming attraction—of implanting surveillance devices in the homes of millions of Americans in order to gauge, read "control," their daily routines and habits of of life the better to know how to market specific products—it says here. The name given to this kind of fac-finding by surveillance is data-dredging, a scientific name for your business is my business. After all, what will it hurt to watch your day over our corporate monitors?—if you have nothing to feel ashamed about. And the electronic method beats polls, market surveys and the like.

The pernicious bureaucratic Elite will demand a kind of perfectionism that works in conformity to political symbols, namely, to the edict to worship the Earth, to save the darter snail, to salvage the protoplasm of abortions for science and cosmetics, to chasten Bible thumpers, to glamorize official philandering, to equalize poverty world wide, to demonize and demolish past heroes in America's history as irrelevant old white men, and to enshrine foreign prophets and seers like Mohammed and Zarathrusta as "our kind of folks." Conformity will also make the condom a national symbol of "caring about risk," will place a bounty on skin color like animal furs and will make Justice wear the nightgown of privacy with more plea-bargaining and trials by Media intervention. Conformity already teaches that Excellence is shameful because it makes others feel inferior by comparison, it having risen above mediocrity. The State has already taken upon itself the power to snuff out whatever human endeavor it disapproves of in the evolutionary name of planning for the Perfect Man. Equality by whatever means at whatever the cost is a Utopian mantra. Our inferiorities in certain accomplishments has mad us feel bad. It is up to the Federal Government to make us feel good about ourselves, level the playing field, punish the achievers when they blow the whistle or get out of line, mock excellence and praise mediocrity, and turn the grade schools into academies for experimentation in educational theories guided by school officials of vast authority but little understanding.

The personal liberties of Americans are on the decline as a result, say, as a consequence, of the State's interference in the private lives of its citizens. The State has invaded our lives through the increasing swarms of officials annointed by no one to manage this depraved business of social control of the citizenry, each new administration adding another agency to rectify some problem that were better left to the people themselves to correct or to resolve. The State in its unspoken arrogance would fix men's problems for them, as if they live in a broken society and the State is incumbent to do so on the presupposition that thle citizen lacks the intelligence or the initiative to fix matters himself. This is the liberal creed. Can one find any other attitude than arrogance in so demeaning a pursuit toward the Perfect Man? Remember that the Supreme Court has endorsed the quasi-scientific dogma of evolution, which necessarily includes Man's ethical and moral evolution. They who have lived by rules of evidence find evidenciary what is and will always remain a grand theory: evolution. To enforce evolution as the only theory taught in the schools, the Supreme Court must accept hearsay as evidence. For examples: Nature transmits mutations, carbon-dating is not ruined by water seepage, and similar bone structures do not serve similar purposes but demonstrate evolutionary variations, such as the fin for the wing for the hand. These pieces of hearsay, claptrap evidence pontificate the grand theory but plead no case for any other theory, such as Creationism. To plead the contrary views is to accept religious myth as evidence.

We now look to the Federal Government, the State, to define for us not only wht is scientific but what is evil, such as a dislike for another person liberals call "hatred"; or unethical, such as hiding money that ought to be taxed, or such as the obliteration of freedom of associaion in a corrupt and litigious denial of such free asociation to one if not to another group of citizens, such as the Boy Scouts or Bishoprics free of sodomizer leaders. That is how the Socialist Party of Hitler's Germany began—preferential association as racial exclusivity. The Supreme Court's liberal compromises place its rulings somewhere along the despotic's contnuum toward the Perfect Man. Laws that restrain a person's unlawful conduct are, indeed, must be, a transcending phenomenon in Mankind's evolution. They are but temporary measures to insure his genetic survival for the future Utopia. Genetic engineering waits in the wings for a caring: Elite corps of scientists and bureaucrats, who will attempt to fashion their Perfect Man in a test tube. Children being raised on the blatant absurdities of Man's evolutionary perfectability will succumb to genetic enginering in future years, out of pride and after the eradication of all moral inhibitions.

If Mankind is therefore perfectable, with fewer and fewer crimes occurring, fewer wars and less visible destruction of the planet, the results of the work of psychopathologists as well as environmentalists, we can then look forward to the slow relinquishment of his obedience to all laws in deference to his personal self-disciplined liberty on the rise, inasmuch as the laws and their embodiments which have held him in check for some seven millienia can at last be removed. Anarchy will become rarer and, like a shed skin, rid him of his rebellious desires, lawlessness and his discontent. Ultimately the selfless creature of the Perfect State will emerge and any and all laws that formerly governed human conduct will have been eliminated long ago. The Supreme Court has committed itself to this vision by its removal of religious obstructions in the pursusit of that Utopia, including itself The Supreme Court is willingly on a course of self-destruction, for their presence will be needless in the evolutionary society they have helped to create, sustain and perfect.

It follows then that the paradisical co-existence of the Perfect Man with his fellow Perfect Men, a relationship secure in all its Utopian "tolerances," will be benign and harmless and morally innocuous, that is to say, *innocent.* This is a marvelous optimism whose greatest value is to affect today's cynicism; cynicism is the blindness of the weak and the defeated. Of course, that is an ideal society, but one ought to remember that any person or institute that accepts evolutionary dogma at face value predicates this vision. One cannot accept the evolution of biological homo-sapiens without accepting his moral and ethical evolution as well. The inherent logic of this supposition, this axiom, leads one inexhorably toward lthe Perfect Man.

If these sorts of evolution are taking place—and if Man is no longer a spiritual being—then contemporary America is today in a state of transsition in which the innocent are constrained to stand idly by while the more violent, lawless malefalctors work through their evolutionary malfeasance stage, striding from the forest at last and into the light as politically right, just, compassionate and "caring," for the world to witness as true **Egalitarians.** Anxious to see that they compete successfully for the power to govern, the Media will see to it that criminals get their full measure of "caring" from the people, while the victim's families take care of the vicims of crime. Society in general continues to shut its eyes to the workability of absolute moral laws which have done much to make America one of the greatest nations of all time, its greatness being not so much technological as visionary of Man's capacity for the compassionate accommodation of all who come here, the distant reverberation of Her forebearers. Until some forty years ago, America lived that commandment of Christ—after God, "thou shalt love they neighbor as they self," the two greatest Commandlments. The gradual *Balkanization* of America that results from cries for *"diversity" ad nauseum* means the slow purgation of our spirlitual and moral heritage, for that mantra supposes that the elimination of the real diversity inherent in Americlan society is desireable for its perfection rather than for its unity. True diversity will fall before the cynicism of reality that the American version of Mankind is not factually perfectable and that she must surrender to this growing inter-alienation by way of technological encroachments on personal liberty. In short, ignorance of what constitutes true diversity will give into a pathetic bureaucratic notion of a highly diverse society that hates change. That change, those changes in forced human relationships, in sham *excellnce,* in fostered American "guilt" for the world's ills will constitute Statist counsel for perfection of all Mankind, not just of Americans. Here is where the Globalists will make their grand entrance, the disciplined liberty of Amerilca's *great experiment* having all but vanished from the consciousness of her citizens.

Liberty to the slave is visionary; liberty to the freeman is commonplace; liberty to the hireling is a gratuity and to the alien, it is a scoffer's dream.

The ethical choice does not beggar reason and irrational conduct; instead it abhors what is harmful to others while it expunges proud malice, the quintessential of unethical conduct.

Let no man disdain your love for liberty, especially with subtle offerings for corrupt gain; in his liberality, there is only derision, first of liberty and then of you.

Truth is the true confidante to liberty, honoring her whenever she is in travail.

In order to preserve a country and a people, liberty must not be bled from the arteries of thought, conduct and a conscience.

The despot makes every effort to embalm all final authority. A foolish people will do it for him.

The conscience of a man directs his steps, whether or not he admits to its effect upon him.

If you would permit evil seductions to pollute your will of righteous wisdom, remembering their power to deprave, then tarry a while, drink their genteel poison and die in the spirit at hell's fount.

Try out liberty as a pragmatic pawn for negotiation and you will lose its power to govern.

20. BROTHERHOOD: A PROPHETIC SURMISE

The philosophy of Henry David Thoreau, a revolt against the social order of New England with his faith in the "absolute freedom and rebellion" of the wilderness experience, a rebel who wrote of the "charm of Ithe Indian"—fits like a key in the lock of John Mill's doctrine of the "despotism of custom" as a "standing hinderaance to human advancement"; of the ongoing "struggle between liberty and power" and of man's ape-like capacity to mimic mediocrity. The overview of these two men does not seem to have changed much in almost two hundred years.

Both thinkers extolled the freedom to explore and to discover and to break free from artificial constraints of avaracious tyrants and mendacious government. Both thinkers inferred the capacity of the human mind to recover original innocence without interdiction by wealth or power or custom or God.

The extension ot their thought, derivitive of experience, is that successive generations will become more alike in their separate innocences-meaning their individuality for Mill and freedom without anarchy for Thoreau. Neither man foresaw or could have anticipated experiential liberty outside the confines of their own faith in a natural order of things, being in a word, presumptions.

Just as Thoreau's romantic naivete to justaposition to Mill's pragmatism must lead to an inevitable social Utopia, so did each of them believe that good men have the capacity to distance themselves from their depraved natures. The inference of the latter general concept was that laws that defeated humankind's most receptive and capacitous ability to experience awe, wonder, and inventiveness, whether of nature or of social change, should eventually lead to new forms of cherished liberty for which there could be no miraculous counterpart except creation. Through these forms must all of mankind in one Grand Kingdom of Brotherhood find unity on earth. Benevolence would reign and the laws of natural man would become increasingly responsive to the hidden human potential for goodness of his nature liberated by experience from innate evil. How glorious the perfected society will be! A State identified by its benign anarchy would then produce the penultimate happiness is the breasts of all whose good fortune it would be to be alive then. This, it appears, is the logical extension of Thoreau's romantic freedom and Mill's pragmatic re-constitution of human nature.

These tentative prophesies must today appear absurd to some persons of skeptical mind, however, it is true that many American social planners push their agencies, cajole for budget allotments, proliferate their microscopic rules of regulation and delight to indulge in omnivorous conquests of power upon this very poromise: to wit, that being creatures of habit or corrupted by bad authority, the American people must be compelled to change, to adapt to their State prescribed purification, and to experience for their moral salvation by laws of pennance e.g. apology to God for His inclusion in their mundane affairs like school prayer, the Pledge of Allegia;nce; and ny the redemption of their innocence, under threats of legal acion by the State against parental malfeasors who espouse religion. Electronic surveillance is a relatively new action by Ithe State to make common, ordinary and fearsome all things bold adventurous in American life. Electronic surveillance means to insure the people's securlity inl an almost totlly manipulated environment. Such is reform by inimidation made pervasive by television, political authority and and exculpatory laws that let reform-bureaucrats escape charges of breaking the laws of privacy and personall intercommunication.

Because of this Utopianism, or, more accurately, to promiote it, justice has become correctlive, the "oflficial" (NEA) arts messianic, the propaganda of political conformity widespread, elucation a dismal leveling of achievement to mediocrity and, finally, social Egalitarianism in almost all walks of life, religious ecumenicism included. In this manner of leveling to the absurd by intimidation does evolutionary Utopianism weed out Excellence as threatening and obstructive and as politically unacceptable.

To affect this end of the common Brotherhood of all mankind, lost in their jungle of sterile similitudinousness and conformmity, the bureaucrats with the condescending blessings of Congress, must devise such regulations as well as politicize the conscience and devalue personhood, veginning with the foetus to late term abortion into childhood. These bureaucrats, Planners annointed by liberal politicians, desire to create a New Order of the redemptive perfection of all Americans, the beginning of which shall be repentance for past mistakes in American history. Unconscionable reparations for insults to the British Crown amnd King George III, an unworkable Constitution for old white men, social changes and new laws to benefit the rich, for immoral slavery, for vengeance against Germans after WW—these events require some form of pennance before the world.

Carried over into the marketplace of ideas, in which the State will claim a monopoly in goods and ideas, social repentance will inevitably initiate further encroachments into the most sacred grounds of the family, and into the integrity of private contracts, religious freedom of worlship and private ownership of the land. The invasion of a totalitarian State is already well under way with a virtually one-party Nation—the Democrats bereft of ideas except control—and all powers of press, education, communication and entertainment—the persuasive powers—preempted by disinformation by the democratic party in Washington. Is not the prefigurement of Germnany's socialist labor government plain to see by way of example for America?

The State will mandate in some working areas quotas that affect private conracts. In conjunction with this statist oppression, workingmen's compension laws are destroying small buisinesses. Currently it is enforced medical care compesation, the anathema to small businesses with a limited income in the marketplace. Futhermore, the State is beginning to define the New Age family, bound together by sodomy and the respectabilility of sexual perversion, the whole grounded in a unisex society, a choice hypocrisy. The State has made deep inroads into the matter of parental discipline of their children. Religious freedom is under constant attack by the hostile State, whose minions rather prefer the enchantments of godless chaos in a valueless society to traditional religious morality, anything to reduce stress on fragile human nature.

The State in every way is attempting to prove that its agencies are more loving, more caring of the welfare of Amelrica's children than are the parents or the school, the traditional and acceptable birthplaces for values of virtue, honor and integlrity. The motto for my high school is **Achieve the Honorable.** Nowadays dope and illicit sex on the campus are up and graduation numbers are low. Parental training is lacking—the true source to instill values and self-discipline in the next generation.

Disruptive students will eventually be redeemed from their willful and obstreperous habits by the administrative bureaucratic hand of the Federal Government that tolerates an escalating misconduct, doing so by awarding diplomas of advancement based on academic failure! Already some malevollent leaders are proclaiming that petty criminals are the **avant gardes** figures of tomorrow, worthy of emulation, their violence in neigbhorhood gangs being merely the effulgence of the tomorrow's idealistic outreach youth. The more disruptive the student, the more certain he or she is of graduation from the system, the school being quit of him or her. The price of his diplomaa redeems behavior with the reward of a diploma. "He reformed in the 11th grade."

Furthermore, the State controls the American economuy throughl the Federal Reserve Board, none of whose members is elected yet who in concert bear directly upon interest relate, property loans, the value of the dollar, and the issuance of new currency—which powers are given to lthe Congress under Articlel I, Section 8, of the Constitution. "The Congress shall have the power to coin money, regulate the value thereof, and of foreign coin...." That the FRB prints currency isntead of mintiung coin begs the quustion of whose power is it, The Federal Reserve Board's or the Cogress's. This Board, a non-elected committee of bankers, is intended to stabilize the economuy and confirm the Broterhood of American labor in all areas of enterprise and expense.

What have these statist phenomina in common? Each represents a loss of control by the authorized entity, whether school teachers or the Congress. This loss in every instance represents the devaluation of stanrdards in order to accommodate the gains of expediency. That loss at a time before the change occus betrays acquiescence to bad judgement. A the loan money flows from Washington or from State coffers, the kid in the classroom has been socialized to accept his entitlement in free school lunches. He's bright; he knows his parent(s) is not paying for his meals in the school cafeteria or out on the grounds. He feels embarrassed because he is poor. The State makes up to him for his inferior status. The State has thereby created a Brotherhood of the Poor. With a child-like heroism, he hides his shame from his "affluent" schoolmates.

This socialization in personal liberty and benefits must, to be consistent with the evolution theory of reform, envision the moral perfectanility of native citizens on a personal as welll as on a national level. How can it be otherwise that later generations are stronger biggerr than their ancestors yet are duller in mental accumen and weaker in morall stamina and endurance? The answer comes easily when one lsubstitutes the politticization of the conscience for the "vapid religiosity of moral absolutes." It is commonly assumed that one grows strong morally as the State grows powerful politically. The irony of this supposition is that the untainted morality of the happy savage in his innate goodness can be accomplished only by the progressively greater sovereignty of the State, in the direction of increasing dependency. And that is neither happiness nor a moral milllieu but is *depotism under Statist control*

It is apparent already that the media *personna* who claim to be society's next flank of teachers, first of the children and then of the adults, will show Americans how to reach this marvelous sweetness of a sterile inner life and outward conformity. Their lesson plans will contain the adorlation of thei liberal Magi-CBS, NBC, ABC and the *New York Times*. The social planners have built into their schemes, their ideology to restructure the instituions of society, a cyniucism that seeks release through open rebellion from authoritarian controls of the *status quo*. The mantra for the young is : ***Challenge all authority!*** Outbursts of rebellion have often occurred in the form of street demonsrtations, student rallies and, more subtly, a campagin of disinformation. These happenings do not speak well of the evolutionist's thesis of the triumph of Brotherhood. In this perpetual struggle betwen liberalism and conservatism, the courts remain committed to the theory of evolution in all areas of human life, implicitly so. They espouse the closed system of physical evolution.

It is evolutionary to get rid of God. It is evolutionary to seize a man's property for the common good. It is evolutionary to acknowledge a woman's right to ptivacy by granting her the right to murder her child. It is evolutionary to give felons quick prisosn release and child molesters brief prison stays. It is evolutionary to grant the poor special rights, the sodomists their own marriage institution, the United Nations the right to debase our people and their history. It is evolutionary to suppose that Man is in full control of his own destiny and that natural disasters are the work of nature's laws and are therefore prognostic and treatable—like global warming and earthquake predictions.

Evolutionists, will, of course, lament that these endeavors are only forms of temporary stagnation in Mankind's glorious advance toward tlhe Brothrhood of fixure perfection, a perfection in which the victors will rise to the top, triumphant. The fittest is to survive, so the Hedonists will in all likelihood say, would have arrived sooner on that plateau of benign caring had it not been for bad religions such as Christianity, a malelvolent and angry God, an ordinary human Christ and a corrupt clergy. They are to blame. Lamentably, believers have placed their bets on the anarchist not the messiancic Jesus, who in a sense was more realisltc on the use of violent power. That was Pilate's fear. Yet conscience, the Judeo-Christian Scripture informs us, is the very instrument of their apostacy of moral blindness and idolatries. To some extent this misplacement of faith is responsible for the diaspora of the Jews amd God's chosen people. Also to some extent the violence gives rise to a smeug self-saltisfaction that all is well in Western civilization when, in fact, it is gradually eroding its civilied gloss through the self-will and iconocism of its inner corruption of ts values and its failure to percive of a power higher than and outside of Self. Be that as it may, a New Age liberty of conscience in its purlest form has made the rebellion extracted from it, the harm to Self and of others removed, ane evolutionary standards of perfection attained and acknowledged.

This inner purity of Man is God, since God is in all men, is now in a positiion to challenge the piety of the Saints of old and curse in the downfall of estanlished denominational religion. The charisma of dwelling zapped by a polytlheistic spirit is at last wiithin the reach of all men. Disciples of this New Age fantasy are in a position to dolubt and ldestroy arguments of the established religions. They are able to exercise conscionable ethical and moral choices under all ciricumstances, called siluational ethics, without the courtesy of a church or a doctine or a belief in God extrinsic to Self

They, these good ones, will exhibit a conscience that is so spure in that it can disregard theft as only an inter-evolutionary stage toward **full** godhead purity of motives; and that makes of the ancient dictum against false witness a shibboleth for honesty, real truth; and that casts murder in the guise sofl bad-judement and tastelsss ethiclal choice or ... for the more demanding—murder as mere illusion of mind gone awry and deserving not to ne believed, although requiring psycho-pathologiucal gleneticl tlreatament vy a kind ofl gene splitting that aborts the **criminal mind** and generates the evolutionary perfect clone of moral purity. No doctrine, no outdated moral impediments, no true God is the fated result. Once he be-comes, himself, a god new purity, without the dogma of forgiveness, becomes a permanent change in man's nature to be translated as an evolutionary fact of human perfection.

Even the old saw agalinst covetousness (Exodlus 20:27, the tenth Command-ment) will seem anteduvian, or at least preserved like a monastic gemstone, in the review of the Torah. "Lifeboat ethics" will arise like a sensecent ghost from men's childhood only to be disregarded as a harmless aberration of early moral confu-sion, a dilemma dangled before schoolchildren in the 21st century. Parents? Who will concern himself about honoring them when biological enginerering and stat-utory laws will have restructured the family by means of "hate laws," same-sex parentiang and test tube "arranements" and the enshrinement of State surrogacy, as in Hitler's Germany?

International demands through the United Nations will require that in-vitro babies vorn in surrogate, State-certified mothers,be sent off to police the world. The State will then have become the true Molech. Murder will have become mundane, as it has aleady, and necessary when performed by doctors under State supervision on the foetal unborn, on the near born and on the old. God is already an anachronism to millions of former believers, a call-word for frustration in the

State's accomplishment of these enterprises of human ingenuity and biological invention.

Evolutionary changes are already being achieved. First, by optional and then by mandatory surveillance, the State is preparing to tabulate the lives of all its citizens. Property will be the first to go. Tax records in Washington are already areality. Consumer spending habits will accrue via the internet and data dredging techniques. Thus isl recorded ownership by the masses. Surveillance chips included in the manufacture of houshold appliances is the next step. This insidious device will give the State access to the patterns of living habits in of millions of Americans, nationwide. The monitoring and control over the lives of Americas citizens will not be complete until Statutes that prohibit entry of a man's dwelling without probable cause and a search wlarrant from the proper court are struck down or ignored totally, as in todays warraantless searches for terrorist connections among innocent Americans. One receent Attorney General has already led the way in this un-Constitutional invasion of the citizen's dwelling place, an odious crime practiced by King George Ill's gentlemen soldiers. Have we come such a long way as not to know the difference between 1775 amd 2001 (2006)?

When the State, by proxy, owns the property of all but the most private iteme in the household, lwho will dare to raise his voice in protest against State proceedings preemptive of private property and the State's revocation of that happiness that private property brings. Will those who do possss no property then be mollifed by the pain of the possessors of same by their deprivation? Indeed, who among the evolutionists has ever mentioned "happiness" as a component in the Brotherhood life of the Perfect man, a status necessarily envisioned, implicitly, by the US Supreme Court when they have totally purged the *nuclear famly* and the circumstantial evidence of the evolutionists? Perhaps happness will drop out somewhere along the evolutionary time-line as a mutation in the human psyche, like our gills and our tails.

Finanlly, there is adultery. Americans already consider it simply another a-moral lifestyle. We are on that road today, to re-define procreation, and to accept the reality of sexual perversion, being touted as a just a variant kind of marriage. Siuce the evolutionists consider Man to be a mere animal without a soul, his sexual habits can be relegated to the reproductive processes of the animal breeder; and grossly immoral deviancies such as homosexuality, lesbianism, necrolepsy, incest and beastiality will be redefined as merely tasteless bad choices. By changing the *word referents,* tlhe liberal courts and press eliminate the moral aspect of sexual deviancy and therefore contribute to the evolutionists' dream of the Perfect Man. The God of believers is a sovereign God who will not be mocked. Their ethos of moral choice is on a collision course with thel New Agers.

For most Christians who claim a resource of power to reject Molech's seductions, their rejection of the New Age philosophy of man-god and their refusal to comply with Statist orders that contravine God's Word will make of them outlaws in a largely hedonist Humanistic society. Around them the scoffers at God and the practitioners of deviancy will flourish mightily within the sanctuary of tolerance, with or without Brotherly love and complications of dispute with the new amoral State. The Perfect Man will be the one who tolerates all human depravity, but when the legions of hell come to claim his soul and his life, who will defend him?

As the wind blows and bends the tree, so do the adversaries of liberty gather to shape the fibres of the wood they'd distort to their evil will. Street riots to intimidate justice are of that sort.

A people's liberty ought to be tantamount the loss of their lives, for what is to be gained in slavery but mere existence?

Do not try on liberty like an old garment for it is sure to tear where the greatest neglect has occurred.

The liberty to declare war is a defective use of politiclal power if not all advice is courted; and an immoral abuse of the capacity to decide when God plays noi part in the decision.

If you would defame America then you must regard your liberty of conscience as worthless and in its place subtitute the will of reason alone under state mandates.

Liberty is rearely bargained for without crippling its moral strength or ethical purpose but fought for, it acquires the mettle of its martyrs.

21. WISE AUTHORITY AND A CYNICAL PERFECTION

Since the gala days of the Garden of Eden, Cro-Magnon man could not be depended upon not to injure or to bring harm to his neighor, or to live out his life immune from injury by others of his species. Obviously such sufferers down through human history, in war and in peace, have found little merit in forebearance. For, after all, it was in the preservation of territory for a hunting preserve or for distancing between enemies that the hunter-warrior and the herdsman-farmer, that Essau-Jacob relationship began and property acquired boundaries. There were obviously local pragmatlic ordinances of social control that came later among the Germanic tribes, the city-states of Greece and the Emperors, pro-Consuls and Tetrarchian Courts of ancient Rome. In the days precognate to modern history, however, a time when the god of Ancient Hebrew faith had revealed himself, one was constrained not to hurt another lest he efface God's image and/or incur pain or death by stoning The French Revolution denied the wisdom of forebearance, as did Islamic tribal injury against the accused in Middle Eastern societies. In our own Revolution, the Colonists minimized the fact of consanguinity in tempering their hatred for British rule.

The reflective law of compassion's wisdom has always been that one ought not to take vengeance upon another but ought, instead, to seek accord and leave retribution to God. The Judaic saying ofl "an eye for Ian leye, a tooth for a tooth" was never a trival expression of unwise action. Again, a man must not let the sun go down on his anger, butr he should go and reconcile himself with his brother nefore offering his sacrifice to God. The Apostles Luke and Matthew and the sagacious King Solomon, in Proverbs, have much to say about treatment of one's enemies. Under the New Covenant Men are urged to be peacemakers, to practice love as tolerance and forebearlance. These solemn innvocations for humanitarian conduct existed before and after Christ walked the earth. They exemplify the possession of knowledge of the truth of compassion turned to its just application, to the enemy. One may wonder why the shepherd David did not chose a peace accord with Goliath, the lesson of the rejection being that wisdom does not always mandate peace.

In human his history once again, as controlling authority became concentrated into the hands of fewer men, usually the militarily and spiritually powerful leaders, trival chieftans, and baronial antagonists, laws proliferated to deal with increasingly complex human situations and relationships, pragmatic case-laws that confronted problems of everyday life and their solutions in the ordinary affairs of men and not of the gods.

Because modern-day judges have, in the essence and implications of their decisions, found these laws of protction and betterment to be evolutionary, that is, optimistic for the improvement of society and the criminal involved, it was but a short step of reason, extending down rom the Enlightlenment, for men to consider themselves enlightened visionaries of the evolutionary *philosophy*. That had to be "progressive" in the inevitability of time's contintinuum. For what other thesis would fit the expanding mechanisms for meting out justice? If men were not sgtriving to better their condition sociologially, they were at least becoming more controllable. In short, common men were evolving judicially toward a quasi-perfection. The proliferation of laws was, in effect, humanizing society, refining its members toward perfection and not toward degradation. Illusory or not, that was the premise that gave rise to many humanitarian traditions and institutions—like police protection and medical care. Political theoreticians such as John Stuart Mill might counsel a utilitarian approach:—if it is useful conduct to promote social welfare, adhere to it; if not, dispose of it and all customary supportive laws. Thus, since reason was inherited ny nature, its rationale was to reject undesireable laws. The pragmatic societal results wsere held up as illustrative of evolutionary survival. On the other hand, while the Enlightlenment was a major advance in human understanding, wisdom's application of known truhs to life actually never kept pace with intellectual attainments in the bodys of philosophical speculation by lsuch men as Freud, Skinner, H. G. Wells or William 1 James. There continue to be the social evolutionists of stature. Their theories outran social achievement producing what is called *cultural lag.* The perfection of man is not identical to the Perfect Man, for the former implies improvement in contradistinction to the ideal of the Perfect Image of God. The theories of these several men imply both the static insights into and the measurable"improvement" of human behaviorm but they are blind to the endresult of Perfection would ldeny any such vision as a Perfect Man. The theory of Man and Society evolution must, if it is to be a credible philosophy, embrace the ideal of human perfection. That is an evolutionary concept whereas *improvement* is not.

The United States Constitlution has imposed constraints on the authority-power of its various offices and its triumvirate branchs to inhibit them from the commission of explicit injujries to the people and to individual citizens.

It is a document fashioned solely for the individual citizen working in concert with his fellow Americans. It is not a tyrant's tool. The Amendment process illustrated by the Bill of Rights is the major inhiition against those "abuses" by Big Government that take the form of onerous micro-regulations and threats of supervening Federal agencies. This behemoth of power in Washington, DC belies the perfectability of any part, group or individual of the electorate. The citizens still battle violations in the form of warrantless invasions against home and privacy in America. Big Government seems to contradict the theory of human perfectability, a reality the roots of which extend down to the violations of citizens' rights by the king in Colonial dlays. Are we to say that wisdom can be applied to authority only in the presence of legalistic threats against the people.

Or, is our litigious society exemplary of a denial of man's perfectability and, coincidentally, of the theory of evolution that embraces this promise?

If the people of America are volitionarily moving toward perfection, as the US Supreme Court tacitly affirms by its mandating that the theory of biological evolution be taught as an exclusive closed system in the public schools, certainly then the bench warrants to investigate for criminal evidence should be considered by the people to be invasive abuses by the policing agencies, which can then be waived as the grounds that they are an endangerment to the perpetration and survival *of the fittest* test. Ferrit out the culpable accused and bring him to trial so that evoluionary progress can go on. Find a way other than invasion to discover the necesary evidence and leave the "advancing" people alone. One cannot have it both ways, that is, that the accused if convicted and rehailitated shows forth proof of his implulse or motivation toward perfection. The question still remains as to how an accused person can demlonstrate improvement toward perfectability. Rehailitlation, it would appear, answers this question. It stilll leaves out the engine to move a person, or a society, toward perfection. The ambivalence of the Court ruins the prohibitory attack on the Perfectability argument.

The thesis of Man's evolution toward perfection has brought the ever lenient criminal justice system to abet and support the *fittest,* as the victimizer, the murderer, the rapist, the extortionist as demi-gods of liberal intransigence whose exprerience is popularized in public for its sensation. A crime often promotes high profile interviews. Although criminal conduct is tacitly condemned by the public at large, it seems to be applauded by the Media and even extolled by the Court system. No? Then ask: how often Is the crimsinal not punished for his crime but is admonished in such a way as to make him seem fittest and once again strong enough to stand among his fellow citizens as a *survivor?* Hlis survival lheroizes him in the public's eye. The absurdity of the theory of evolutionm is evident in our criminal justice system wherein the criminal is reformed, saved or rehabilitated and "returned again to the lmains stream of society." Indeed, our justice system recognizes the validity of the evolution theory when it exempts certain classes of citizens from confronting the *survival test,* as the criminally insane and the new born (2st term) citizens. Justice for them is mitigated or passed ny altogether to permit the pregnant mother to live and the abortionist to survive as the fittest, the trashed infant the weaker and therefore, as a social flaw, honorably discarded.

Under actions by the Courts that exempt the culpable for whatever reason, the authority of criminal law becomes a *detente.* And any indemnification for the helpless victim of a crime becomes, instead of jusltice, the sword of vengeance.

For it should be seen that it is far less cruel to the victim of a crime for the court to mete out the full justice to the criminal than it is for the judge to subject the victim of the crime to the survival test once more, gliving to the convicted the repeated opportunity to assault society and again be captured and imprisonr for his deed. Just as there are repeat criminal offlenders, a victim can sustain attack more than once from the same criminal. It is the leniency of the judge that has permitted this recidivism to occur, as if in the name of justice but actually as a survival test of *the fittest* of the vicim rather than the other way around, the survival of the criminal. While the *survival of the fittest* is not a plea to indulge the criminal, still his perfectability, his curability, his redemption toward a better person (reformed) lies at the back of the mind of the liberal judge. The criminal court thus masures the salvic power of justice rather than the punitive power of the sentence. Such a twisting of the ends of justice belies socliety'strust in the court system, a trust that as a man sows so shall he reap. Of course, what he reaps is an extension and flourishing of that power which, criminal when proven, yet is his right as one of society's *fittest.* The same cannot be said of the victim, for whom the court is the lawful intercessor.

The State must involve itself in these agencies of rehabilitation, education and criminal oversight (like parole noards) that will promote th perfection of society's aberrant individual. Here we are talking not of moral perfection but of survival stamina that is both physical and mental. Indeed, such stories in the Media are now all the rage. However, the State has applied itself, through social entitlements and custody programs, to correct the destructive force of the revolving court penal system in our society ... which has freed child avductors, abusers, "stalkers/' neighborhood gangs and drug smugglers-netherworld activities that erode the culture's strengtlh and deprive its people of happiness.

These transgressions are hardly different in kind from those of the Cro-Mlagnon culture of conquest by might and violence and fear. The Book of Proverbs, the ancient Vedas, the Hebrew Talmud, the Koran, the Code of Hammurabi, the Gospels-all, in one way or another, reveal the retributive power of justice in the power of their writings. Their authors condemn as corrupting to the soul the evidences of everlasting human depravity. But, contrary to Western justice and in particular to our own system of criminal justice, these admonitions to the human spirit point to Man's corruption and not to that legalistic, quasi-scientific notion of his ultimate perfection and the end to all forms of human depravity. Who, then, is right: the evolutionists or the prophets of evil?

It is interesting to note that whenever some crime of heinous proportions breaks into the news, religious and irreligious people do not pull down musty court rulings to find the answers as to *why*. They look to their religious leaders to help them to clarify their thinking, to point to moral paths, to unravel for them the eternal conflict between guilt and innocence, sin and righteousness, punishment and forgiveness, and contrition and restoration.

Who other tlhan God has warned men about unequal balanceweights in the scales of Justice? Who informed them that is it is wrong to steal? Who has condemned their desire to drink to their glutinous fill of wine that bites like a viper? Who has denounced emvy, false witness that are found in suits for defamation of character? Who has condemned sloth and covetousness, crux ofmostwelare claims? Who has denouced idolatry that leads to the refusal to accept accountailiy for one's actions? Since wrong and right are no longer taught in millions of American homes, the courts are consequently compelled to redefine them in terms of the injury, the consquences brolught upon society by harmful or injurious behavior. Proof of the wrong is not the standard of morality or ethics but the degree of calamity suffered by the victim marks the balalnce of the scales of justice. In other words, a mode of conduct,such as driving while drunk is not wrong until the accident occurs the contrilutory cause of which is inebriation. The philosophy ot that approach o moral conduct, truth by consequences, is:that it is all right if the driver can get away with it. He can no longer blame the accident on his startled horse.

Furthermore, the corrective to bad behavior often follows the act as proof not that the act was immoral or unethical, but that the results thereof were unfortunate, as if chance were the major contributor. The upshsot of this inverse line of reasoning that starts with the result and works backwards is that the courts have taken upon themselves therapeutic and exhortatory duties. They and not the insructions and examples of parents in the home have become vehicles of the evolutionary theory that it is not the inner change of the individual's perception and his life that reorder his attlitudes and his thinking. Jlust the opposite occurs with the imposition of juridical power to the misbehavior. The Court replaces the father, head of lhe household. Law replaces faith, spiritual change, renewal of the mind and changes in conduct. It has become the business of the State to establish that a violation of social-law results in a penalty for wrong as the substitution for the natural law of right and wrong that works through the conscience. The State can accomplish this restructuring of the man if it assumes the role of God or plays an assigned role of surrogate to the father. As for the courts, they possess no salvic value to promote perfection yet they must appear to endorse its possibility. There is an optimism, yet a delusory hope inherent in this notion of Man's evolutionary perfectability. The liberty to innovate, to experiment and endure trial-and-error is involved in this optimism.

The American courts of more liberal persuasion especially those dealing with juvenile crime and domestic problems, taken togfether with *avant guarde* legislators, would "level the playing field." They would smooth out life's problems with another Federal agency. They would voice the miscreant minority desire for nirvana by conjuring up its image of plenty in the hands and coffers of the more affluent and, in so doing, remove from the path of the "deprived ones" all those ancient and immoveable impediments that have kept them from becoming perfect in stature and in gain—sooner rather than later. The attempts by social anarchists to restructure centiries-old institutions, like marriage and the family, represent attempts to demolish the obstacles to individual ambition, outlawing the institution in the name of libertine freedom only to accept total tolerance of their iconoclasm as the only condition for social change. Such iconoclastic acts seldom consider in their apostasy matters of virtue, of honesty, thrift, moderation, loyalty and self-control. They would have society bend the knee to their rebellion.

While the Federal government has grappled with great numvers of disruptive persons and situations, the so-called "dysfunctional family," drug addiction, child and wife abuse, abject poerty, violent crimes of one kind or another within our highly mobile sociledy, it has assumed the roles of priest, Salvationist, counsellor, savior, gravedigger and many other roles, ever urging the common oeole to conform to its benign guidelines of government and ever encouraging them to reach out toward the intelllectual purity and objective ethnicity of the controlling "elitists," most of whom as public *gerus* in think-tanks and on television, biased toward the liberal outlook, consider themselves to be society's legitimate teachers of the future.

Each step in the direction of social elitism and ethnic cleansing has led the people further and further away from the time-proven dogmas of moral absolutes, the authoritarian knowledge of the ages appliable as wisdom to today's life issues. Each separatist step by the actions of liberals in lthe Government, liberal judges in the courts boths the Appeals Courts and the Supreme Court, and by the liberal Media, has cost Americans a particular liberty. Freedom of Association is today under attack. An example is The Boy Scouts of America. By the rules of Members of that orgnization, they and not the Federal Government have a right to control their their membership for moral reasons. Religious liberty is under fire when children cannot express their faith in a public forum, whether that forum be the classroom or at public ceremonies. Images and symbols of religious significance are barred from public display. The insidious and corrupting agendas imposed in the name of "political correctness" seal off freedom of expression, while intimidation is the cannon of enforcment. The secularization of the nation that is today well under way in the name of Humanism threatens to replace our traditions of Judeo-Christian orthodoxy, the moral and ethical underpinning of this nation, with a hardcore athiestic and spiritually empty worlship of the law in the fallible hands of Man as the only vehicle for social change. The Law lies totally within the purview of lthe State; therefore, the laws of the Ancient Prophets will no longer have any validity in modern America. That prohibition rules out the Ten Commandments as a moral law. No-fault divorce, retrogressive indemnification by jury tampering, and *situation ethics* are examples of this mounting acceptance of un~accountability, in attitude as well as in avoidance. Man would perfect himself by his own devices. He could achieve nobility as the image of God without God. He would find liberty sacred only when he adjudicates its applications. He would otherwise mock those who luarrel with his Humanistic liberal faith as rellics, useless and obstacles to the glorious advance of human wisdom and comity.

Accompanying this inversion of traditional moral values is the perversion of common meanings of the English language. One can, by changing the **referents** of words, (in the mind) turn the meaning of life, its values, its sacredness completely around so that foetal death means tissue loss, murder means death with dignity, amnesty means forgivness for crime, and the public forum means public for some but not for everyone. Christian Fundamentalists, one of the most hated groups in America because of their belief in the inerrancy of Scripture, are told to "get real," which means to submit to circumstances without a whimper while the reality imposed is the reality of others, that of the Humanists whose god is Man himself. One might, by his very refusal, run the risk of being called *mad*. This kind of possession was commonplace in the Soviet Union where the insane asylum was the destination for political objectors. One might continue with the malapropisms: disease has become a problem of the environment or physical short-term impairmet, homosexuality is a lifestyle to be granted special protection by the State (law over morality). Cheating in Govenment is put under the microscopic scrutiny of another *committee investigation* that implies a mere questionable guilt.

These rationalizations often couched in deceptive legal language—the opportunisms of *non sequitur*—are fabrications that deny that they are, in actuality, sociological mutants upon our system of justice and its laws for over 200 years old. Challenges to the law, such as occasioned by bribery of Congressmen are not evolutionary; they are flaws of character. They do not denote Amercians' march toward perfection endorsed by cynical judges and opportunistic Supreme Court decisions, such as *eminent doman* decisions. They, however, have helped to establish an ineluctable corrent of mindless, instinctive social abandonment of morals, under the control of evolution-minded judges, legislators and teachers. Evolution is depicted as "change," subverting the naive to believe that we are moving inexhorably toward human perfection. Give the activist judges and the liberals another thousand years to reach that Epiphany of virtue. It promises that the old is bad for the new and the less said about the old the better. Moral virtue—what other kind is there?—is a *bete noir* with the accountability of conscience its keeper.

Liberty of conception, choice and acting is not exclusive to an elite corps of thiuk-ers. They belong to all free men.

Malice, envy, vituperation and deceit cannot of themselves dislodge Liberty from the Halls of Justice. But let them amass themselves in a surevellance without moral cause and they will deliberately destroy the rectitude of a intentioned slogans of pride and power will fill the void, to the dismay of an inert or an ignorant citizenry. Seiure of the land for the power of the State is one such example; acceptance of a political bribe by an evious lien government is another. The corruption of the democratic vote cannot be excused.

Hear ye! Liberty like a torch flame, will go out unless patriots tend its fire, shielding it from the winds of hate, envy and alien sabotage.

Freedom and Liberty seem synonymous yet Liberty of speech and action cannot surive in the absence of that toleration which is freedom; nor can Freedom long sustain itself without the presence of the other two doctrines or credenda.

The still small voice of Freedom is the conscience of millions of American citizens acting in concert under the law.

Liberty is the juxtaposition of the capacity to think, to chose and to act with the reluctancre to conform. Each of these is under the tutelage of social disapproval, lawful duress and the court of the conscience.

An inalienable right does not prescribe an ethical decision or a moral path of conduct. The right is the authorization, not the actuality of the liberated choice.

The right comes not from Man; it comes from God, the divine source therefore, within the context of the Constitution it ought to govern decisions and the day to day conduct of a Republic's ways of life. For our Forefathers believed that our liberties of conduct could not be sustained by a people acting without moral scruples and ethical values.

22. THE POLICE STATE AND CIVIL LIBERTY

The police represent the people as an extension ofl their will to remain secure on their persons, places and things (4tlh Amendment, US Constitution). Constitutional protectionist guarantees of the first Ten Amendments and applicable court rulings by the United States Supreme Court justify their presence. Moral conduct by the ordinary citizens rarely encounters police interdiction and when it does the alleged wrong omitted is not often a clear mistake. Police power can be a fearsome engine if corrupt. They do not act to represent a regime in democratic America, although by their over-zealous law enforcement they can appear to be despotic.

They, however, are not an ajudicatory body; they are not a court of law out in the field, on the streets and in communities. Yet individual citizens and their sympathizers have, in the past, resorted to the doctrines of "fair treatment" and "equal justice," that issue from the 14th and 15th Civil War Amendments in the Bill of Rights. It serves no constructive purpose to emphasize and to deplore constantly how majorities in a community give vent to their frustration by drumhead "trials" on the streets as vigilante acts of vengeance, leading in the past to lynchings while making mere vandalism their presentation of evidence in the name of justice. Community-watch groups serve to avert crime. Their consensus of the facts, *ex jure*, is the social interprertation of what peace and order and preventative-justice mean, they, knowingly, being the enforcers thereof. When a community of citizens dares to enforce the peace by condemnation of the police, taking the law into their own hands, their rebellious actions tend to erode their own concept of justice and to make ineffective the existing police protection.

If the State is despotic it can make some kinds of harmless conduct appear to be criminal, eg. unlicensed parental control of their children in public, in deprivation of the child's rights. As freedom becomes, in the eyes of thepublic, the license to censure and the leglitimate agents of justice appear to be powerless against criminal assault of various kinds, the State begins to decide for us, *viz-a-viz* the television, what is decent and good or unethical and corruprting. Socal approval or disapproval of immoral and unethical conduct, as the smmons of dichotemous power to judge, existed in the past when the non-activist judges handed down severe rulings and parole boards did not allow a shortage of beds to guide their decisions. In evidence before the 1960's, today that power of moral decision is relegated to certain groups in the community, religious congregations, service organizations, and to a small conservative element in the Media. The State, however, by its egregious assaults on public morality has usurped the authority of conscionable behavior, the power of the God-given conscience, and in its place has put a cold, caloused and calculating authority of the Humanistic religion of Man-god power. Were this not so, situation ethics and on-going hostility toward Christians, in particular and toward moral conduct in general, would not have arisen, except more covertly. For the potential enemy of a consccionless State, so history has shown, has been Christianity and its martyrs. In a dictatorship, as iln Afghanistan and Iraq, where right and wrong were State decisions, one man's enclave of evil schemes and intentions brought injury to an entire population by means of starvation, class warfare and vicious acts of terror.

Where the State thus usurps the people's right of self-defense, the extension of which is police power, the State fields its agents to harass the people and to make dangerous, if not illegal, all such measures which signify that right—suchl as gun ownership—acknowledging the primacy of local police control over events that appear to threaten the authority of the State and the peace of the community. This prioritization of police power was never intended by the 'Framers to strip the power of self-protection from the people; the former merely augments and reinforces the latter. When the Justice Department, for example, uses the FBI with its fire power to capture and destroy common citizens in their attempts at self-dlefense, it has acted a-morally and unconscionably. Then US Marshals are brought in to control and to enforce the law of free association for purposes of education. In brief, the State has acted a-morally. When Federal troops are mustered to threaen and to shoot students who refluse to knuckle under to a judge's order, the State has acted a-morally. When the paratroops are brought into a town—as happened in Little Rock in 1963—to enforce a ruling ol non-segregation, instead of mandating that the local police do the job, the State has acted a-morally. In these instances the right of self-defense capitulated to a tyrannical Government action which, acting not out of conscience but out of a questionable method of law enforcement, the State elevated its authority to the level of oppression thereby denying to the citizenry their right to defnd themselves—a right vested in the authority of the local police. Only when, in fact, an uprising or resistance to a Court's order constitutes an insurrection does the President have police power through his use of troops. Previous labor strikes and the bonus marchers on Washington have brought out the troops, by Federal order. Yet the use of Federal troops to enforce the law should always be the last resort. The President sent the troops thereto prevent a riot while the Federal Marshals saw that the law was enforced in Brown v the School Board. The local police would have proved inadequae to quell a riot, for or against the Governor.

To the extent that local police power gives way to Statist authority, which means troops of US Marshals or contingentss of the army or Justilce Departmet Agents, the power of the people in self-defense, vested in their local police, becomes null and void. And the militia, tolerated and mandated by the 2nd Amendment becomes illusory, first when the State usurps the police power of the people, and second, when they are caused to surrender their weapons for self-defense, which, the citizenry being armed, constitutes a terror to all tyrants, including ours in Government.

Nor does the genesis to subjuate the people always come from the State. It can emanate upon the demaogic words and vitriolic actions of anarchists within the community as an larmed insurrection. In America it is a truism to say that justice is established to protect the citizen from harming others or himself, or from injuring him. To accomplish those ends the police enforce obedience to the law. What is not always clear, be it in a village, small town or city, is that the citizen does not possess a total freedom to do as he wants. Mill's philsophy would have proved too Utopian and anarschistic for modern America, reflecting as it did the 18th century Enlightenment of radical social agreements.

Implicit in the first Ten Amendments was the role and actions of the individual citizen's conscience. In the Declaration of Independence its authors and its composer Thomas Jefferson inferred the conscience in its appeal to a sovereign, and to direct the people toward freedom,. In "appealing to the Suspreme Judge of the world for the rectitude of our intentions," the Founders layed their charges before the king. This confrontation illustrated the conscience of the people's rectitude versus the unconscionale power of the King, who represented the State of England. The charges meant two things: (1) a civil war against one's own countrymen, and (2) an intention to secure freedom regardless of the other side.

Taking the matter of personal liberty to the extreme of individual action, we find that if a man is an anarchist he must certainly be one by his own understanding of what laws gird State actions, amd what lawful pursuits he rejects, otherwie he engages in the malevolence of a child or he is mad. He has rejcted the conditional presence of liberty for the total absence of those rights of free speech and action, liberty and right being interchangeable, one with the other's corresponding act, as to cry, "to arms," the shouter then raising his firearm above his head in the Public Square, shoot a passing tyrant. Liberty infers an accounability for one's actions or they are without any meaning, just as the right of self-defense has no meaning once the State takes away that right by its use of prison and judicial authority. The anarchist is devoid of that accountability. He has no right to enjoy any right, becaue he has set aside all rights except for those of brutal mahem, bloodletting and hostile mischief that he might give **frail** rein to his malevolence. No anarchist has ever practiced benevolence toward others; even his comrades are suspect and he, and they, seize raw power before the public's recognition that he is, in deed and words, a nihilist who promotes outlawry.

Street anarchists are the chief opponents of the local police and in their vitriolic malaise they would set up and establish the despotisms of their own selflhood and god-men, like the supermen of Fasclist Germalny. They would and do then rule without laws, an oxymoron of meaning. For if the right of self-defense—and we are dealing with police power here—is a right given by the State, then it becomes no longer a right but an edict, a command of the oppressive and conscionless State, a tryannical imposition, a false right.

The Nihilist's seizure of a right is the first step toward despotism. In our country, religious freedom constitutes that first step. Such a police power lacks the conscience of human will and therefore exists outside the bounds of adjudication as moral right or wrong. The pleading of the proud, authoritarin and tyrannical human beast then becomes that "the state can do no wrong." So it was with King George III. For if the State usurps God's authority, then moral choice and moral virtue are dead as guiding lights. One needs but to ask: Which Court in America today validates and certifies a law, by its decisions and rulings, that lacks a correspondingl morality? I affirm that the US Supreme Court has gone far in the direction of doing so by its approval of late-term abortion, its acceptance of those most heinous acts as symbols of freedom of expression and privacy, its seizure of private property of one citizen and giving it to another, its purging of the conscience from relgious expresions of faith in public, its enforcement of the closed system of theoretical evolution without factual evidence, its mandate that the State possesses the power and the authority that are superior to those of the natural parents; its deliberate and diabolic intent to redesign guilt to assume the appearance of victimization, and to imitate at least in our Liberal courts of today, an the overreaching authority that belongs to a sovereign God.

For the Supreme Court is not interested in moral virtue or morality; its function is to interpret the law without the spirit of soul. Matters self-defense for the lower courts, have no hearing on their lofty plateau of judgement. Yet every case that reaches the highest court bears somewhere along the way of its progress of adjudication an individual moral choice that merits condemnation or deserves grace. Where that choice happens to be the chosen use of a right to self-defense, a police power never surrendered by the people to the police, moral action enters in. Thus moral choice has become a practiced and an exclusive right, not of the State but of the people.

Only time will tell if the police can resist the temptation to nationalize themseles in the name of efficiency, a better cooperation between States and communities in tracking criminals. For to the extent that the authority of the police agencies is dispersed nationwide, they cease to represent the common people of America, the source of their authority. The concept of mass policing then occurs. Who in the Government, other than the Department of Defense, will have oversight of the balance between police power and surveillance-tracking methods? Will the computer fix and regulate and legitimize that power? It would appear to be so with the invention of electronic data-mining. The police can then readily become agents of a Centrist Government answerable *only* to its own bureaucrats and corrupt politicians while yet pleading common-cause of their protection of the people. Such an expansion of police power summons the Soviet notion of a Central police authority, a KGB Bureau of police surveillance and apprehension, perhaps then a Gestapo-like agency, without the brutality, to defend the execution of the President's homeland-security policies.

Nationalization ol the police in America, a great "army" in blue, means a corresponding dependence upon the State and its agents. Electronic surveillance of the people is already a reality, a means of invading communication at the option of the police, exclusive of a warrant in certain situations—seizure of drugs, detemtom of probable-cause suspects of a crime. What agency other than a court is prepared and empowered to block politicization of the police and provide oversight in the use of sophisticated surveillance techniques? Is the FISA Court sufficient—when it is used? Who then can or will call upon the local police to defend him? And, following this delegation of police power by the State through corrupt or overly-ambitious politicians, the citizens' right of self-defense will rest theoretically in his own hands. This shift in the focus of authority seems to mean a distancing of the local police from the citizens.

There will always be local problems in which the police ought to be called; but due to response time-lag and inability of some communities to upgrade their police with new members and the latest equipment, the effect of police power on the stability of the community will be nugatory, almost as if they were not there. The computerized cop will fill this breech and to greater and greater degree become his own court on-site. With an increase in the power of the Federal Government to control local situations will come, as it does even today, greater pressure for gun-control. Attacks upon the integrity of the police are attacks upon the citizen's right of self-defense. No theory of cultural mores can diminish that Constitutional right—except by a practiced violation of privacy under the fourth Amendment. *The security of one's person means the right to his privacy. That right cannot be separated from his self-defense, with or without a gun, the former under the 2nd Amendment.*

The protection of his privacy is a right the citizen shares with the police. To the degree that the authority of the police is diminished, anarchy will find expression and with that loosening of societal-control and personal maldiction in some of life's complex venues—tax gathering, property rights, tainted contracts, bribery and "influence-peddling," political extortion, voting 'irregularities" and drug peddling and usage—there will come threats to human life and security which the police are sworn to protect against. Have we not learned from the bootlegging era in America? Will the cry then be "to arms?"

Do not treat your personal liberty as a trivial gain. It was won by blood of heroes and martyrs.

Unrestrained freedom is not the exercise of liberty of choice but is the wanton disreard for all choices, since the action issus from caprice, impulse and blind obedience to emotions and, lately, radical violence of religious extremists against Amerians and Jews.

Religious liberty is the soul of America. From it have come all the compassionate institutions of our society—hospitals, child labor reforms, healing arts, protestant justice. It posits Man's likeness to the image of God. It denies that men are naturally good, kind and loving.

Seek not to know evil or it will overcome you either with its perfume or by the sword.

The loss of liberty to a people is the triumph of their witlessness and their pagan self-worship. True liberty wears humility with honor and seeks wisdom with understanding.

23. LEGALIZED DRUGS, PROFITS, CHOICE OF BURNOUT

It will not be the increased availability of drugs that will reduce their unsafe, deceptive illusion. The exact opposite phenomenon will occur. With the increase in supply due to the desire of the suppliers to maximiz to meet the market demand, they will invent new avenues for the importation of cocaine, drug of choice. Numerous tunnels recently discovered between Mexico and the Unirted States attest to this smuggling cunning. Smugglers and sellers will effectively retain control of the trade. Their monopoly will put a lock on high prices regardless of the quality or the quantity coming into the country. Natural human depravity will not tolerate this kind of *laissez faire* without its finding the means to even greater profits and, in grisly alliance with death, occasion the loss of many lives through drug use and cartel violence. The decriminalization of psychogenic drugs is, in effect, a concerted attempt by addicts, some doctors, and by the AMA lobby in Washington to testify as to marijuana's beneficial medical use. But, if experience provides any insight into human nature, decriminalization will not reduce addiction or cheapen the cost of drug use or medical care for the addict. Removal of legal liablility will only enhance and increase drug trafficking in this country and provide police and hospitals with many new cases of addiction.

What are a few of the consequences spiritually and pathologically of legalization that argue for the rejection of this proposal? The lawfully permissive use of cocaine will reinforce the social acceptance of a pernicious evil. What today is a crime exacts from the *user* all choice but an obedience to the toxic addiction which, having caught its victim who is now euphoric, will no longer tolerate free personal moral choice in matters that require fine judgement and moral discrimination. The need for money to support the habit will lead to robbery and criminal violence as, gradually, obedience to the habit demands enslaved changes in behavior.

The well known "enslavement" consists of the chemical dependence and, wlith the ingestion and satfisfacion of the poison, to the bondage of will, moral liberlty of choice, rational cognition and aclear conscience to discriminate right from wrong. Not one of tlhese capacities is fully functional when the drug user is in a state of euphoric stupor. The discriminating usefulness of the cognitive intelligence is not visible durinng the period of intoxication, nor is the clear-thinking faculty to chose other options or to feel one's own emotions. There ocurs a patlhological numbing of all the senses. Mortal death is the result; the crippling of the intelligence is th product the "burnout" is a suicidal death wish.

The uxer is lss the offener of society than is the pedder who, now permitted to sell what is presumably cheaper though not inexpensive, and finding the market expanded, will not compensate with a lower price per "hit." Instead, he will in silent conspiracy with others—since the network of users is in place and available—agree on a set price which, likethe splitting of stock shares into halves, will, if initially lower, rise again with each half meeting the old; market price. The increase in availability of thehit will doublethe cost to its victim.

Such a cheap absurdity of legalization should be apparent. The investment of free choice in the retention of the drug habit works to destroy the user's rational will power, thus making him more subject to profitable medical attention for his prescriptions and his accident prone vulnerability. His habit excludes alternative lifestyles/The religious conversion-drug use is a cult-works to attract linto his confidence and vicinity those who share his addiction. As the police, hospitals and society, generally, all know, the addict must, himself, sell drugs or commit robbery for the money not just to support his habit but those dependent upon his income. They, too, are victims of his habit. He must somehow increase his income from his job performance, often in the entertainment industry. It is wishfull thinking to presume that legaliaation will reduce the usage. It can only reduce the the use'sr police arrests for having the drug while at the same time leading to increased accidents on the highways that put the drug usage on a causal par with alcohol. The AMA does not see beyond their diagnostic vision in the matter.

These powerful drugs empty the mind of reason and therefore of the mind's rational choic The user of either dlrug, LSD or Cocaine, hashish or derivatives like "ecstacy", or "harmless" marijuana, becomes literally **mindless.** And if the drug is "mild," like marajuaana, the dope user's choices aee liklely to bcome childish and obscured by delayed sychomotor responses to environmental stimuli. Therefore the liberty of free-willed choie cognition lacks evaluative realism and cogency, just as a few ounces of win will impair reflex actions and timing. Consequences become momenarily obscured. The euphoria assists in blocking out correlative experiental mememor. The delicate, fine sensitive tissue of the brain, can take only so much abuse from a "politically correct" chemical, correct because it is acceptable by mass consensus. The lowered resistance to drug use is due partly to desensitization by the liberal Media, who tend to trivialize marijuana use. The liberty to chose a gradually higher-potency drug or their combination gives to the user the suicidal power to self-destruct. As a consequence of this "indoctrination," he becomes a prisoner of his libertine choice. In time the addict will drift toward self-destruction, at which point the liberty of free will, a gift from God, is emptied of all mening. Narcos use their so-called "free will." their "liberty" to enter hell of the drug addict.

Liberty is rarely an automoatic respose to an issue or problem, since its derivative of free-don invites consideration of alternatives and consequences.

Once discarded for material comforts and dependency on the State, liberty will atrophy in importance to the people. In its place will come "correctness," conformity and social approval as authoritarianism and cultic personality like-ability.

The value of the right, or liberty, of moral choice is not in the absence of controls or dogmas but in the presence of options.

Keep liberty, the freedom of personal choices, enchained by bureaucratic regulation and you will make of it a mawkish, obsolescent and old falshioned anachronism. Liberty will then draw its justification from bureaucrats, not from values.

There is no liberty" in mob-mind or riotous violence. The freedom observed is the freedom of the predatory beast to roam by instinct and would extol and emulate this kind of ani= mal "morality." PIETA has absurdly assigned moral choice to the animal world; man is the killer for food.

24. LIBERTY MERITED, CLAIMED, NOT DOLED OR SOLD

Many are the criminals who after being freed from our prisons resume their lives of crime. Habits of the past, prison contacts, the return lust for profits and hedonist pleasures contribute to this recidivism. The records of repeat offenders support this categorical statement as to statistics and to individual crimes. Today, however, there is in our counry a climate of *sentimental forgivenes* that is intensely self-congratulatory, while it reflects the ignorance of the true meaning of criminal reform, namely, that the felon while in prison has adopted a different, a new, standard of values which prohibits and controls him by the synergistic operation of moral conscience and criminal law. Activating forces of evidence, innocent-plea bargaining, jruy verdict or extenuating circumstances pleading assemble during his sentence-time. When he is released on parole, they join with his desire to repeat his former criminal activities. This is the rationalization of the freed man who, speculating on his past, dares to repeat its mistakes. To the warden and society without insight, the fiendish actor has been rehabilitated from proven sinner to qustionable saint.

Yet, true "renewing of the mind," the inner transformation must be internal. Being genuine, the change does not condone or include "acing as if changed. The staunchist skeptic will disagree that such an innner change can come about only by a religious conversion that is spiritual more than it is intellectual. Yet all other change is challengeable deception and a false mask. Not all the psychiatric treatment in the world can effectuate such a total change of mind, attitudes and conscience ...

This is the illusion of modelrn psychiatric "medicine," that such changes can be wrought by man alone. Extended into politics, politicians will plead that their programs will "heal our country." When, however, God is excluded from the from the public forum, and psychiatric medicine, for so it is called, fails in attempts to revive the conscience to deal with moral choices, the victim of moral amnesia can only retreat to his former redoubt in the security of his ignorance. He is easy prey again to the drug dealer.

The people have observed the relative ineffectiveness of shortened encarceration, corrective parole and prisoner lawsuits against prison officials as means to remedy prisoner behavior that effect a change in him. At the same time, compassionate leave and holiday visits, the upgrade of the "animal syndrome" together with conjugal visits, prisoner television and game rooms, taken with a whole complex of otherr rehabitation programs, as group therapy, prayer sessions, outdoors games, trade school, etc. have made of punishment an effort of salvation . Our rehabitation programs have made of the State a messianic engine for saving the souls and the lives of hard-core prisoners.

God in the above ways is presumed to show His salvic power through rehabilitation. This had been true in some rare instances—Charles Colson of Waterate break-in being one but then he was famour before was sentenced. The obvious failure of rehabilitation practices is inevitable in the present-day prison and the criminal reforms espoused by evolution activists. Of course, if reform were a total impossibility for man, then that would constitute a denial the central purpose for Christ's crucifixion. Athiests fail to see llany connection anyway. In the long view, the reformist results of sentimental sympathy remain inadequate and sterile of actual criminal reform.

Prisoners do their time under the frequent assumption that the trial judge misappropriated their liberty or that the judge and jury irrationally condemned the prisoner to exile. Sentimentalists of reform and liberal pundits who feel personally outraged by incarceration of any form, and in particular by capital punishment, make the present-day kinds of "unusual punisment" appear to be crimes of torture—the long incarceration in "the hole," political disenfranchisement, separation from famihy and friends and deprivation of exercise and yard freedom.

The prison reform movement, however, would give to these popular modifications of ancient retribution of revenge, the redemptive status of restoration. The guards can be called to account for their mishanding of a prisoner although not often in Federal institutions where the most hardened are kept. Where some degree of leniency is practiced by the warden and his jailors, these change are supposed to represent social enlightenment. Detainees during wartime are locked up under a different set of rules and discipline, the Geneva Convention.

Despite these civilian prisoner amenities, criminals repeat their crimes when released. After all, goes the reasoning, are not religious confession and absolution somewhat the same as a convict's having to endure these terriible ordeals—their imprisonment being a kind of wrongful suffering that correlates with retributive justice if not absolution? The criminal is thus relieved of his sense of guilt by a false compassion of Stateist forms of power, of forgiveness by virtue of his parole from an all-powerful state, of criminality expunged as an unintentional, evil act and not as a mistake. The former one is immoral, the other a bad choice.

There has come about as a result of these modern-day perspectives an almost total perversion of the significance of punishment for crime, the State representing itself in a manner that proclaims that death for a capital crime is now *"cruel and unjust"* is anti-Constitutional and made rational only by the liberal Court's changing the purview of law and punishment to imply the State's "forgiveness"! Imprisonment has the significance of the criminal being forced to sacrifice himself for his crime. All who agree will weep at the prison walls. Liberals in the Media, especially, and in the Universities consider capital punishment to be legalized murder and a shame upon a society that regards itself as compassionate, if not Christian. Often these reformist conscientious objectors are the same radicals who find nothing immoral or cruel or depraved or destrucrtive of civilized society about rending a baby in the womb of its mother, in the process urging society to approve of the act and the following "humanitarin" donation of the remains to of the unborn infant to medical science, as for Parkinsons diseae. How blind and grotesque and bloodied over by death's pal cast has our vision become!

One may conclude from the above commentary on prisoner "rights" that personal liberty is never freely granted by the State but that it must be earned or, at lesst, waited for in line. In those circumstances the misunderstanding of the prisoner's liberty arise from the fact that Mankind is ceaselessly and with cunning pleasure inclined to do evil, but that he is progressively getting better an better morally. That subtle yet "indisputable" improvement is attributed to changes in his environment, both inside the prison walls and in society outside. Yet, the increased crime rate among repeat offenders, the recidivist rate, is evidence that no matter how carefully the lawmakers craft our laws and make changes in our system of justice and restrucure our prison methodologies, the inbred tendency in men to do evil will forever appear and repose in our nation's life, irrespective of changes in the environment. Jobs will not eliminate robbery. Prostitution will not eradicate rape. Religious idealism will not expunge the crime of extortion. When God gave to Man freewill, He witheld the knowledge of good and evil to protect him from his own self-destruction. The evil was already in place by way of satan's rebellion and a third of the angels whom God pitched into outer darkness. The evil that God shielded from man was begotten in heaven by the Angel of light, Satan, the evil of vaunting pride who also had free will. The test of obedience configured forever the character of the individual man's will. Its nexus was human pride. The will to sin meant the end of mankind until Christ's atonement of forgiveness. Belief in Moral evolution makes the Cross irrelevant to modern-day man. His pride rules out submission, as it did Satan's.

Must we, under these "backward" circumstances of social denial to potential criminals, tremble with the fear of crime? I think not. The Christian community whose roots certalinly are pre-Revolutionary, will say that men's innocence can be restored through the salvation of his soul, making him righteous before God. Yet we have watched religious leaders cavort and gambol and fornicate like the wildest seamen in port. This human flaw, this will to imperfection as an obsession to do evil, still proves that the laws of authority in earlier America, laws that accepted personal liberty in character, deed and covenant—the Constitution is a covenant between the people and their government, under God—sufficed as the basic law of the land until recent decades. The out-of-sight banishment of moral values especially in the public schools is now and will again be hotly debated. A people cannot deny their roots. Meanwhile, the liberal agenda of "values clarification "and "sensitivity training" have proved impotent to control social rebellion and crime in the public schools.

Both weaken the moral fibre of American society. The upshot of these dangerously sentimental programs is that the onerous is put not upon the egregious offenses of the programs, but upon on the lack ofl higher teacher salaries. Don't change the behavior of the children by reminding them of moral standards. Make new laws that will remedy these forms of "child abuse." eg. institute mandatory homework at home, limited television, study discipline at home, and generally better parental oversight of their children's learning, at home and not on open house night. The environment of a Utopia cannot change human nature. Even the finest teachers cannot goad laziness into action or indiffeence into attention. For contemporary children expect by cultuaral TV indoctrination, an element of entertainment they have not found in the fantasies of great scientific and social experiments, and in the great discoveries of man; for these are are the greatest entertainment of all!

The shaminism, the borrowed New Age mediational simplificaion of life, ateempts to impose a Humanist philosophy on young and old alike that will not produce the result of forebearance toward others. The Humanist spoilers promote in concealment the moral suicide of society, first, by severing the taproot with America's own history by rewriting American history, and, second, by indoctrinating the next generations in the false belief in America's cultural and moral inferiority. This disposal of honor is a direct result of the egalitarianism that affects one-worlders who suppose that no one country is morally superior to the next. That's fine if voodoo is one's means for change, or the *final solution* is the way to prove Aryan superiority, or that slavery is a benefit to both the North and the South, or that Caesar deserved a second chance by way of Mussolini.

The rust of medocrity-thinking and evaluation of citizen pride is silently at work. It is blind speculaion to assume that the evolutionary hypothesis inferred from Thoreau's romntic happy-savage concept will ever give birth to an intellectually and ethically pure specimen of **Americansus Evolutionus.** Teachers may try to kindle self-esteem in their students, based on dumbed-down classroom performance, lawyers may attempt to engineer vast plans for biological unity, and preachers of Scripture may expound on the doctrine of brotherly love. But men cannot bury their wont to do evil, to tolerate corruption with the sweet, siren voice of atheistic Humanism. Man-god advocates, if left in control in our courts, will wreck the ship of a strong and morally harmonious society, as is becoming the case.

If, however, there must be some sort of benign final authority to govern America, and an interpretable Constitution supposes that life's diversity is a given, then the dominion of that authority will be atheism as it invades the lives of the people. For men change and they are corruptible and devious and shewed to escape responsibility and to promote self-grandeur. The prowess of Humanistic atheism will become militaristic and its *zeiltgeist* will be one of absolute synchronology, Liberty will give way to total efficiency and conformity, a fully computerized society, the end of which is today *political correctness* and the denial of the values of our Forefathers. One cannot force a living being into the mold of a rapacious sense of personal power. He must be educated to assume dominion by which he finds his first alliance in the State. That is the task of our university professors and, in the grades, liberal school administrators.

That such an evolutionary State of perfection is achievable is the philosophy claimed by the United States Supreme Court today when they give their ongoing support to the theory of evolution. Recent radical decisions regarding religion, abortion and property attest to that slant in Court opinion that envisions a more perfect union, not by representative government but by "judicial tyranny." The Court cannot pick and chose which theory, the evolutionists or the Creationists, it would lend its authority to. And so the matter of orgins presupposes only one theory to be valid for skeletan man as well as for moral man.

That final benevolent authoriy must insure that the people do not harm one another by its insistence that crime is either to be tolerated as bad-choice *mistake,* or the punishment be so mitigated by charming amenities of imprisonment that the whole episode of a crime, trial and sentencing can be written off as simply another and darker, lifestyle, the "cruel and unusual" fact of imprisonment. Plea-bargaining will become a thing of the past and the power to pardon and to grant amnesty be increasingly manifold. Tampering with the mehanism of guilt and punishment will trivialize many kinds of crime, as doctor-assisgted suicide—to cite one example and crimes as symptoms of mental disease, to cite another.

A corrupt judiciary and court system will make this transformation entirely possible. New laws to insure a restructuring and impact of punishment will require, momentarily for a few years at least, the Stateist surveillance of all activities of the citizenry. Even now the social Planers are attempting to set up that scenario by insisting on miulti-cultural homogeniety and political conformity. Mediocrity and attacks on elitist excellence are on the march. The Americlan traditional, or nuclear, family, being "elitist" and authoritarian, is daily blasted by missives that range from pornography to wifeswapping. These common evidences of moral decay among the people are like the softening up barrage before the actual invaision and the invasive linkages beteen the bureaucrats and the media moguls are many and intricate. Somewhere in this brew of power-grabbing, the individual citizlen is getting lost. His moral compass needle, his conscience about things he had been taught as right or wrong, is deflecting. He is assured that the technicrats and the Humanists will deliver him by their elecrtronic ways to keep better track of him—by the exploitation, for example, of his consumer habits with the latest telchnique called *data dredging.*

Washington bureaucrats have increasingly made matters of personal privacy, their concern by urging that the Congress pass laws to better control the intrepreneur and his "suspicious" actions, especially if he conducts trade withs the Middle East. Indeed, so immense a gulf of suspicion separates the people of America from the Federal bureaucrats in Washington, DC, a gulf that was never brided even a by FDRs popular fireside chats, but rather was widened by his weakening thus effectively neutering American morality. When an impersonal State authority colllapses from its own rot, there come in its place highly invasive bureaus which, by threats and fines and imprisonment, begin out of envy and corrosive greed to work at our former liberties as though they were of no great significance. The bureaucrats count only their centralized power as beneficial to, and homeletlic for, the people. Remember that Caesar gave his citizens of Rome bread and circusses to appease their unreason over his power. The bureaucrats will look for groups to hate and to scapegoat, those who oppose their Humanist revision of Americas history and abasement of moral standards in the name of tolerance by law. The multiplicity of their rules increases their power, while the people intuitively sense the loss of theirs, accompanied by a growing disrespect for and distrust of Washsngton Government.

Let us carry the plot line further. An unhappy and frustrated State, discontented still with its crushsing might brought to bear againt individuals, always individuals for effective State control by intimidation ... will install a reactionary military force to work with the local police against the common people who have failed to attain the degree of motivation and cognative purity the State demands. The educational systems throughout America will become the real scapeoat for this failure at redemption, at intellectual and ethical, moral and racial conformity, to effect, stateist notions of evolutionary inprovement. We see this taking place with all the hoopla about school test scores.

Tjus, our own Revolutionary vision will appear to have come **full** circle, ever more so as the influx of the children of aliens overload the school systlems and make their polylglot demands upon the corriculum, dissatisfied with America, jealous of her wealth, contemptuous of her values. Millions of them and their parents will be anxious to seize liberty without a struggle, as an entitlement; while the indigenous people, both native and naturalized, will fight this invasion as a bureaucrat prostitution of earned freedom. Imigration is most commendable when the immigrants with gratitude wish to adapt to, not to remake, their new land. Yet they are too proud, these aliens, to feel grateful. The proliferation of cultural islands insults the host and provides only sterile soil for liberty's growth. It also provides the source for an ignorant yet a volatile rebellion of the kind that is foreign to America as a Republic. The last thing one wants to do is to attempt to lbuy them off, for they understand not the significance of their liberties under the law—or the blood spilled to gain and to preserve them.

A man who whips his ox unmercifully shows less understanding of freedom than does his ox, which understands the freedom to graze.

Political propagands exploits the people's ignorance of their heritage, of liberty. It will not thrive in the face of an historically informed citizenry.

Liberty is of little concern to those who are dependent upon the State for the course of their lives. Therefore, liberty does not flourish in an Oligarchy, a Dictatorship or a Welfare Society.

Treat liberty with indifference and you cultivate anarchy. Treat her with disdain and you prosper war. Treat her with contempt and you eventually enslave a people.

A right without responsibilities is form withsout substandee—and thus its appeal fails before activists and image-makers.

25. THE POLITCALLY-CORRECT VERSUS THE CREATIVE

Individualism does not require eccentricity in order to be unique. It's an astounding fact of contemporary society that most human enterprise not revolving around "conventional wisdom," "political correctness,"or the "socially acceptable" in speech and conduct are actually thought to be deviations from the *normal*. Few will disagree that what is "normal" does not attract unusual attention, yet transfer the customs of one culture into another and the normal instantly becomes abnormal or un-customary to the host culture. That is because a society finds comfort in its usual practices and is stunned or stricken with curiosity to see cultural practices ourside their own mores and standards. This kind of rigidity is at times intolerance, although more often it is a form of curiosity.

Increasingly, televiion is establishing criteria for the normal in areas of variant cultural norms, by televised history, by on-site photography abroad, by revelations of how other peoples live. We should expecd television cameras to do this important work, since it is a prime teacher and condtioner of our American culture with all its diversity. Normal, however, is a word that is being replaced by wisdom which, in its everyday usages, indicts what has been considered traditional to be palpably false. The entertainment industry has indoctrinated its vast audience into strange and alien mores, global in scope. The venerated name for this constant onslaught against traditional institutions is *political corrctness*. The changes wrought by this shibboleth challenge are subtle and poisonous to inventive, creative, curious persons who are exposed to expositors of this damning mindset. The young are most often affected; older generations scoff at the idea of a paradignm of "correctness," especially if politics dictate its content.

Cautious phrasing, a delicate use of words, an over-sensitized expectation of resentment, an inbred reluctance to take orders for the sake of concience—these constitute the reistance to any kind of enforced "correctness."—as if "correctnss" in the sense of polity involved a special wisdom, even if labeled eccentric by critics. For example, "mutual consent" refers to a courtesy agreemenl, "intolerance" demands *license,* "playing field" is an empty symbol for combat arena, "separation, as church from State, indicates a *prohibition,* "morality" refers almost invariably to sexual activity, "foetal materal" describes an infant in the womb, privilege means a categorical *right,* lifestyle means whatever the user says it means, and *correct* describes an agreement with whomever the user choses as or her standard-bearer. These examples can be used as forms of intellectual dishonesty by which the user often intends to convey a corrupted version of the truth.

Eccentricity in speech, as a dialect, is cultural and discernable. True eceentricities like malapropisms, schenecdoche, verbal inventions, anachronisms, new-fangled concocktions, barbarisms and fetishes of the language all seek to invent, to be deliberately *different.* There is in them a liberty of intellect that gratifies the inventor though it may bewilder the hearer. Eccentricities of language, however, have earned a place in American slang for which there is ample proof.

There is in the uses of these variants of "plain" language a freedom of cognition. It is not proffound for someone to slay that these variants represent and connote in any way a kind of ethical use of the language. One cannot ascribe an ethical or a moral significance to any of these variants, yet, the gerus of political correctness wince, turn their backs on, eschew, denounce or in some instances express disapproval when any of thee variants is used in a politically incorrect manner, as if the user means some sort of slander, or bad mouthing, or harm to the hearter. There is room for complete freedom of language within the bounds of an accepted civility; that should be the only balancestone. To ascribe bad-ness to any one of these is to slander the user by treating him as loathsome of speech and unmerited to express his thoughts openly. Bad can mean bad sometimes and not all the time. A bad word by itself has no absolute moral value of right or wrong and can consequently be replaced by a ood word, which may be more inviting, pleasant and accptable. The discretion, however, should be the user's and not the oppressor of the English language.

Social tolerance by lothers of an eccentricity is a measure of the experiential range of the person and of the sophistication of the society. Foks in a culture who try to shackle the language demonstrate not the cospmopolitan but the provincial culture that they reall are. Political correctness is exceedingly provincial and dishonest by mandating a language acceptable to all yet esclusive to none. Many collegiate intellectuals are are quite provincial in this regard, they who have lived in the metropolis all their lives and sholuld knew eterby their exposure to cultural diverssity. Small rural towns, quite understandably, rarely invite, or accept, the wierd person to live within their borders. This provincialism has no sure solurce except community acceptance .The point here is that free choice in a democracy ought never to beg for a handout of acceptance, not even from the *politically correct* activists as a test of integrity, whether in choice of words or in open dialogue.

Exclusionary tactics by any majority within a society reflect the egalitarian attitude that all men must speak with equal precision and color, an attitude that leads to a kind of nominalism of entrenched enlightnment reason, in a word, to mediocrity ... The minority of the eccentric persons may, at the same time, voice a desilre to level the majority and call it equality. It is, therefore, imperative before any meaningful dialogue can begin that the speakers agree on the meanings of the referents, the words they use. Anything less is babble and leads to confusion in the minds of all persons. Issues of nationl sovereignty fall under the purview of this declaration.

But, again, true egalitarilanism is a philosophy since it can be encforced only by law and not by 1 moral censure. Just as there can be a tyranny of the majority, so also there can arise a tyranny of the minority of one, the tyrant. This nation was founded on the morality of the inalienable, the God-given, rights which were premised first before the Constitution of the State was enacted by Man. A Monarch by divine right was onlytolerated before our Revolution to overthrow the Divine Jurisprudence of the Crown, Theocratic governments have caused many troubles in the histories of nations. (Matt. 28:17; Rom 23:11) By tlhese verses and their experience with King George III, our Founders were informed that the people needed laws that were morally reflective of God's authority but enforced and trnsliterated into moral law for man's use, benefit and enjoyment. The language of our Constitution discriminatses and establishes right government from wrong government and that is a moral preconception of civil conduct and authority. Not being Humanistic, it is not "politically correct."

The degree of tolerance that Americans demostrate toward aliens, let us say, is directly related to their adaptability to what is unique in others. The obverse side of this observation is that conformity makes comrades of us all, thereby all too often squelching talent, ambition, "uniqueness" to accomommodate the commonplace and the mediocre, surnamed the "politically correct." In this way an egalitarian sociey does then bring injury to the integrity of human individuality and personal aspirations.

The question arises: if the artist is more innovative than the reader, in the verbal forms of innovative content and highly exquisite inventions in character, scene, circumtances, ought not tolerance for the "eccentric" imagination to be fostered, helping to initiate and provide a climate, an insurance for creative works that provide new ideas, new art forms, "findings" if you will, in kinds of radical aartistic representations that are comprehensivle to the average reader-observer of the work? This is a major purpose of a university, to promote what is different, not what is correct. For often what seems "correct" is eccentric in an obscurely innovative way.

Original work can be the resuslt of experimentation possible *only* in such an environment, as, for example, an inventive reconfiguration of old or known data; the the radical combination of discordant elements, as in poetry; and the borrowing from other disciplines in suport of a radical hypothesis, as moion picture art has evoked fantasy in painting and *visa versa*, as scientific cloning has drawn poets to the infinite subtle shadings of The Self or to the word "identical" to describe likeness. If a lcreature can e cloned, wlhat is to vbe slaid abolut plagarism or in=beeding dddor the replication of light waves into sound waves or the value to animal husbandry of ecloning, if there is one? Is there not a danger in this contemporary urge to "scoop" God by redefining nature and nature's expression by way of language into patterns of "political" acceptability? Or have not politics een carried too far?

Within the atmosphere of this sort of creative social laboratory, hypothttical variations from norms and known truths are, or canl be, descrived as eccentric, or plauslibly different. It is usually the dull mind that impugns orginality in order toexcuse its want of the samel attribute. It is society's accommoditition to what is different, the presence of liberty in mind and spirit, that allows the imagination to create a work of art, ply, painting, poem or piece of music. Here the eccentric, the novel and inventive and singular appear within the context of the works' exciting content.

Internal eccentricirty, one might call it, is the cognative variable, the comprehensive choice, between right and wrong as those choices refer to moral values. A creative work that ignores order welcomes chaos and so irrational and incomprehensible; having neitner intention nor direction, it is a-moral. Much modern art depicts life as meaningless and chaotic and irralationall.

It sometimes represents the artist's suicide of the spirit.

Contrariwise, conformity to the traditional requires little reason, Non-compliance may give rise in the execution to lthe critics' acclaim of the work as "extraordinarily different," "sensational," vbeyond expectations" etc. These superlatives are attempts to identifys true origisnality, that is—like no other. Tey should alwlays ve suspect, for that perceptiont takes time. It is a value-judgement based on the history of the particular art form and its practitioners, the examples for comparison. Various schools of art in the past have illustratsed this action-reaction among painters and playwrights. Conformity can be progressive; in politics it is called Reactionary. Fixing the *status quo* as immutable always gives rise to challenges.

In politics the most pragmatic way to break the grip of conformity is to litigate in a way that shatters the voice and the preference of those entrenched in power. Public forums in the media, partcularly in radio, have this capacity to topple barriers to eccentricity, that is to say, to the truth. For the Eccentric often carries the torch of noble Visionary and ageless truths. These forums can readily, as they have demonstrated, mount the barracades erected by the members of the the popular, the profitable, the unassailable.

The eccentric vision or crusade or outcry must have moral content in order to valiate the claim to values. Attacks in the arts have been called, as in politics, reactionalry. That is a word to which mongers of propaganda attempt to discredit "decadent" values with the *nihilism* of moral suicide; with god-like conundrums of when life began or when death should be allowed. Those advocates coming from all walks of life in America are the missionaries of death by their proscriptions on life.

Yet strangely, the old values persist while the characters on life's stage change. The newcomers are outlaws. Their non-conformity to custom and convention is not an act of outlawry. But absolute moral values are not necesarily represented by the *status quo* either. So it is there seems on occasion to be a tyranny of the majority that makes of the eccentric writer, poet or painter, an outcast with the banishment of his work, conformity can otherwise be the devil put on the back of an "eccentric" artist by the smug and pious conformists around him. Moral discrimination is blind to dress and manners. The values remain while the choices are personal and creatuve, lyt ecause of novelty alone, solicit dddddddoppossli-tion, evoke the criticisms of false originality, of an "eccentricity" in graphic, pictorial expression that is mediocre. Sholuld a poem, novel or play voice a moral stance whatsoever ... or does it really matter that the originality of the work offends—or does not offend—a tradition of expression by its a-moral judgement on life?

Right is not the indulgence of pleasure and *wrong* the inflicting of pain. Instead, *right* considers the justice of an act and *wrong* the character of the retribution.

Ethical choices between right and wrong are not always clear-cut. In these cases it is better to abstain from acting or to wait for new evidence.

Liberty in the affairs of men is most often impugned by fraudulent overtures to a-moral freedom; that is, to anarchy.

Treat liberty like a stepchild and it will remain barren of great deeds and moral example

Because of valor men win laurels in combat.Because of moral righteousness they win accolades from the pious. Because of liberty rightly exercoised and brought to bear, they share annony-mity—which is a curse to the impious and to the valorous a platitude; but a gift to the grateful who love liberty.

26. TELEVISION AND CULTURAL HOMOGENIETY

Television is gradually, season by season, *commonizing* the American people, reducing them to talk with the same speech phrasing of the interrogatory style, and to adopt similarities of political idiom, to mimic sit-com blaze manners and behavior, to imitate dress codes of corny nonchalance, to feel envy of the upper middle-class~the dormeered Cape Cod Cottage with a two car garage and two storeys—and yuppie dress-code apparel, cosmetics, entertainment of crude swank, two-year old utility vehicles and liberal notions of political outrage. _Standards_ is the the word for this kind of viewer indoctrination. Deviations from these images, these assaults on regional and cultural variety native to the American scene are considered to be the effronteries of incorrectness, whether or not political. While to conform to these television images is thought to be, subliminally, socially correct. Such everyday TV images, often modeled by anchor persons, are typical nowadays of common America vulgarity and tastlessness in all areas, dress, speech, conduct. Often the language, profane and obscene, nonchalant with sophisticated intention, is insipid beyond repetition. Those who write and produce these televisionl feature themselves to be the teachers of the New Age. To conform to their standards is savvy, is "wisdom" of a high and acceptable order. This specious absurdity of empty adulation goes on and on.

The medum is stirring together American idiosyncracies of social situtions and cultural types into a polyglot mixture that represents neither ther greater America nor even its regionalisms, cerainly not the classes of persons depicted. Only news stories somehow keep the continuity of American customs, lifstyles and native values relatively evident and recognizeable. The television industry, in its dramas, is making up its own small provincial world of stock stypes with stock emotions, stock ambitions, stock reactions, stock face expressions and voice intonations and gestures. The stylization of America is in progress. This is the America that reaches foreign audliences and accounts for much of the enmity against our people.

But so what! One might ask. Sheer escapism, not reality, certainly. The virtual reality episodes are more like mockeries of reality, scarcely true, unique and original representations of American life but rather impostures upon reality. It is evident to more intellilgent viewers, or shall we say, more objective viewers—that American life is seldom so brashs or so blaze as the mouthpieces for writer propaganda expect us to believe is the case. The images of on the screen are fraudulent caracatures of real life counterparts whose emotions are stockpiled and type cast, as I've said. They are symbols of affluence and grotesque distortions of the "typical American." But the viewers, of course, have the right to edit their own watching.

Much like the films of the 1930's television is fantacizing America and in doing so is replacing old values with other values, the New Age Humanism of man-god centrality and relative virtue, all he while appealing to the consumer who is the ultimate godhead of both the indusgry and the marketplace. The main thing, apparently—on the prime-time shows at any rate—is to make 'm laugh or cry. The fantacizing must stir the limited emotions. What is a wry smile, what is a tender caress or a nod of wise apprehension? Why should violence be applkauded and/or laughed at—a man slips and falls on a banana peel as if to advertise a brand of non-skid carpet or a floor wax or a brand of shoe-wear. The vulgarity and coarseness are appalling to the sensitive viewer. Talk not of "political correctness!"

In order to accomplish their ultimate sebacious end with a serialized play that lasts as long as the ratings hold up, the writers and actors "conspire" to create visual enactments of those new values which tend to make television characters beast or god or boor. The males are nerds, devils and beastial, the simpletons if they are not gangfsters; and the females are goddesses of a kind of supreme intelligence whose charms inspire awe and envy. Propaganda stereotypes who appeal to a *movement* of one kind or another, the feminine extremists, the multil-culturalists, the environmentalists. Along the line, I have often wondered why characrers in a play don't turn off some of the lights in the room. An why the straight man who is not macho looks like a papaer mache yuppe manikin. If not that, then he is cast as a perhistoric cro-magnon in either looks or actions for a clown who is able to do tricks for the sale of a product.

The typical telelvision play is demonstrably weak in social insight and crudely powerful in its subtle slander of traditions; normal i.e. unexciting everyday relationships and values for living. Basilic honesty is one, true manhood is another—am idenltity crisis in America; the centrist family is yet another distortion. Loyalty is replaced by commendable promiscuity. Adultery is *tres chic*, marriage of a man ;and a woman is old-fashioned. Philandering has replaced marital love, selecive misconduct and pampered children have replaced filial obedience and ordinary, child-engnendered fun. Frugality and thrift are the discards of prodigal waste or laudably-stupid enterprises, like sabotaging the lives of a dozen people in the isolated shipwreck-island in hopes that "The Admirable Crighton" exemplifies a new egalitarian socialist society.

Glitzy success has, indeed, replaced drab day-to-day mere existence. Modesty in houses, dress and conduct has yet to replace flambuoyance and "conspicuous consumption" with its 30-thousand dollar cars and second-floor mansions, which hav to be heated and furnished, swept and kept from foreclosure. Genuine regional modes of living and idoms of speech are ignored in favor of a studio non-language and a studio-generated theosophy of slang realism. The stereotypes continue apace. While 90-year olds continue to ski on the slopes, the over-tenderized, solicitous habits of stereotyped careomg fails to regard folks over seventy years of age too old for anything but the rocker and am old-age pensiuon. In trasnition themselves, physically, they would foist their identity crisis upon both the elderly and the very young.

Ringmastering has replaced child rearing in domestic dramas. Serendipity of melodramatic incidents in the plot has all but blanked out accountability of motivation, from doctors to junk yard dealers. Sometimes the antics of the story are funny, more akin to slapstick ; at other times they are banile and rarely ever clever. Recorder-type profanity and non-language that follows non-thought have replaced the intelligent dialogue of the "old movies," and have obscured much of the phonographic/photographic realism of contemporary television electronic drama, almost as if it did not pay the producer to create sound realism in his video-storly. Still, the brain-washing plunges on.

The integrity of the TV watchers is at risk. The contrived and stagy fantasies belie the common-sense attitude of most Americans. Surprise! We are still a nation of common horse-sense, Yankee traders. That, lhowever, flies in the face of the false values of the sit com. The inveterate viewer is elevated by a kind of hypnosis into thinking like his TV set thinks—another member of the family, the impact of which drives moral conscience underground. Right has become wrong and wrong the right way to live one's life, conducl one's buisness, family life, romance, rear children. Burgeoned by Ithe television, the cell phone has become the family doctor, priest, cop and therapist that gives immediacy to needs and soothes stress while conjuring up false security. It often nowadays defines relationships.

The *commonization* of Americans through their telelvision fantasies has lowered the barriers to immoral conduct. Constant connection with the tube cannot help but do so after 40 to 60 hours of watching, week in and week out. Cognitive thought and social perception are mysteriously destroyed or reduced. When the rape of a man's wife is fodder for comedy before the eyes of the watching audience, that is gross and highly offensive. When a teenager turns up pregnant and her condition is a subtle invitation to return to innocence thus to elicit the humor of ridicule, that is offensive. Quasi-criminal is a new word. As such, a scene joins force with the actual rapist in our society; the fiction character monstgrous act of the real felon. Any treatment of such a crime desensitizes the public. Child aduction, re3peatedly screened, so dulls the conscience that the victim receives no help from passersby. The television has in its own dramatic way to desensitize the public. The government and trial lawyers and the overactive trial courts with activist liberal judges have intimidated the publlic. Who wants to get involved and sustain a multi-thousand dollar law suit by involvement in an immediate crime? When the criminal is the victim, why rescue the real victim if that is possible? Again, Robbery is glamorized by real-men villains whilest the police are often suspect if not villified. All of these dark antisocial fare are barbaric and insulting and degrading. Many popular television stories intended to entertain are a rebuke to a civil society.

The political "sexual revolution" would never have gotten off the ground were it not for the impetus given to it by televisions situation comedies. Illicit sex has been made to seem funny and abortion trivial. Marital infidelity is *deja vu* and thrilling; fidelity is humdrum and confining. Violence is pathologically thrilling and non-violence is obsequeous and timid. The sight of blood does not pique compassion but instead excites a craving for more. Empitness, all is emptiness, such gross atonement for conscience leads passsive-aggressivce segments of the viewing audience toward the abyss of dangerous experimentation and calloused disregard for others around them, sometimes even their best friends. The hand-gun symbolizes the new-found disregard for human life on the screen.

This *commonizing* of large numbers of Americans by television fantasies has produced a scornful and censorious attitude toward tradition and institutions of an historical America. Woman, the extremist femininists, lobby for sexual devia-tion, "manhood" for themselves and total emancipation, just as some men lobby for death and on demand, absolute religious suppression and a connubial same-sex lifestyle. Television is not, of course, the sole or perhaps even the main genesis for some subliminal and increasingly open desires, bul it is patently a viral carrier for them through its news selection and prime-time stories.

Television's ubiquitous show of originality in creative "investigations" is fan-tasy driven because the real Amerfica offends the liberal creators of the show sce-narios. They are responding to targeted consumers who patronize the advertisers. This we know and yet the gist of product consumption has largely extinguished any dramatic presentation of moral virtue on the electronic screen. And the images thereon have actually influenced legislation to such a degree that they have, by the means of spot commericials, produced a promotional vehicle for spe-cial (politcal) interests. Fantasy and reality mingle and in the minds of some TV watchers become as one. The lifestyles of today's America, where they replicate the abomainable stories, characters and images on the screen, are cancelling out the moral values of bygone movies, honesty, loyalty, true courage, courtesy, civil-ity. The purveyors of profanity dnd toilet-stall language mark the water levels of such prettied-up television swill. The shame is that among a functionally illiterate television audlience, who knows the difference? *Tolerance* has become a vice, a word that used to be synonymous with consideration; yet now it is a used as a weapon of slander, hate or indifference. Moral values are up or grabs. At least a number of late-show television writers seem to think so. If they think virtue is undramatic, they should check into the nearest prison and try saving a soul just for the expeerience. Liberate a condemned man by showing him the example of a God who keeps His covenants. For that that failure—to keep promises—is often the source of malevolence in our society. When you take your driver's licensr test, you are acting out your intention to keep the rules of the road. That is a covenant, an agreement, an enforceable contract with greater society.

Withhold liberty from the slave and you engender visions of his inalienable right to chose freedom.

The Justices of the United States Supreme Court consider themselves the final arbiter of the right and the wrong side of a valid constitutional challenge. Yet their moral discriminations suffer from the absence of any higher authority than themselves, despite lip-service to a God. That consideration is a a matter of appeal to God. The conscience is the spirit, of the law of a divine directive.

A political judgement that slanders the character of the adversary has only truth for its defense; otherwise it is the defamatory use of free speech and liberty of thought.

God granted wisdom to our founding fathers because they feared Him. Their human agency reflected their parents, ministers and schoolteachers' training. There was liberty rightly instilled ino young minds.

Freedom to act is constrained by just laws, while the liberty to make new laws is annointed by God. Mammon, by ironic illiusion, is often allowed to govern.

Moral precedents direct and govern only. They ought not to tyrannize, because free choice is that libelrty of conscience which all men possess.

Retribution is punishment only for a crime and ought not to be confused with correc-. tive measures by the application of mitigating circumstances.

If the right to life is inalienable, then abortion is un-Constitutional and the procedure is evil, the immoral destruction of a hallowed gift of life.

27. CONFORMITY COUNTERFEITS LIBERTY

A people do not ordinarily abolish by tacit consensus or by way the need for or the practice *of a* time-honored tradition. It would be hard, for example, to change the pracice here lin America of driving on the right side of the road. Or, filled with a number of insoluable complexities would be any attempt to mandate that the bioloical parents of a child must, because the State so decrees it, surrender up its offspring young to an agency of the State, to make of politicians headmasters and as of bureaucrats baby-caretakers.

Conformity, on the other hand, does not in and of itself suppress freedom of conscience and action so much as it affects and shapes them. It is unconscionable and dangerous to violate a principal law for the use of the road, just as it violates nature's prerogatives for parents for them to abandon their children to the tutelage of adistant State agency. But it is in abdication of a privilege or of a right possessed by nature's continuum and oligarchy that liberty becomes conditional upon the will of others, as a consequence of which, claims of outward visible freechoie counterfeit the reality within the fee holders, the parents in the latter case The errant driver as well as the irresponsible parents share this utilitarian charade of tradition. In either case, one is compelled to appear congenial or normal or "like everyvody else," for strange though it may appear, there are those individuals who would prefer left-handed driving and others abdicate parental involvement. The latter is especially true in contemporary America. One only needs to study the causes of head-on-collisions and the incidence of avandoned children in orphanages. The point is that tradition matters, and that its violation is not liberty of choice but rather programs for disaster.

When this nation reaches that point where it requires no reason for its traditions, it is headed toward cultural decay, stagnation and from thence to deterioration morally and, finally, to death. America's reluctance to condemn or discourage immigration has kept her spirit of adventure, her cultural vitality and her will dynamic among all other nations, outstanding for those reasons. At the same time, when a people, with all Americas diversity, lose touch with their history and the purpose for voting and so vote thoughlessly or not at all, then they will eventually forget the reason for their doing so. If, also, they have money and relative contentment, fewer will be inclined to go to the polls to vote. Their cycnicism, a defeatist attitude and indifference all will represent the *status quo* that customarily resists changes that threaten that contentment. Voting will then seem to them to be a useless charade and meaningless exercise even without the liberal Media in their state of competitive greed making elaborate poll predictions and, until recently, before Western polls closed! In this way we will see basic liberty of our free Republic government transposed into a mere litany for belief in a way that foretells the end, or the trivialization of political choice and open local discussion of candidates and issues.

Having reached this demoralized juncture, the people will then look to the courts and not to their personal or legislative choices and decisions to instal new officers into government power. When the society thereof considers the high courts of the land to be legislative bodies, called Judicial activism, it has ignored or overlooked or remained ignorant of the Constitutional structure of checks and balances between the three branches of our Federal Government—and of the States' governments as well, which fundamentally replicate the Federal structure of power. By his shift in the people's perspective and understanding—as demagogues and politicians lusting for more power reinforce the radical change-there diminish to the point of obscurity and then oblivion, except for token respect, the veto power of the President and the Congress, the selection-power of the President to appoint supreme Court Justices, and the power of Judicial Review to outlaw certain legislation. For the people will have learned not to care. "The politicians are all the same. What does it matter?" When the people have lost the social conscience that perceives the United States Constituhtion to be only what is has become, an "incorrectly" limiting instrument and controversial impediment to "social progress"—a view some Senators lately hold—the power of the people to control their own destiny their basic law to insure its safety will have been irretrievably lost. That noble document will have become irrelevant to a modern age.

The real danger embedded in this attrition is, of course, that entrenched political-legal powers vested in the State, the Congress and the swarm of bureaucrats in Washington, will deter or postpone or expunge certain liberties that spring from everyman's moral conscience. That conscience can pretend, ans solicit others, to be a-moral; a status marks its extirpation. Freedom of speech, of association, of movement, or participation are, eacn of them, liberties that Hitler banned when he declared himself a blind, resurgent Germany's Reichfuhrer. The irresponsible attitude of the people toward their personal liberties placed them in jeopardy of their loss. This is nowadays especially true when freedom to vote our conscience is scorned, as it is in American where less than 50% of the eligible voters—or scarcely that number—turn out to vote in a major election. That attitude and deportment is repugnant to a free society and odious to patriots. The inert *no* voters would have no right to complain of a *coup de etat* by a tyrant. Their response would be retrogressive nd certainly not remedial. For in the wake of indiference would follow the cries of national anarchy as in revolutionary France. Amerlica's founding Patriots blocked such a destructive outcome with a plan for stability, freee intercourse beeteen the people and self-directed happiness.

Right versus wrong surely is a matter of conscience in its various social involvements and applications, to which the courts in America are ready to respond as plaitiffs may require. The adversaries of conscience, the Egaliarians—they are at one extreme of a social political correctness; while the Chaotics,

I shall call them, stand at the other, for they have plied their philosophny of a moral nihilism in a similar manner of appeal, chiefly however, to obtain a consensus of what they consider a "true democracy," the social conscience achieved, as it always must, by acts of terrorism. This plight of affairs would then, though it does not yet, represent the totally Humanistic State in which Man is god. Faith of the terrorist in Allah is a delusion; he is god acting on his own initiative. In contention between those two extremes of social plausibility, represented by the obdurate Legalists and the unrequited Zealots, stand those who crusade for conscionable moral choice in life's affiars. They are not compromisers; they are decision-makers. Theiy are not social re-constructionists; they are patriotic adherents to one guiding construction, the Constitution.

As a derivative of their contest for governing authority, that of the Statist Humanists and the docrinaire lawless Nihilists, there arises the logical question: whether or not there can be two *rights* of a moral choice confined within the parameters of one set of circumstances, or whether, for example, the citizen should have, for example, the absolute right to desseminate pornography, or wnether or he should bow to the State's pedagogic command that it is not good for the people to be deluged wsith "objectionable" material. Notice the conflict of competing *objectivities.*

The Supreme Court of the United States has tended to extend certain personal liberties, Roe v Wade being one of the most celetrated, while prohibiting othner personal liberties, such as liberthy of religious expression in public—though the High Court's hypocrisy is most evident in this *oberdictum.* Silent to persuade the people of another other side to the issue, the court has posited confusion as to the meaning of *inalienavble right.* For the choice in either of these two rulings is either a moral decision or it is an authorization that lacks morality. The people do not perceive how the cancellation of an inalieanable right can be immoral yet legal if the law supposes that its basis for reformist interpretation of the law is a ruling reflective of moral rectitude. What about the *right to life* involved in medical practice wh;en, against the Hyppocratic Oath, the aborionist undertakes the socially-tolerated late-term abortion or doctor-assisted suicide? Again, how can a Supreme Court ruling excise a freedom such as religious rexpression in a public forum when less tlhan 100 years ago it was legal and tolerated. In defense of this decision, can the High Court still claim its Constitutionally mandated abortion ruling to be moral? I deed, the Cour attaches no moral significance at all to the aborion ruling for women's rights. Indeed, why should murder e anyone's right, or liberty, in conformity with feminist lobbyists.

If all statutory decisions conceived as rulings by the Court must be tolerated, is the impress of their legality—or their illgality—not our concern, that of the people? Must the conjectural opposition among the citizenry close their eys, so that the Court becomes an arrogant legislative body working outside the traditional virtues involving honesty, duty, loyalty, integrity, work, reverence, civil respect. In case appeals when the Appellate Judges evade values appertaining to personal and corporate virtue, precepts belonging to the people since our country's beginning, there then can be no justicableness or any pretense of rigteousness characterized as germinal or integrsal to the Court's sfuling. By the emptying of a decision of all its moral import and substance, the Justices thereupon politicize the virtue of moral choice as an illusion. By degrees the people lose their grip on their virtue that may be inherent in the *law per* se;and they become mere worshippers at the shrine of the Liberal Court's innovation. Never was this intended to be so. Our Founders believed that our laws were made for and useful to a moral people only.

Let us now examine another area of controversy, freedom of speech not in words but in symbols, such as flag burnsing, fiery crosses on front lawns, euthansia made acceptable by repetitious practice, bombing innocent street bystanders—to name just a few of these symolisms. Other more innocuous ones are visble symbols of Veblen's "conspicuous consumption," in an afflluent age. What about the "speech" symbol of a decapitating bomb. Does not liberty make demands on its citizens and draw lines of prohibition? For a society toremain free and unharmed and fearless, it must m;ark the bounds of expression. A terrorist bomb no more symbolizes speech than does the bark of a dog. It symbolizs an attitude—hatred for the victims evem for those unmarked by hostility who die by the bomb's blast.

As for true freedom of speech, it is generally overprotected, the liberty thereof being a moral choice. Yet who will set the limits if not Man, claiming injury or God enforcing righteouesness? Mortal man resorts to violence to resolve that issue; while God's judgement is ever present. The right of the unnorn receives comparatively little protection, that is, the authorized right to be born, a symbolic right possessed by all unborn babies and a right mandated by nature and nature's God. But who, what agency, what individual in the circle of its horrors is willing to surrender that right in place of the infant? Does not the mother-too-be seie by her will alone that mortal's right to life? Does such a question not then vecome a matter of pre-natal murder. To think otherwise is insane.

The doctor who crushes the infant's skull and sucks out the brains by his technologically upscale machine, or dismembers the infant in agony within the womb with a high-carbvon steel cirasse is committing an act of murder. It can only be said in defense of such doctors that the infant had a moment of silence before going to its Maker. The truth of free speech and the truth of free-born are consistent inalienable truths, but censorship and free-speech as well as abortion and free-born share the value status of a divine right. Man, the imposter, puts out the light of life and of the truth by his vicious barbaric extermination ... Censorship in general and abortion in paricular are both tyrannous. The choices of moral "right" and "immoral "wrong on an issue cannot co-exist either in the law or in practice. The woman's right becomes the infants *wrong,* the demagogues right becomes the censors *wrong.* One symbol cannot be exercised and prohibited while the other is tolerated. On some issues, such as the above, compromise is impossible and conflict is inevitable. The sentient eing cannot be partially born. The infant is either born or is murdered.

Nonetheless, two kinds of conformity are usually evident in a free society: conformity to custom, which includes clothes, cars, homes, the stuff of affluence, fad and manners. And comformity to the laws—which carry within them elements of command, duty, oligation and civil respect. This latter conformity shows itself in attitudes and agreement between compatriots. Case laws tend to legitimize these agreements and attendant duties, since they, above all other laws, speak for the people. Statutes can often extirpate such compromises, while custom long oberved can assume the power and rightness of the written laws, as the case laws and the adjucatory rulings by the courts.

Under the first kind of conformity of appearances and possessions there is rarely actually any violation ofl custom, fad or craze. Conformity is acquiescence, and it is instituted for some non-legal social purpose or cocde. Almost all of the people enjoy this option for their happiness.

But under the second kind of conformitys violations frequenly produe crime, suicides, bodily injury and great unhappiness. The tyranny of enforcement resides not in the impersonal laws of the court, as such, but in the moral conscience of millions of individuals who, misinformed or misguided by a humanistic a morality, act in concert without vision. Protection of our environment is one such instance. Now it is a compromising vigilance for terrorists. Yesterday, it was safety in the wsorkplace and labor protectionist laws, as for children in the mines and women in factories.

Iit is a deplorable reality that Liberals hasten to condone many a crime on the grounds that society is the fundamental cause of the criminals act. And that, therefore, the perpetratsor ought to be forgfiven or his sentence lightened. The tyranny of a politically incorrect ruling by a lower court and Democratic pressures to take a sott stance toward minority-committed crimes echo the wisdom of the Marquis de Sade, that: the pleasure in evil ought to be recognized and accepted as a part of human nature. This Humanist philosophy is destroying ourt judicial system, since it predicates that moral standards ie.e the virtues basic to character, ought to have no part in social choices or political decisions. A man's skin color should free the prisoner, just as a little girl's pregnancy can be blamed on her neighborhood. The Marquis de Sade activists bear within their humanism a streak of cruelty when they inveigh against moral absolutes, for they endores a kind of evil snobbery which says that the criminal only wanted to be thought of as a good person. Therefore, punishment is an infringement upon his happiness and his inalienable right to enjoy life. The Sadists cannot brook any value systems of right and wrong being connected to the political power structure, for such holiness descries the States omniscient and omnipresent thrust to maintain its one party lust for power. Therefore, the predominant party either leans toward sadism in its treatment of the oppressed or toward enlgihtenment in its acceptance of all-controlling reason.

By the simple elimination of moral conscience from the equation of crime-conviction-punishment, thereby skirting the *reasonable* critique of right and wrong in the criminal's conduct, those same Sadists attempt to ignore or to remove the operative conscience—which they will call tyrannous—and instead extol New Age Humanists' wrongs disguised as self-satisfying, good, fair, comfortable and equal. They do so in full conformity with bureauctratic quotas and mandamus lawsuits to overturn the people's will expressed in lower court rulings or by a vote of the people as on a challenged *referendum.* In such instances the state acts as a tyrant to deny to the citizens their absolute right to protect themselves and to localize their government as an extension of their collective will.

Criminal attorneys, responding to clear-cut substantive evidentiary indictments—as a mother's murder of her children or shootisng of her husand—want their clients to appear both good and moral, a persiflage which the liberal press is quick to exploit editorially, For said client, often viewed as a felon victimized by society or a bad home-life or by a childhood molestation or a poor level of nourishment or, indeed, being the mindless instigator of an unreasonable choices ... the insanity defense ... has attained a state of general irresponsibility. Therefore, though not innocent, he is not guilty of the alleged clrime. One can readily see how Enlightenment reason, applied to a heinous offense, lifts the burden of choice from conscience, when, all too often, the crime constitutes a violation of the conscience of society's dissernment of the case.

Customs of conformity can, of course, be changed or deviated from and they often are. Nowadays, conformity doth make saints of us all even exonerating becomes the plea to overlook a serious violation of statutory law, such as rape when the body cannot be found. DNA is contemporaneously brought into the deliberations and verdict not simply to free a convict of both his bad conscience and his crime, but to indict the court system for its imperfect adjucatory machinery. And to give new hope that serous crimes like murder and rape, high treason, can in the future be shown to have faulted the system and not the criminal. It may then become quite easy to counterfeit the crime as totally circumstantial and outside the pale of acceptable proof. How can this be? By changing the dimensions of what is and is not considered to be, and therefore is not, called **criminal** By redefinition of the criteria for judgement, not by God and absolute moral values but by the humanist State and its changeable ... its situational value judgements. That is not to say that the State is, under these dicta, a theocracy, for such prescribes the submission of all laws and Institutions to the control of the clergy ... The counterfeiting that occurs will be based on the State's philosophical mindset of its people, en masse, by of what constitutes *bad* and what *good,* what benign and what evil. Thus doth the State attempt to usurp the citizens' right to self-determination and his expectation of integrity from the government over him.

Whenever the law seems to be oppressive and despotic, and empty of meaning., the soldiers of the thought-polixe, nowadays the Liveral establishment, will respond to public pressure to enforce conformity. In this a depotic regime has the character of compelling conformity by the use of economic force, political force, and para-military force by the police.

Moral choices, however, resist change and compromise, this reesistance being the chief reason that Relativists and Asolutists, alike championtheir their ultimate worth is as guides through times of gturmoil and uncertaisnty, for they each would compel a moral order that may or may not be divine but in a free society has the characer of governance by choice and conformity by election. Liberty under a despot, a State's a-moral order to enforce by might, is therefore an illusion, whereas under a secular constitution instigated by a moral citizenry, Liberty real to the citizens. The morality that underlies Liberty in this country, still can be ascribed to a Sadist, supported by reason alone, but it cannot for long be counterfeitted by him in the absence sof moral strength. How long will bribery last in the Congress that involves payoffs by lobbyists and deception of the people by their Represenatives? Conformity to such agreements sustitutes unlawful licence for Liberty, making the latter a counterfeit of freedom of choice.

Thought-control is the pulse of mind enslavement by the Liberal media, by idealogues and those misguided but vocal zealots.

It is achieved by the censorlship they claim is to anhor. It is denied in the piety they would eschew and in their arrogance which they do not see.

Encourage liberty and you discourage the spoiler. For you assume that you are free to call, and the other knows he is captive to his passions.

Liberty thrives where tyranny contends, for its true strengths is unseen, its evidence is a gathering force until oppression.

The capacity to make a moral choice does not always accompany the liberty to do so. since the one involves a nascent rationality, the other a tenable though pragmatic decision. The slow wheels of justice are a case in point.

Liberty is at times scorned as obscure by him who wishes to hide what is most visible, his wrongdoing.

28. POLITICAL CORRECTNESS V. MIND, CONSCIENCE

Conformity to pop-culture ideas and political correctness are today synonymous in American political paradigm situations—like offician caucuses, meetings, panels—and political discussions *extempore*. The Liberal pop media have perpetuated the ironic notion that conformity is the best example of political insight and understanding, as, for example, a quota system for qualification in almost any capacity and the obliteration of the edge of talent and achievement in order to accommodate mediocrity, especially in pedagogical and creative enterrpises, schools, films, academics, licensures and awards. America still porssesses a guilt complex born of slavery and disbelief in a God who forgives: this is the Liberal position on American justice. The truth is that America's diversity belies all charges of widespread racism, the Liberals would have the people to believe otherwise. This places Liberals in mind-control.

The political correctness syndrome supposedly, according to liberals, carries the stamp of majority opinion that cleanses neighborhoods, communities, institutions of individual errors and unacceptable attitudes. The stance is **Messianic,** meaning salvational, a philosophy to rescue the ignorant and disbelieving public from their errors of thinking and their unacceptable behavior. The Liberals would police the thoughts of Americans, especially Conservatives. Who dares to argue with the majority about the relevancy of the Ten Commandments when the Fourth Estate reflects the correct viewpoint of equal opportnity for thieves, adulterers, god-worshippers, coveters, in the face of unequal effort to achiec excellence or practices of illegal ventures, added to a multiculturalism tnat wars against itself? Conformity to popular buzz words, euphemistic expressions, conceal bias. **Political-correctness,** one word, is a way to signify loyalty, as to a groups such as to homosexuals and Fundamentalists. **Political-correctness** signifies a conformity that totally lacks the tenure and ring of freedom. Such conformity bears within its thinking the logic of irresponsibilithy. In darker areas of the human psyche evidenced in mob mind and street riots, there occur the spontaneous flareups and conformity to what is screamed, shouted or assigned to be fair. Enforced conformity iw always negative. The very word *fair* is, however, without any legal significance. It is pejorative or it brands as a *word.* In the law of equity it assumes a regretiable status: the negotiability *per se* of what is legal in import, the result of the compromise being described *as fair* when the result is often highly subjective.

In politics, **political-correctness** means that it is correct to say of a candidate … or of a person … that he or she stands for changes yet without his or her having to define those chnges or the opportunity to do so. One must use the **politically-correct** phraseology. Here are examples: the "broad-based contributions" of the American people mean the middle class taxpayers; a politician who "seeks the welfare of my constituents" can refer to almost any kind of give-away program of the regulation; to "turn the cosuntry around" is an empty promise that appeals to the usual financial frustrations of many citizens. A politicisan whose words have the euphonic sound of rehtorical greatness will imply, where expeditious and opportunistic, those maxims of comfortable political comformity—the prospaganda, the slogans that replace independent thinking. Into this category falls political correctness, yet but another name for sloganeering, properly called *propaganda.*

Politican Action (PAC) committees are the exploiters of sloganeering. "Uncle Sam Need You" was a popular slogan intended to raise money and troop enlistments in WW I. The "New Frontier" of President Lyndon Baines Johnsin, "I've been on the mountaintop" of Reverend Martin Lsuther King; "We have only to fear fear itself," the pithy saying of FDR for the Great Depression. "We will build a bridge to the twenty-first century," was a slogan of President Wm. J. Clinton. These electioneering campaign and political-movement sloans served one major purpose: to animate the citizenry to respond to a candidate or an incumbent with votes and money and commitment. That is all well and good. But they are also inductments to accept the premise that acceptance and conformity affirm one's patriotism or religious belief and this, without giving the matter much more thought.

Deviations from the slogans of a "progressive tomorrow." "the New Frontier," "the War on Poverty," "global economy" and "save" the planet ... the trees ... the whales ... the endangered species—all jingoilstic propaganda puts its pressures upon the voters' loyalties, then to their consciences. People often respond to their inate generosity without their enquiring about its morality. That can be a good thing and widespread in a nations whose people are instinctively compassionate—if the cause is morally just and human. The hidden irony in the politically correct syndrome is that it often contravines their instinctive judgement, for better or for worse. The unfortunete aspect of this response to popular judgement is that millions of citizens who try their hardest to conform to politically correct language, inferences and concepts so as not to offend anyone have already trashed their options and the power of their personal opinion choices and free expression, onformity rules out moralityHared of Christianity induces the coma of conformity without reason or with substitute myths.

Thus, exposure to media opinion and to Hollywood producers,dirctors and high profile actors and actresses ought always to be guarded. The liberal "thinkers" in these media will attempt to project calamities, specious warnings and polled poilitical policy-resuslts in order to conform the rightness of their judgements. Inclusion of tyrannies like Libya and Communist Red Cina into the Human Rights Commission of the UN is one such instance. Using the psychology of projection, they attribute to the enemy composed largely of conservatives the shortfall in their own attitudes, often amounting as it does to a colossal bigotry. Example: conservatives hate illegal aliens because they are different.

Because we are in the main a trusting people, made so by our open, free society and therefore vulnerable to attack, it is easy to lead Americans about by their symbols, the buzz words and clever phrasing by sideshow hucksters, the which I have already alluded to. Many of these liberal sloganeers occupy seats in the Conress, in both houses, they who are importuned and supported by the thousands of lobbyists who put their thoughts into the legislators' minds and money into their coffers. If one wishes to hear sloppiy thinking, poor judgement and unethical counsel, he has but ti listen to members of the Congress speak. Newspeak, double-talk, innuendo and lies are the currency for all too many; while others appear content with committee work and cloakroom exchanges, letting only their voices speak for them.

Why ought the conscience to be violated in moments of "crisis" on lsuch issues as perjury under oath or the ovstruction of justice by a clever defense law-yer, or campaign oratory, or the slanderous abuse private information—when those "crises" can be and are precipiatated by a political conformity that is expected of incumbents in political office. Unananimity is the bellwether to suc-cessful legislation., proof positive that an act is good and ought to be passed—good that is, before challenged and taken to the U.S. Supreme Court. Yet why this vacillating on moral issues? The liberation of oil fields in the Persial Gulf was just as moral an issue as was the liberation of the Kuwait people, for the moral reasosn that our weaponry and armed forces interdicted phenomenal hard-ships to the American people in lthe form of lost jobs, health care, the continued operation of our schools and hospzitals, and winter fuel and transpotation needs. Our intervention in Kosovo was sheer oulawry; we had no moral reason to bomb Helpless Yugoslava, United Nations soldiers not being salvation or morality to a beleaguered populace. It was only in the first instance when we invaded another country that we did so to combat evil, to be sure, but most importantly, to fore-stall a complex of circumstances that would have harmed our own nation.

In the last analysis, conformity to global peace does not exercilse or demon-strate the dictates of what is morally right. That truism cannot be shunned or concealed or ignored. Conformity of action that is animated by a moral decision produces moral consequences, usally. In the Genesis story of Joseph and his brothers, Joseph was thrown into a well, described to his father Jacob as a son killed by a lion, yet craftily, for them, sold to a trader caravan. In this instance, the cruel and immoral conduct ofl the brothers was reconstituted for the good when Joseph, by the Pharoah made Prime Minister of Egypt, was able to supply sacks sof gain to his vbrogthers in a time of Judian faminne. Only God has this prerogative, to allow an evil to take place that ultimately brings about good con-sequences. Providence, not chance, governs in the affairs of men.

Liberty is an abstraction, and an ideal, but robbery,malice, injury to another, cheating in government and in edcation are not. They give evi-dence of the devaluation of liberty as an action of responsible, premedi-tated choice.

Liberty rarely consoles the evildoer because it rejects out of hand his self-fulfillment in the wrongful act. Moral values are not the result of

magic or transient opinion but are given evidence by ancient wrongs committed by men against God, against society and against themselves.

There is in every ;man a conscience, obscured, caloused, seared or dwarfed but never totally exterminated.Those who commit crimes have usually overruled, or violated, their consciences.

Allow no man to convfice you that peace is more honorable than the moral conflict between good and evil; that comfort is more desireable than sacrifice of com fort, that self-justification is more commendable than retribution payed for a wrong.

29. GOVERNMENT CONDONS THEFT-*SIT COM*

When the Federal Government protects criminal extortion in the form of inflated bid-contracts, calling the arrangement *freedom of contract,* government agents perjure thieir administative honesty. The chief reason for such dishonesty is that the lobbyist who "swings the deal" has only his corporate interests to consider, knowing all the while that he *ups* the costs for a project for which a corporation lawyer team will defend him. They can lawfully attach their contingency fee—in defense of over-pricing—to the costs of the project to the Government. Loser pays double. That's theft from the public treasury, a non-defensible crime against the taxpayers that lhas been practicd for so long the manipulation of public funds is deemed lawful.

Professional interest groups Hike the American Medical Association and the ACLU are no less culpable in the game of bribery, which inevitabvly involvs the self-interests of the lobbying parties involved. Bribery can be defined as "sweetening the pot" with a lawful attachment that is most often engineered so that the elected politician, purchased by lobbying groups, whether Senators or Congressmen, remain in office for indeterminate numbrs of years. The bottom-line question is, why ruin a good thing?

Yet, it is said that progress in civilization is due to "enlightened self-interest." The word "enlightened" may mean for the "pubvlic good" or perhaps for the "public's good." House and Senate Finanace Committees, caucus groups, intent on spending taxpayer money, so that the allotment for such and such a project may not be wanting in the next fiscal year, are all a composite of porkbarrel politicians who do not consider that the interests of the nation come first.

No, it is the voters of his or her State that come first, regardless of the obscene expenditure for a trivial land often needless State project. From worm farms to bridges to nowhere to the study of the mating havits of fruit flies or of relationshiups between *doubles in* tennis.... More thousands for a trip to Borneo to sltudy the greater chlorophil content of Equator deciduous trees and, by all means, an intensive investigation of the matling haits of the common Southern firefly. Citizens who count precious dollars to survive are robbed of hundreds of millions of dollars everyyear by porkbarrel politicians, a crims which taxpayers accept in silence. For these political highwaymen come like thieves in the night. The practice of such disingeuous theft is tolerated without complaint by the common citizens of our great country.

Nor do the facts which these studies, these "scientific" investigations, discover serve to enlighten the people or, the members so the Congress to whom the Porkbarreleers must report, if they ever do. These are the insider wheeler-and-dealers who conceal, among the pages of the national budget, somtimes running into several millions, the narrow interests of railroad ridges, lapidary studies, and long-ago paid-off hydro-electric debts. It is a safe assumption to say that most members of our Congress do not read the Federal budget but, instead, let aides read and condense it. The lately-enacted line-item veto given to the President acknowledges the porkbarrel abuse but does not correct it, and probably never will so long as our leaders lack the integrity of truet statesmanship for their office.

There is a slight-of-hand that goes on here when "fifteen millions of dollars can be spent for the UN Population Fund," 4.4 millions for a railroad crossisng in Springfield, Illinois, "84,000 to study "why people fall in love," "250,000 to research sweet potatoes, 16.8 millions to "operate the National Agricultural Library, 2.7 millions for a fish farm in Stuttgart, Arkansas, and on and on. Up to 10,000 pork barrel projects, in fiscal 2006 amounting to unacconted-for billions of American dollars were squandered for porkbarrel projects that kept a legislator in office with his constituents' votes. This is nothing more than a purchased legislature, a bought Congress, bribery on a massive scale yet unchecked. On and on the ripoff goes. Nails for a government project cost $1.75 apiece!

This kind of knavery is criminal on the part of vendors and of the Congress. All members are indicted as accountable because these criminal bribes have occurred with their knowledge or their personal participation. Corporation CEOs, who increasingly disavow loyalty to our county in deference to an increasing globalization of American industry—it is they and project managers who are involved in these and other acts of blatant thievery from the American people.

By its unethical and immoral sanction of such wholeale extortion, the House of Representatives, closest to the people, is the principal responsible party and clearinghouse for government contracts. When our Representatives thus stand behind felonious extortion through taxation—of these corrupt expenditures, without representation, they are guilty of cirminal offenses that are scams in th multliple, and, at bottom, are violations of Constitutional representative government. King George's marking and stealaing tall Carolina pines for his ship masts was no worse. The British taxes without representation were a leading cause of our Revolution, yet those taxes were no more encriminating that today's current leglislaion for sale with bribes.

The cashing of bogus checks, *kiting* it is called, already known about; the abuse of franking privileges was another similar crime. But these are small items compared to the President's sale of our high-technology equipment, much of it secret, to communist china for money for his presidential campaign. The corruption of Johnson, Carter and Clinton, by their sale, barter and giveaways of America's wealth, drips both slime and smell. There are the campaign kickbacks, payoffs, if you will, for campaign contibutions to anl incumvents war chest. Also, there are the expensive vacation trips abroad, phoney junkets for offical purposes to other lands, all having, in their concealment, made of the Congress a mask for criminal activity. Yet the power of the Federal Government, the *State,* if you will, protects and shields them both from scrutiny and from prosecution, which duplicity outrages common sense and the integrity of the American people. How often can we be deceived before we grow cynical toward Constitutional Republicanism and the enumerated liberties of a free people and either clean our House or take up arms in rebellion against such corrupt acivities? The Second Amendment implies that right, much to the astonishment of elitist liberals practiced in grubbing money from the pockets of taxpayers.

These repeated assaults on the moral strength of a people are corrupting the next generatioin who look on, by the toleration of the frauds perpetrated against both generations. They constitute the numerous wrongs of these, interdicted and condemned as they are by numerous laws, the which support the absolute commands of God that: *Thou shalt not steal.* Small wonder that the U.S. Supreme Court wishes to remove the law agalinst stealing from the minds of Americas schoolchildren. Their own hypocrisy is abundantly evident in this matter. But then, Americans in the aggregate have allowed this surreptitious kind of corruption to thrive because of their indifference. Their pretense to tolerance of the thievery taxation is accepted by almost everyone, their evolutionary belief in human goodness and perfection and their failure to attack lthe problem of legislative theft has created a culture in which dishonesty thrives in every area of American life. This is especially true with the failure of liberal churchmen to emphasize integrity in human behavior instead of a situational morality and ethical "adaptation."

Cheating in schools is endemic, on colleges exams, in the grades with ready-made reports, tests, clever electronic answer devices and inter-cultural supply and demand of examination answers. These venues accord with hating by the President and, by some some; members of the Congress and their campaign organizers. Semantic euphemisms such as *remembering my constituents* and moral cat-calls such *as you've got to lighten up* and, *what is, is,* have replaced moral conduct in the American character. Our liberties in this country are slowly being eroded by such mallpropisms *as fair conduct, rigfht thinking, the choice of experience,* and *it's just another opinion or its "curious sor its "clevcer sor whatever excuse feosters general acceptance* These are all significant gambits that indicate moral corruption and ethical lapses in our ways of life. The majority of the Congress, I am convined, regard *moral relevancy* among its members, not as wrong but as a satisfactory legal considieration for themsellves until election time. That kind of tolerance is crimianl derelection of duty to lead. What voices rise to protest robbdry of the people disguised as "cost overruns" or the *political correctness* of special protections for selcted deviant groups, or "entitlements" for illegal aliens, the which costs tasxpayers more money. Can a Nation long endure if its leaders ignore the doctrine of moral accountability? The decline of ancient civilizations say **_no._**

A man horn in freedom, if a criminal cannot waive his right of defense under the laws of liberty without his imposing self exile. 11 he is convicted, he has done so through his self-elected crime. If he is an anarchist, is so through his destructive choice. But if he seeks respite from the burden of responsibility that liberty imposes on him, he defrauds himself with an illusory freedom.

30. POLITICAL POWER AND LIBERTY

There has never existed a society sympathetic to and engaged in slavery without there concurrently being a conceptualization and the open practice of personal liberty enjoyed by the non-slaves. *Liberty* is inherently presupposed by its absence expressed in the institution, authorization and regime of slavery. The powers of the United States President, exceeding those of ancient monarchies, reflect the practice of pre-civil War slavery in America by its very position as one of the three

Branches of Government under the Constitution. Article II, Sec. 3 gives him the power to communicate to the Congress regarding the state of the union. "He may on extraordinary occcasions, convene both Houses or either of them" and in case of Disagreement between them, "he may adjourn them at such Time as he shall think proper." That lin itself is an extraordinary power given to the Executive Branch of our government.

Article I, Secion 2.3 enumerates Legislative powers "excluding Indians not taxed, three fifths of all other persons," a prohibition amended by the Fourteenth Amendment—this reference (Art. I, Sec. 2.3 being to slaves within states where the "peculiar institution" of slavery thrived. Thus slavery from the beginning was "white man's burden" socio-politically, morally and spiritually. Its very existence corrupted the ideal of a pristine liberty for all men, and challenged the doctrine of "inalienable rights," foundationnal to the Colonists' Declaration of Independence.

President Lincoln was the first President to articulate with any exactnss the bifurcation of America's freedom-slavery population. Yet the black man's plight was more than an indenturement. In America his enslavement, rooted in the cotton economy of the South, was antithethical to the concept of liberty in its denial of free choice, to the man of color's full access to the Bill of Rights. Not even the-Civil war brought sa full and remedial retribution for the institution of slavery . Until the Civil War, it seemed that slavery was a silent issue, not because it was not visible and known but because the leaders of the country suppressed all consideration of the social antipode to freedom. It was chiefly the abolitionists, clergymen and lay leaders who called slavery wicked and immoral and who brouht it to the forefreont of challenge to America, consistent with the major cause for the Civil War and with Lincoln's 1863 Emancipation Proclamation. Not until Brown v Board of Education in 1953 were Jim Crow laws and the notion of equal-but—eparate challenged in the Supreme Court and decided in favor of black integration in all areas of American life.

The powers of the President deal tangentially with incarceration, e.g. pardon for a crime, or the communtation of a sentence for a Federal offense. Although imprisonment is not slavery, its presupposition that a man can be denied the rights of a freeman did not at the time appear to many to be analgous to slavery. A meager sustenance, limited liberty and punishment for attempted escape aligned criminality with the fact of black iamprisonment on plantations, casting a shadow of a false alignment across more than one hundred and ififty years of Americas racial strife. Certain figures of the Civil War years ought always to be remmvered for their participation in the black mans fight for personal liberty—the abolutionists John Brown, William Lloyd Garrison, Harriet Beecher Stowe; the escaped slave Frederick Doublas, Harriet Tubman, Rosa Parks, Martin Luther King, Jr. They survived, as their spiritual descendants survived. With the draconian pronouncement of the Emacipation Proclamation and the Civil War Amendments, the 13th, 14th, and 15th, mandated liberty for former slaves and their future successors. Liberty for the black man was given a new infusion of hope. For almost three-quarters of a century, however, the concept of libertty had lacked moral validity and practical reality for most of the nation. The white man who embraced slavery had corrupted his conscience by ilts repeated violation in the name of economics in a cotton economy. The black man continued to affirm that the God who had tendered to settlers His "inalienavble rights" had not forgoitten him, whilest the war itself had bared the soul of America. Slavery and liberty had stood side by side since the 17th century. Virginia colonists prohibited slave ship importations in about 1716 in an attempts to abolish slavery. These early efforts were partially successful, for the one colony but not for the others. Also, Plantation owners encouraged procreation for the one purpose only—slave labor and, generally, they fostered the illiteracy that discouraged protest.

There was an ambivalence about liberty throughout the country mid-19th century. Demagogues and abolitionists saw Lincoln as a supporter of a political system that condoned slavery. Not even the Emancipation document issued late in the war, 1863, could effect these attitudes sprung from Lincoln's resolve to abolish slavery and save the Union at the same time. His detractors saw in Lincoln what insrrectionists have always wanted to see-a lust for power, the re-emergence of a fearful suspicion put upon Washington that he intended to become another King George III. Indeed, the violation of moral conscience plagued many an early leader who did, in fact, keep slaves: Thomas Jefferson, Washington, James Monroe were among them. Each man in his own words and ways condemned slavery while he particpated in it, howsoever ruefully or reluctantly. By way of example, however, none of them freed his slaves until after his death. Owners of small contingents of slaves did in fact free them before the end of the war, providing the manumitted slaves promised to take up arms against the North. Degreees of enslavement did indeed exist in the chief border states of Missouri and Kansas—sometimes called "freedman" States—by virtue of a bargained option in exchange for Statehood.

Reason became servant to excuses for conscience's sake. Manumission by other slave owners, in numbers a small minority in the South, did occur when morality dictated, some owners sending them North—where they met a similar prejudice—or keeping them as indentured servants. A minority of blacks had leaned a trade—carpenter, mason, bricklayer, iron smithing, for which they were given badges of their trade to be hung about their necks for identification. Not a few remained near or on the plantations as hired help; for where could the go when given their liberty? Their right to vote was far distant, for they owned no property or civil rights Thus did liberty mid-19th century not only impinge upon politicala power; it was denied to the powerless as evidenced by the Jim Crow Laws that were enforced until the 1960's CM Rights Movement. The power that liberty draws from suffrage is that divine power given to a government annointed of God and therefore anwersable to Him. The institution of slavery was a usupation of that power. Sharecropping failed to indemnify the freed laves, a mule and an acre of land keeping them impoverished.

Yet men will have their own way. The power of the Senate when it became a Constitutional reality in 1789 bore a faint resemblance to the British Houe of Lords comprised of a landed gentry, that august holdover from inherited power that belonged to the novblemen of Feudal times in England. The power of lthe Senate was aristocratic in origin, connected to land ownership among the Colonial burgesses. They who wrote the Constitution owned land. Yet that power was at the same time rooted in the ideiolgy of freedom historically conferred by its autocratic actions, a power not given by men, although it appeared to be so, but was thought to have veen ;bestowed upon them by a Deistic God whom they accepted as a non-interferring Sovereign over all the affairs of men. Liberty in settlements prior to the Revolution was the fruit of property ownership and of the omnipresent consciosness of the cruel, bloody calamities of European tyrannies, not the least of which was that of Napoleon Buonaparte, and George Ill's war against the French.

Many of the perceptions of America's founders were theocetnric; they were passioantely convinced that God-given reason could, and ought to, resolve conflicts in political polity. Jefferson's years in Europe brought the Enlightenment home to our shores. The origin of the Congressionl prayer to open it session began during the days sof the Constitutional Convention in Philadeophia, a tradition that acknowledged the personal belief of the fifty-five delegates in a Sovereigh God. As a matter of historical fact, most of them ere Episcopalians. The Mayflower Compact pledged the lives of the immigrants to a settlement founded under God and with His provision for their welfare and lives Plimouth was to be a fully communal effort. Theirs was a God to whom contmpraneous mankind owed the glory of his true and discoverable nature, which included "natural rights" estowed upon him by their Creator. These were the "linalienable rlights" of the Declaration of Independence. Not being Secular Humanists, whom else could they appeal to as the source of liberty? There was no conflict between faith and Enlightenment reason, since both ;had their genesis in the single Diety of Scripture.

Furthermore, they believed that justice should be based on operable laws of Christian moral pobity and conscience, and that it was the nature of all men to do evil from which he ought to be protected, the evil in their day being the wickedness of kings who fomented bloody wars and corrupted the power of both religious and secular origins. The Colonists and early patriots in American settlements practiced a certain meekness in their lives and committed themselves to the Protestant view of God's world, aproachable through Scripture and town councils, the minister of the settlement usually if not always sitting as arbiter in legal disputes and infractions of civic morality. Hawthorne's _The Scarlet Letter_ has depicted this scene with dramatic clarity. One of Nathaniel's forefathers held court to condemn Salem woman as itches, for the discrace of which and to dissociate himself the author dropped the middle E from; his own name.

The Enlightenment.was the ideology of appeal to reason for solutions to rational problms. An experiencied skeptiism, formal learning and everyday pragmatic solutions would eomvince men's minds of the rational dread for their English king Gesorge III and of a Parliament unresponsive to their petitions for justice. Rationalim was the legacy of the Europea Enlightenment of Hobbes, Locke and Descartes—not that it had never existed before but that it should become the tool of greatest secular reliance, confirming and supereding even the time-tested moral values. This tendency toward an a-morality was the beginning of today's secular humanism. Liberty on the other hand, looked to God as well as to men's experience for its values in the operation of governent and in the conduct of the people under that government.

Nationalism could nonetheless—so it was believed—be used to enlave the people to adjust pragmatically, and to apply the accepted absolutes of the Judeo-Christian ethos, even in contention with the skepticism generated by Enlightenment reason. Yet under the impress and eroding influence of scientific humanismn, those moral values of our Founding Fathers have, even today, been replaced by forms of valueless license in private as well as in pubic life. This _conformism_ betrays a statist desire to conrol the masses. Honesty has been stretched to accommodate self-will for personal gain more than for public benefit. The "thou shalt not" of the Ten Commandments have been supersvened by; a bloodless and impotent directive from the U.S. Supreme Court which, as an organ of the government and instrument of the State, has compromised moral vaues to make way for relativism. One size fits all—the axiom of relativity is the pattern for human behavior. Therefore, all moral values as are found in biblical injunctions that relate to particular personal integrity become empty rhetoric.

And, equally in education, *conformism* is especially evident in pedagogical circles where the minds of children, yet unformed, are pressured to conform to adult paradigms of mastery in composition the result of whcih is that a child gifted in narrative and descriptive mental imagery or in music memory is condemned to failure for a lack of natural lability to analyze, compare and conjecture in thesis/antithesis mode.

The House of Representatives assumed the role of moral lawgiver—with much more complexity and with different structuring due to census apportionment—that was handed down to them from the House of Burgesses in Colonial governments. They were the Senate of the Continental Congress for some ten years and were the unicameral government of the country before the Revolution. The Lower House of 1789 established a body that was analgous to lthe British House of Commons, but was invested withs more direct management power and a presence of competency that acted upon the will of the people by their votes.

When slavery was confronted in connection with the Constitutional right to vote, the Congress's abuse of the power of liberty did, as a consequence of that abuse by disenfranchisement, remind us of the political ideal, while the "sin" of withheld enfranchisement was explained and practiced as a tolerated wrong in the life of the country. That ambivalence was never corrected until the Civil Rights Movement in the 1960's. The Jim Crow laws mocked at the equal protection of the 13th Amendment, while for millions of white Americans consciencd chaffed as prisoner of a social-racial wrong that was variously defined as "agrarian demands, "economic dictates," and "landed wealth." Liberty for one hundred years after the Civl War was thus rarely partial, equally, to slave posterity and born freemen in the minds of both Southerners and Northeers. Color was alll that mattered.

The checks and balances written into the Constitution inevitably disclosed old clashes and conflicts of interests, of lingering remnants of intercolonial disputes and fears of a malicious and corrupt Federal Goverment that might again oppress the people who had not yet convainced the world of their capability for self-government. Yoked as they were by consanguinity, they faced the tasks of unification grounded upon fundamental cooperation and sympathies as joined States, as separate yet united politicl entities.

The House of Representatives was logiclly the voice of the Nations conscience. Absolute moral values euphemistically called a "code," were as much a part of America's thinking about life and its practice in villages and cities as they were indigenous to the people before the Revolution. Most Americans probably Idid not want to think aboutl the irrational coexistence of liberty and slavery. They believed, almost universally, that the "white man's burden," the "problem" of race discrimiathion would resolve itself "in due ltime." But the conflicts and the contradiction, morally, was there to defy the righteouesness of the Hebrew Deuteronomuy law and the Christian Beautitudes Jesus.

Then again, our independent appointive judiciary is our contribution to our own undertaking of a regulated political body. The tension exists between independence and regulation. If the nine U.S. Supreme Court Justices seem to represent ancient Greek and Roman aristocracy, that is chiefly because their critics can find scant signal cause most of the time to rail against their manner of justice—the political indiffeence of ancient Noblemen. Thus were the terms *liberal* and *conservative* too general and amorphic for one to use in imputing an objective morality to the court. It's true that the Warren Court was criticized for being too liberal, but then embedded in the case law and statues of our judicial system moral conjecture and opinion has always been a given. This, I believe to be true. Nor has there ever been a "rabble" in the European sense of peasantry to confront the High Court of American "aristocracy," which to a singular French critic appeared somehow a dereliction, he who was unable to separate himelf from the French revolutionary *deja vu*. The French had no plan to replace its aristocracy and her noblemen. We had a plan to replace the Royalists and the King. That is the major significant difference between the two revolutions.

The fact is that all three Branches, their departments and committees were designed to work together, providing that the elected and the appointed did not forget the divine source of their power and its transmission to the people as "inalienable rights." For neither the Legislature nor the Supreme Court could call themselves plutocrats or nobility in order to gratify our enemies at home and abroad with the stamp and status of inherited powers of an idle justice

If these structured relatioships of the 1798 government are as legitimately viable and morally sound today as they were back then, taken with a continuing dismantlement of the freeman-slave mentalithy, what can be morally wrong about our personal freedom of our conscience in its exercise over the liberty of choice and action that Americans have come to take for granted? Do—or should—those distant pre-Civil War connections as well as mistakes in antebellum society, in any mealsure, so overshadow liberty's fundamental honesty as to reduce its effectiveness in politics and life? Ought the corruption of slavery to sit in perpetual judgement upon American life? Ought the immorality of that evil institution to play the godfather to contemporary social issues of racial lharmony? Or must we, as Americans all, sublmit to an overwhelming sense of guilt for sour past blunders and, mocking our forebearers, apologize before the world for a false humamness and visible generosity and honesty as a people? We are today going through that apologetic phase, fueled by liberal distortions of both history and current events to force them to accord with their cause of universalism. In short, the Revisionists are forcing the education and publishing establishments to distort and rewrite America's history to accord with their biases instead of with the truth of our past. There is a deeptive intent, a fundamental dishonesty in this nationwide Revision of American history, as if to purge the past of such dangerous and irrelevant old aristocrats as General George Washington, Thomas Paine, Jefferson and many other of our great Nation's Founders

We are a sovereign people accountable first to God ... if we stand in the light of traditon; and then to our own conscience llif we acknowlede moral absolutes. Indeed, murder, extortion, rape, pediphelia, infanticide, obsession with deviant sex and drugs, with the occult—all belie the existence of any moral righteouesness among us. But that is no true. In fact, we know for certain that those dark passions are violations of our way of life, that they actually tend to destroy the operaton of conscionable liberty by all the citizenry, its presence, its meaning and its power. They transgress the laws of a well-ordered, sane, civil socety. When neighborhoods shut own because of crime, that reality is evident. When the police are impugned and attacked, our right to self defense is attacked, even as our personal liberties are also attacked.

The colossal error both naive and sentimental of our time is, it appears to me, to attribute this eradication of old moral laws and absolute values to the triumph of evolutionary law. The New Age *gerus* have worked diligently to bring about this transition in principles, substituting an irrational, anarchistic self-indulgence for morality. Leaders in this collapse of moralty are Hollywood, the liberal media and the ACLU. However, tlhe trimph is one of decay over life, a kind of social and moral/ethical entropy. The courts, for their part, have willfully and bonsciously attempted to separate out the immoral evil course of unlawful conduct from the socially beneficial and lawful and in doing so give to judicial leniency the aspect of progressivce compassion. Their juridical work has, in fact, been made retrogressive by the endowment of the criminal with the charisma of the "fittest." Why does society gobble up the criminal's book of confession when he publihes his angst of wrong, as a $10,000 reward for his pentitence? What a mockery of justice, what a farce of reason, what an insult to intelligent people! One answer to that questin is that the public envy the criminal's fame, his stature beofre the law! Why else would such lenient activist judges extol the criminal and

categorize the crime as a-moral by putting the felon under the tutelage of rehabilitation? In the main, such activist judges subscribe to the philosophy that mankind is perfecting himself toward an ideal good and a more perfect society.

Jurists would restore the right to vote to life-time prisoners for the same reason
that many of them would give the vote to illegal aliens—"entitlement"! Why
should adult criminals be corrected like naughty children? astivist judges query.
Or crime, generally, be calculataed as sensible to *reduction—reducio absurdum*-by
medical intervention? A sick criminal is not a criminal at all but an unfortunate
victim of his illness, these judges lament, whatever that may be construed to be.
Or the criminal is the victim of unforutnate childhood of abuse. Where is the law
in all this, the moral defensibility, the justice of reason unimpaired by sentimental defenses of imaginary causes—a twinkie diet, a childhood abuse, a tyrannical
father, poverty, obsessive fixation, an over-protective mother, a hyper-thalmic
condition, obesity, thoughtless vengeance justified, uncontrollable rage as reme-
diable habit, and, lately, *bipolar disorder,* the camouflage for manic-depressive
schizophrenia. These are the ready-made alibis of defense lawyers and amenable
jurists who cooperate to weaken law-enforcement in this country in the name of
tolerant evolutionary progress.

Even if the courts, the trial courts and the appeal courts, try to read morality
into the rulings on crimes that were the result of childhood deprivation, or poverty or a bad neigbhood-gang influence, or any number of other "plausible" alibi
circumstances, do judges' words silence the evolutionary clamoring for a more
liberal justice, ever more lax and blindly forgiving? This dishonesty must stop
somewhere or the laws of the jungle on the city streets will become the accepted
commonplace, as they have already in some of our cities this day. The courts continue to cling to the evolutionary theory of mankind's improbability and eventual
perfection, this in the face of his propensity to do wrong, to break the law, to
"sin." Absolute moral laws are thought by many to be antequated. In their
absence in schools, government and homes that exists an atmosphere of limitless
tolerance that has converted Americ into a criminal State where licence to coff at
laws is becoming the norm. Be aware that unbridled tolerance will lead to tyranny, and that a continued violation of conscience by a formerly a moral people
will lead to rebellion against both common sense and established and settled
social institutions. The family is presently undergoing this ugly and graceless dismantlement by the sexual-deviant lobbyists, willing clergymen, community supporters and by the schooling of adolescents in poly-sexuality, the which can only
lead to beastiality and incest. God does not annoint evil to serve His will.

There is am authority-system of social approval and condemnation that is simultaneous with and parallel to case law, a pragmetic and humanistic body of social practices that are not laws *per se*, the which people are ever increasingly taking for settled law and that control their lives. The liberal media foster this subculture of what I call *presumptive law*. The authority of the courts has become a kind of sanctuary that has coddled criminals when ordinary persons in their right minds would not do so, th standard of "fairness" which the law itself uses to estimate the motivational logic behind a crime. The typical lenient activist judge, more often than not an pretending Samaritan, instructs society by way of his instructions to the jury and his ruling, not to be too harsh on the criminal. Even when the accused is a repeat offender that same judge will frequently mitigate the sentence by acceptance of a plea bargain based on extenuating circumstances, real or fancied. Or he will find a flaw in the pleading or a fact not discovered to the defense that throws the case into mistrial mode. More tlhan one liveral judge has thus acted so as to win the plaudits of his fellow liberal judges and the aapplause and support of the liveral media who helped elect him to the bench. In this manner he instructs by precept and example, assisting to bring about a diminution of moral persuasion and ethical conduct, his influence on people's lives being subtle at first and then more bold. In this manner activist judges have helped to build a whole generation of cheaters, bribers and extortionists in legislation and in common-law contracts. The re-interpretation of the law to make it relevant to the case is today undermining our system of justice in this country.

Some judges, lacking either conscience or discernment or both, underestimate the teaching power of their words on the citizens. Old societal laws are broken or revoked outside the pale of legislative power to make the law-trespass, for example, the invasioan of one's home by the police or other officers acting under color of duty. Doctor-asssited suicide is gaining in juridical appeal and common acceptance. The infanticide of late term abortions has won acceptance by the highest court in the land, to their shame with the legal consent of the Court to murder, the mother-to-be complicit with the doctor and his abortuary staff. Malicious conduct fed by a continual mill of pornography is overlooked if it caused no spilled blood. Rape has become a thing of the past, almost. The eventual emergence of the cruel, sadistic attitude of life as meaningless when possessed by the aged or the helpless is coming into vogue. And liberal judges are tending the triworks of a system that more and more is agreeing to expunge the morality of human life's inherent value under God. That is Statism of the especially heinous and virile sort that is intrinsically evil. It is as though such judges admired the murderer, for example, for his survival strengfth in the face of his sworn oath of office to uphold the law. Th upshot of his thinking is either that the applicaion of the law must be changed to accord with *evolutionary pietism* or the court musf find a proper excuse not to apply the law but rather to use censure instead.

The nations past mistakes ought not have the power to destroy personal liberties, as of association, of free speech, of contract and of religious worship in the public forum, just so long as these mistakes retain their indissoluable character as <u>mistakes</u> and not as prophetic laws invented by legislative liberal courts. But such is not the case. Selected groups with certain standards for membership are ordered to overturn their rules for membership, the Boy Scouts being one. The character of good English is corrupted to allow for corruptions of meaning and unnatural, i.e. syntactical, foul vocabulary. Television instructs in this venue. Contract quotas, irrespective of candidacy qualifications, are still in place across the country, this before the fact that freedom to form contracts has made of America a great merchantile nation.

Religious worshp is relegated to the junkpile of freedoms in America when believers threatena liberal equanamity and arrogance by their public mention of God and Jesus Christ. The "separation" doctrine is a myth that continues its implacable presumption as binding law. Yet, withal, our past mistakes ought to stand in history's shadows as reminders of our humanity and our commonness of origin, and as has been said often, that our roots are buried in early lawful immigration. Surely, too, were the Commandments of a Divine Creator—a part of America's heritage—accepted by the men who understood their rationale and the dependence of their liberties on moral and ethical conduct. They also foresaw that those liberties empowered just and conscionable choices outside the chambers sof government.

The Founders of this nation did not forget that the rights which came to them were inalienable—could not be taken from them—and therefore supernaturlly given as inseparable *natural rights,* that endowed them as leaders with not only a lawful and constitutional relationship to their compatriots and to their government; but also estblishing through them a fiduciary relationshp with a Divne Creator and by the ordinances of the Christian church and the words of Patrick Henry, Washingrton, Jefferson, Lincoln, Madison, Adams and othners, vocally allying themselves in spirit and power with Scriptural truth. Although this unspoken religious *compact* is much disputed in today's pagan secular humanistic society, the historical fact remains that America drew upon divine authority for her establishment. Primary documents, letters, diaries, speeches and sermons all attest to this salient fact. What keeps America from being a deistic society is that the actions of her government do not impinge upon any particular Biblical precept or clerical dogma. The *influence* of the Ten Comandments is implied without being invoked except to say that common law has long recognized their import and their impact on humanity's wont to do wrong, at times to promote evil.

On the premise that they, the citizens and the President are equally-empowered to vote, and they, as single citizns, carry with him or her, when they go into the voting booth, the commonality of their power with that of the Chief Executive. Each casts his ballot as in an act ot free choice, each potentiates the power of the other that is lawfully bestowed. There can be no illegal voters, whether aliens, condemned criminals or the under-aged. Thus are the consciences of the people no less divinely endowed than in the conscience of the President, who of necessity is better informed though no more powerful to stand and act as a voter. This is not so among dictatorship "republsics," where the tyrant's vote is equal to that of all the people as a mass.

Ideally, the voter is a micrcosm in his rights, duties and responsibilities of those held by the President, whose control of the macrcosm of the nation is the apt expression of the citizen voters' more circumscribed yet more opportunistic liberated power. Only in a dictatorship is the citizen deliberately disenfranchised and stripped of personal opportunities to grow and to manage his life. How inspired were the Framers' efforts to equalize men's power at the ballot box from whence all democratic power issues. Riots in th streets that are said to mimic true democracy are not representative of the power of the people in a republican democracy. The rioters are mere effulgences of self-interest bent upon looting and destruction or illegal force, the shameful work of anarchists who dishonor the credo of responsible citizenship. Their credo is to destroy, not to institute, to terrorize, not to inspire, to kill, not to create, to force, not to plead. Ten to twelve million illegal alien invaders of our country intend her no good, only their own.

To achieve this societal estate, idyllic before the rest of the world where it is both scorned and coveted, the American citizen whether naturalized or native is braced and armored with his right and duties under th Bill of Rights of the Constitution. And may we always acknowledge that heritage with gratitude. Those inherited gifts give to him the power of ancient aristocrats, protectecting him by their enumeration of his rights, while the enumeration of the powers of the Feeral Government, ideally, keep the power of th State at bay from th citizenry. The fundamental impetus and thrust of the U.S. Constitution is to put limits on Federal Government, a lesson learned under British kings and European historical turbulence and wars. This protection does snot provide for the intrusion of any religious body into the common people's government. Visits by the President to the Pope are not to be interpreted as acceptance of Popery into the American institutions and the people's power to govern themselves. Street marches organized by the Catholic Church are anathema to our history and our way of life. The Civil Rights marches led by Dr.King were protests for rights guaranteed by United States Constitution, no more, no less.

When the citizen participates in governmen by his vote, and by his accession to the laws that govern society, he assumes that ancient aristocratic power for his self-defense, enabling him to challenge any wrongs done to him by others. Why does this need to be spelled out? Simply because the increasing power of the Federal Government over our lives has obscured the power to act that is; held by the citizen. He all too often waits for the Government, the State, to furnish him with the opportunity to protest. It is dangerous to a democracy for its people to hold their cause for protest in the cooker of fear, therefore the street marches in protest for Civil Rights had this advantage in the 1960's.

Yet, too, he who acquires as a citizen the power to accumulte reat wealth without its seizure, holds also the power to defend it from premptory seizure. That is largely true at the present time, though the radical environmentalists have made it their propaganda to condemn personal property as ethically degrading. So much for their joy in existence. The owner of property also has the right to pass that wealth on to his successors as beneficiaries of his labor in life. For this reason, if for no other, the present Supreme Court indulgence of greed for the seizure of property under the dictum of *eminent domain,* is volatile, unfair, Marxist and prejudicial to the fundamental freedom of our citizens to own property without peremptory seizure.

The ordinary citizen enjoys the power to secure for himself and his posterity a measure of comfort and security beyond the schemes of avarice, and at a level exeedling that of aristocrats of old. It is commonplce for a man of modest means to own superb ranchlands and a fine home. He can also furnish himself with self-protective weaponry and acquaint himself with a system of justice that is founded upon equitable law and the ethical precept of honesty. These are just some of the powers, privileges and benefits that are his as a common citizen.

It cannot be gainsaid that he is the true aristocrat in his power to delineate his government, its expressions of power, its rules that affect him and its representatsives to whom he has access and a forum for grievances. Ours is an open—and a vulnerable—society. Were his rgihts not inalienable, that is, were they given to him by fallible and changing men in government instead of by an infallible God, he would never be secure in his liberties. And he would forever lack political security and social confidence in the conduct of his life. Indeed, Communism garrishly illustrates this truth of the fallilibliity of human directions and destinies. Its perfect Proletarian Man is today awash with alchol, defeat and unproductive ennui.

The politically active, i.e. voting citizen is the genesis of the power of self-government. Alarmingly, however, that power is being slowlyl relinquished to Statist powers in Washington, despite the predisposition by oral transmission and textbook history to think of liberty as perpetually defensible and enduring without struggle. What do illegal aliens from dictatorship cultures know of this struggle, this enduring freedom? Mexico is one of those cultures. On the other hand, to the extent that the qualified voter refuses to vote, thereby participating in the experimnent, by just that small step does the power of Ms autonomy as a citizen recede and detterriorate. Self-government is not sustainable wthout citizen voter participation. There is nothing, not even the force and effectiveness of the Constitution, that is automatic and an assurance of his power as a citizen if he refuses to vote.

His individual power supercedes that of the citizen of the Athenan State of Ancient Greece. His power trumps that of the individual Roman soldier and citizen who lived under the legal codes of Ancient Rome's Caesars. His power far exceeds that of the French citizen who, today, lives by the decrees of the French Premier and his cabinet. Yet he surpasses in brilliance and inherent diplomacy those powers of the British common man who stands virtually unprotected before his Parliament and his Prime Minister. None of these regimes, these organizations of government power gives to the individual citizen a power equal to that of the average American citizen who holds in his hands the power to oppose slavery and age-old Feudalism Such societies would would be a curse to the "great American experiment." It is the glsobalists who nowadays scorn that political power that is dependent on national sovereignty; they do so out of a deliberate insistence upon the surrender of personal liberties, upon a assumd lack of worldvision denied to our Founders, and upon a deliberate malevolence sprung from the two evils of envy and hatred of America. Madison, Jefferson, Washington and Hamilton were men, all relatively young, who realzied how precarious is personal liberty when fostered by an insecure Federal government and an uncontrolled power center, made so by its dependence upon alien powers such as the United Nations.

The Framers by virtue of their Judeo-Christian heritage, introduced into our Funadamental Law the brilliant concept that disagreements in purpose and polity must be shared between the three Branches of Government. Obedience to that law should then induce, instill and promulgate conscionable choices in leadership and legislation that have an absolute value-base in rigbt versus wrong value-judgements. For human values governing personal conduct that shift and change with every trendy and fashionable predisposition lead the people only into the wilderness of dismay, confusion and fear. Furthermore, that power held by the indivdual citizen *viz-a-viz* his vote makes him accountable to his country, to his fellow countrymen and to himself, for it is the expression of his willingness to submit to the laws that governs his social intercourse, and to his personal responsibility for his actions. That is his "contract" with society as a citizen. At the same time that is the openness that makes him, as a member of American society and culture, accessible to demagogues, to the militarists and the special-interest zealots who eschew their own citizenship. The Globalist, for his part, is willing to be a countryman and a "sunhine patriot" if all looks and goes well. That is his pragmatic outlook on life.

The axioms of self-government, whicn insure personal liberties of speech, association, contract and the vote are: that republicanism begets power even as political acquiescence begets corruption and death. And that power without effective controls, by laws and by a system of justice, invites chaos and tyranny and, on the international scene, invasive war. Such truths did not germinate in a social vacuum. Neither would the sight of war, riots, murder and all their bloody offspring have curbed men's choices and given moral character and direction to his actions by example. The American was never, perhaps until the 1960s, a natural imitator of old-world corruption precisely because his moral perceptions and inclinations had been inherited from the Christian ethos of his history and because of geographical sepatation of America from Europe. Henry James, the American novelist, saw this bifurcation of morals. Indeed Europe has for two hundred years looked to America for this moral transcendance, though imperfectly transmitted to us from the 17th century Puritan-Calvinist creeds. Europeans have tested us for moral leadedership, whether or not we have fiillly communicated our understanding of moral vision to a fratracidal and suffering humanity. And where we have failed to do so, the Old World has scoffed at our feeble and hypocritical paternalism. They do so even today. We have been mocked as regressive and prudish and naive. The prostitution that is legal in the Netherlands is illegal in the U.S. The bribery accepted in Mexico is unlawful in the U.S. The preemption of power by one man, as in third-world countries is outlawed in the U.S. Our stable Adminstration conrolled by Constitutional law contrasts with the quick-change Cabinets in Premier-dominated France. Child labor as practiced lin China, is illegal in the U.S. Pedophilia and child prostitution are are outlawed in the U.S. but acepted in Jacarta and Euroasia. We know ... but we outlaw. That is not naivete; that is wisdom, and may it always be so!

Whenever America's leaders look to Europe for example and guidance in ideas or ways of life, that same leaders in the Supreme Court and Congress tend to retrogress and are made corrupt and blind. Bioethicists in Holland have secured their Tribunals endorsement of rational suicide by the help of doctors. In France, dangerou experiments with abortion chemistry are still under way, even as the socialist government pleads for free enterprise. The Russian people have lost the their way in the penumbra of Proletariamism. Intertribal warfare and the lack of laws to instil hygene and foster medical care are lacking on the African continent. Tribal leaders have murdered hundreds of thousands of their own countrymen in Rowanda. The oath of doctors in Germany is first to the State and then to the care of the patient. England's socialized medicine is almost a total failure. One must finally ask, after looking over the world, what does globalism have to offer our people?

Must we adopt the Medieval practices of a world court that allows no defense lawyer to intervene, no due process, silent imprisonment without probable cause, guilt before innocence. Certain American citizens would have this nation go that route, into abyss of Feudal darkness. Not even profit, the icon of big international corporations, can reverse the moral degeneracy of the Nations of the world. As his own humanist god, Man can do no better than to imitate himself; he must otherwise install tyranny represented by a global oligarchy. Count on it that terrorsism will used to enforce that "solidarity."

Therefore, the power of the American citizen is the power of his privileged liberties, not the rant of a benevolent government that likens God toa pagan shaman, Holy Scriptures to firelight tales and the faith of the people to romantic delusions. Any attempt to reduce the American moral presence in the world to the level of neo-pagan culture, mediocre in her achievements whenever aligned with false standards of "fairness," is insulting to the person of intelligence. An amoral science, regardless of how ingeuous, clever and extraordinary, does not replace the faith of our Fathers—or else we waver and shrink before things of the human spirit and conscience. Today's egregious distortions of the "conscience of America" defames our history. Is euthanasia the answer to guilt or to pain and depression? Is "disposable" man the ultimate throw-away which a caloused, ignoble and thoughtless societly claims the right to discard in the name of *utility*. Have the unborn no defensive right to life? Is "quality of life" the final law by which a doctor or a court judges the worth of a human being? Do corruptions of alternative sex enoble our spirit, enlarge out freedoms and reinforce the character of our people? Americans are the progenitors of their own icons before a sovereaign God for the worship of which we have yet to face future consequences.

Human conscience unimpacted by, uninfluenced by moral standards, will unerringly chose evil, transliterated into all forms of self-satisfaction, some benign, others corrupt and harmful or wicked. But do not doubt that evil is a reality. These moral and a-moral choices almost always lead to conflicts with others that scorn and deny injury, losing the spirit of liberty in the generral unhappiness, as incontemporary Russia. In its clumsy and inefficient efforts by legislation to correct men's hearts and to give soul to their ambitions, to bestow wings upon the imaginations of the people, that the State fails to be the Messiah. False wings feigning liberty willl melt under the sun of reality, and the *Icarus* of humanistic glory will plunge into the moonscape sea of desolation and lost spiritual hope. Such a flight is today headed toward the ethos of a false global unity and harmony. If *globalism* succeeds in all its insidious scheme for overrule by the United Nations, alien minds and ambition will usurp the personal liberties of the citizens of this great nation!

The law of wisdom is the rule of honesty. It is unwise to defect to the chains of power by deceit.

"Sensitivity training" promotes self-indulgence. Sadism and suicide are the fruit of this kind of self-indulgence. life will not always bend to your sensitivity or accommodate your preferrences.

Separate profits from liberty of choice and you offend the spirit of *laisses faire*. You at the same time undulge the latter without restraints, to the endangerment of moral action, and you misconstrue liberty as license.

The evidences of liberty in action, thought and choices in men's lives can be the evidence of good deeds—liberation of a people, compassionate care for the suffering, and greater tolerance for the unpopular protection of the weak and the *good*. It is cynical to disdain Samaritanism.

A false liberty will console men for their ugliest misdeeds while commtting its progeny of self-gratification to oblvion. In this struggle liberty is a delusion manipulated by guile and by cunniung.

31. ON COUNTERFEIT LIBERTY

Incidents of violence in a free society mock representative government as if it were a kind of inept social control augmented by police power. The wild, chaotic acts of violence in the street are not born of the law or any coherent crusade to change it but are spawned by a spirit of anarchy. Street violence speaks for instantaneous reform whenever the message can cut through the smoke and the din and providing there is a modicum of leadership. Banners that prclaim aspects of a cause are various, tenuous at best and often misleading. They are but mere identification markers that appease the cry for explanation and justice, the most common plea behind street violence. Yet even among wolves there is a hierarchy of authority that is absent in wild street clashes.

Far too often the message is madness, turbulence, confusion and abandonment of all pretense to wisdom and good judgement. Marching abreast toward justice sounds noble yet represents a phalanx found mostly in romantic novels. The fires, the barracades, the looting, the hurled stones, grenades, the gunshots and water jets all issue from choice, wicked to the point of destruction. While nehind the rage and violatile mahem are radicals bent on destroying what they would render impotent and harmless by death. Riots are the harbinger of death and the tyranny of pent-up rage given the semblance of comprehensibility by slogans and propaganda, the symbols of some lofty ideal which runs counter both to a just remedy for a grievance and to liberty that promises protection for the excitingly different, the innovative and the daring.

The mood of a mob has been called "mind" whereas mob actions lack the character of intelligence in all its aspects. The violence of a riot is not an act of liberated free-choices by thinkers and planners with ordered minds in search of answers, the oversight and control lacking in the French Revolution. Instead, the mob violence is an action of amorphic group-will and rage in obedience to some half-articulated and vaguely understood minority cause. The insanity is that the riot with its manswarm and the thousand acts of destruction bears little relevance to liberty as a rational response to an alleged transgression of rights.

The nature and scope of the violence of a riot is the inner site of vandalism and does not in the slightest represent liberty that affirms an ethical or a moral decision of the conscience with or without an action in character to follow. Who makes such fine distinctions, if ever any are made in the heat of streert battle? In the great majority of instances, the rioters are attacking the right of self-defense of the majority of the citizens, which right has been extended to the police. One canot champion liberty while destroying its principled foundations.

Furthermore, the violence feeds on either ethnic hatred or on in-group fears within a movement or a cause. The volatility of the rioters reflects their impatience with the *status quo,* their jealousy of its power and their covetousness of the out-group's possessions. In ancient times, these were land holdings and loot of warfare; in more modern times, they are the entities of a society's infrastructure, its communication, transportation, hospital, police and governing apparatus. The Watts Riots and *Krystal Nacht* in 1938 in Germany demonstrated the hidden rationale of hate and death. There is inevitably, too, the psychological injury done to those victimized by the flailing demonstrators. The fanatacized liberty to hurt others is not a true liberty of choice; it is a bondage to hate, the sword is merely the instrument to death. The destruction is simply the abandonment of reason, which is no choice at all but is the absence of reason in the means. Destuction, reprisal and exorcism have no part in the truth of combat against evil; for they are its essence.

Not to be accountable for one's acts is to be an anarchist, an incipient criminal, a potential vandal, a breaker of laws with the open noose waing. Hedonism, the *eat, drink and be merry* motif, does not attempt to set parameters for mutual pleasure, though often the euporia of pleasure finds it a natural end in a stupor of self-indulgence trhat leads to death. The truth of a rioter's justice is his undulgence in a pleasurable onness that is a type of behavior corrupted and distorted, all the more, y money and his sensuous cry for power as opposed to justice. This disease afflicts leaders, great and small. The justice sought is in reality a form of injustice to himself and to others who are lashed to the wrack of Machevellian ambition.

The violence of a rebellion, a more formidabvle and cognitive undertaking than a riot, seldom corresponds in any way to a vision of an amiable practice of liberty among the citizenry. A revellion relates closly to a ciil insurrenction the cause for which are usually just grievances, nevertheless, like riots, a revellion is cruelly divisive and if allowed to gather momentum can precipitate civil war that separates brothers, neighbors and communities.

Fratracidal war and deatrh haunt both sides. There is a continum to such acts of insurrection, for as in a broken trust after many mindless political negotiations, the ideology can get lost in the symbolism., One of the dread results of civil unrest, of fratracidal bloodshed, is the slow strangulation of previously held liberties, the imposition of cultural differences on the host, and tlhe derelection of duty to the host, despite promises to the contrary. The *cause* then necessitates tryanny, for which all too often there can be found easy aspirants.

But the symbol, whether a swatstika, a Cross of Lorraine, or a King's lion does not of itself raise any strident cry for recognition, as often seems to be the case. A symbolism is a reminder; it is used by the tryant, the demagogue, the leader as an engine of annointment. A poerful symvbol, as of conquest or a crusade, is but a device by which an ambititious man seizes sole power and control over the compelling circumstances of defection from true justice. In other words, those who rebel may seek to control the extant system of justice, manipulate juries or if they bribe or are permitted to do so and control weakling or activist judges. Where there is no vigilance, anarchy in the quest for remedial justice, will take over. A true leader can discern the difference between the imposter with a poisonous ambition and a leader with an enlightened agenda for social change. Subtle threats of retribution and intimiation often accompany the imposter of legitimate change who is, in short, the demagogue.

Street violence is almost always a distorted simplification of a symbolic ideology translated into the action of rock throwing, gunfire, bombing and the like. Arson, for another example, is a symbolic purification of the leprous victim whatever his "malady," cheating, ill will, race hatred. Looting, which is often a concomitant of street violence, as in the Watts Riots, signifies the "lawful theft" by suffering "victims" of those who have unjustly profitted by them, although that is usually not the base cause. Lootling is retaliation for real or imaginary material wrongs.

Pain endured by victims of such crude violence, and there are more subtle forms such as euthanasia and late-term abortion, is a means by which the perpetrators of that violence inflict their hatred upon the helpless. Their momentary rage exorcises the demon of want from the human soul—theirs if no one else's. Symbolic mahem and chaos and injury voice the selfishness of a kind of self-righteous anarchy. Its lawlessness is always evcident; its motives are personal to those participating in the violence; the goal is not to seek justic but to exact revengel thus to dominate the enemy. How craftily the *Prince of Darkness* works! There is about violence in the streets an unpreditability and, concurrent with action of storming the barracades, the mob's expression of greed is purified and made almost sacrosanct bby the propaganda of "the cause." Violence in the streets represents the rape of truth, that basic honesty that permeates the democratic community. Where communal integrity in general is missing, corruption rules men's discourse and transactions.

It follows from these considerations that direct "democratic action" as the arm and signet of violence, is directed toward the attainmnent of an untrustworthy ideoeological purpose. Therefore, the action of itself does more harm to a cause than does any mount of counter-reactional legislation or Intelligence action. Reforms by elected representatives sometimes replicate the intentions of violence with bad laws which, in time, iconicize the potential for selfishness of power, laws which simulate the greed of the mobsters and perpetuate the self-indulgence that is intrinsic to street violence. Street violence is, in fact, a lawless intimidation of those leaders who represent a much larger constituency, the general public.

Denial of a permit to march is not censorship; it is the anticipation of a breech of the peace by violence.

Yet within the democratic system of justice the conscionable regard by some men for their fellow citizens is never entirely extinguished when mob rage flares up. Society is, however, injured, and the process of recovery is long and painful and is filled with a mutual suspicion. The entire scene of a riot from beginnoing to end with its cruel and ugly aftermath can be described as *evil*, although liberals and participants will tlry to rationalize away the event as the impatient vioice and expression of justice. The liberty of free speech does not define justice. Nay, moral law and human understanding lead to the articulated vision of liberty. What is restored with great struggle is the concept that fair treatment can be achieved without resort to violence. The caveat is not the inception of truth; nor is the violence. The law is the inception of truth.

Liberty that is tenuously enjoyed following tje action of a direct democratic upheaval or insurgency, like the plebecites of Fascism in WWII in Europe, is an illusory liberty. Inflamned by riotous passion, it anarchy in the streets quenches the conscience for making new socio-political choices. Thus the liberty of expression so vicariously enjoyed vanishes with the cause before the tyanny of the vanquisher. Too, it has ben said that in a Republic the election of a leader may constitsute an election by the tyranny of a majority. The visible option is that the minority can, by due process, effectuate its own will in laws that will be common to both sides. These represent republican conpromises, within which minority voices, not necessarily racial, find thei rrpresentation beyond defeat at the polls. They share their destiny with the majorty of the people, nowadays in almost total disregard for the manner by which the ascendant power took office without violence. This course of events, an election of individuals to representative power, does not occur in Third World countries. Mexico perhaps being a amore recent exception. Widespeead bribery is not excluded from such amicable one-man elections, by fear, by practice, by tradition and by indifference. Military Coups often form up to destroy the new leader, for the powerof organized weaponry is always more persuasive than the voice of the people when power is at issue.

True, it is that there can arise a tyranny of the majority, not however in our country where the three branches of government share and divide the power delegatged to them by the people. There is in America a kind of "machinery" for repression found in offensive rulings by the Supreme Court and the veto power used by the President to cancel favored legislation. But those powers are not oligarchical. Ethic groups enflamed by hate mongers do not readily accept the premise of change, of mutability. Rejectiing history's political axiom *of no vote, no power,* they will often rejecrt the nascent power of their vote and waste their liberty by remaining in tribal enclaves. Such an actuality is today termsd "the Balkaniarion of America." This is another way of decribing the resistance of illegal migrants to ethnic assimilation. Tribalism is Medieval in structure with a religious cleric replacing the controlling Baron. Tribalism denies the free will of guiding conscience. Tribalism defies democratic change, thus it musters to itself the organized church of Rome, corporate power through corruption and lobbyists, and a plethora of new laws to control religion and its expression *per se*. Tribalism is the sledge that will bring down the great First Amendment to our Constitution through **taxation** with athiestic representation and criminaliztion of the bully pulpet to voice God's laws against social corruptions.

The liberty to make choices, in the absence of destructive violence, is a liberty which is not destroyed or even eclipsed by patient reliance upon democratic justice. Our personal liberties remain effective and renewable at the next election and, in America, by referendum, impeachment, High Court rulings or recall. Freedom without these options is illusory and false, awaiting the next king, tyrant or dictator to dominate the subject people with edicts or directives of omniscience. For a society to succeed in counterfeitting liberty, it must first dull and obliterate the idea, then expunge the apparatus of, a free society.

It is not enough to console a man for the loss of his liberty, since he will often summon the demon of vengeance to combat the thief in his behalf.

Keep your personal liberty to charm your slack moments, never putting it out at interest, and you just may extend your indolence to accept a new regine.

A moral conviction about good and evil can never produce an unethical choice and will retain its moral integrity.

The liberty to decide and then to act upon that decision is individualism in action. From first to last, this has been he prototypical passion of the American frontier. Long may it continue before a jealous State!

Keep liberty whole if you would keep life in balance, but let her atrophy and men will seek a delulsory justice that is bondage.

32. TOWNSHEND ACTS (1770) REPEALED—CATALYST OF LIBERTY

Personal "breaking the close" of colonial homes (breaking and entering without authority), secret violations of their dwellings, threatening entry by the power of the King—these criminal acts occurred quite often in colonial times, as they will under an oppressive government, because the Colonists, like all suspicious citizens when overtaxed, regarded the thievish British levies on everyday imports—lead, tea, glass and paint—as unnecessary, unjust and unlawful until they were removed by Parliament. Those tempered and courageous settlers of America considered such taxes as bounty to fatten the King's treasury, the coin of which though scarce was gotten by their own diligence and productive labor.

Also, they felt that such onerous taxation was being used to harass them in support of and justification for the anti-smuggling writs of Assistance employed to ransack homes and ships for Colonial contraband. The Crown, moreover, was using these taxes, the Colonists believed, to pay off the French and Indian War debt (1756—1763) and inconnection thereof, they suspected, and rightly so, that the more they paid in taxes the more feasible it would appear to Parliament and the King to send Britishtroops over to the colony of Massachusetts—two regiments thus being stationed in Boston to enforce harbor closure in retaliation for the infamous Boston Tea Party.

The successful Colonial farmers eyed with asperity and anger the aristocratic class of England who had not had to work hard for their wealth but had inherited it. As for the poor in Britian, there were always the almshouses and other sustenance support from missionary societies, while in the colonies and settlements of New England many adventurers, knowing little about survival in the wilderness and even less about such practical skills as carpentry, fishsing, hunting and timber-felling, they having come over for expected gold and with the soft hands of gentlemen, had died of starvation, disease and winter cold. These calamities had transpired even before Jamestown was fully settled and had begun to flourish. The memories lingered on. A second shipload to Jamestown, fortified by knowledge, made out better.

Colonial artesans were proud of their artesan skill; their craftsmanship, as in making furniture, glass-blowing and candle-making. Germans, Swedes and Dutch had came from the old world via British ports. For these reasons of Yankee ingenuity and imported skills, the colonists eschewed and tried to avoid the taxes imposed by the king and his Parliament. While true that colonial craftsman did not have to pay guild dues, the skills they possessed motivated them to form numerous cottage industries within the towns. Colonial craftsmen prided themselves on their status in a society and to whose skills there attached respect, good trade relations and a practicable income. Bartering was commonplace, a sow in exchange for a new thatched roof, a brindle cow to pay for new fiirniture in the cottage. The Yankeee spirit of tree trade and bargaining was very much alive. Thus British taxes laid upon common goods seemed punitive and harsh and totally unnecessary. Were they not giving back to England finished products—iron-work, candles, rope and soap, not to mention square nails and turpentine, in exchange, via a London's merchant's shipping order, for raw materials like iron and bolts of flax for colonial looms?

Income rather than barter was a thorn in the flesh. For its very absence the Colonists they were made to feel impotent without the power to tax and the means to market the products of their own hands. Curious in its demands and greedy beyond conscience, the Crown set the prices or what to the Colonists made no practical sense. Little gold passed hands between the British here and there in New England where trade intercourse among bretheren of the faith often amounted to "driving a good bargain" with the shippers, handlers and home consumers. Indeed, certain London merchants devised ways to exploit Colonial artesans for their own profit, like price-control and goods-monopoly in London's Trafalguar Square. The Townshend Acts became all the more despicable to the Colonists when they knew that the King and his sympathizers, some within the Colonies to be sure, decried American enterprise for trumping British mercantile glory. This comparison was all the more sharply defined when the Yankee began to build ships tin competition with the British merchant fleet to ship their goods in their own vessels and thus avoid taxes and regulations. And, of course Colonial vessels were not strictly bound to trade with Britslish merchants at British ports. There emerged a triangular gtrade between Liverpool, Jamaica and Boston that involved Jamaican rum The Colonists bore an independent spirit that England feared and watched over closely. The fact was not ignored or forgotten that they, London artesans and the Colonial craftsmen and traders, were of identical blood stock. That consanguniyt made the Townshend Acts eeem all the more coercive, unlawful and impractical.

What does the historian say in response to these complaints by the Colonists, their high ground position, their moral perception of the good and evil of the Mother Country or of their own colonies. Calvinist doctrine marked much of their early spiritual journey. They were thankful to God for His deliverance whilst they kept close watch on the providence of His will for them. And they thrived, sometimes on unethical practices—their dissatisfactions led to the unethical trade practice of smuggling. Tthey smuggled when they could, frequently in Dutch or Spanish vessels and with any country that would cooperate in trade. Without specificity, it was the Writs of Assistance that were designed to frustrate this kind of dark enterprise. The Colonist traders also practiced a smart and ongoing bribery of customs at the ports of entry to England, chiefly Liverpool and London. Colonial traders concealed their "highly irregular" profits gleaned from foreign buyers as well as from Lodnon merchants in expectation that they would be heavily taxed thereupon. The Colonial traders also practiced outright fraud as to the value of goods from the colonies, such as inflated values entered on ships' manifests by customs agents. If English ship captains could practice fraud by increasing the head charge on travelers to the colonies, why then could not the Colonists raise, and sometimes depress, "honest" values placed on goods they transhipped between New England and Britain?

Since British laws still largfely governed the province of Massachusetts—she lost her charter in 1691 and her town meeting privileges sunder the Intolerave Acts—colonial rancor grew against the British governing laws that were patently illegal. No Englishman was ever taxed so heavily, or held in such tight bondage to the Crown to pray for his favor and leniency. Depite these discriminitory and oppressive practices by the King and Parliament, a new sense of freedom, of personal and communal liberty was emerging along the New England seaboard. Were the circumstances of a relatively primitive existence still too circumstantial and individual for the colonial matron, the farmer, the cowherd or Sexton to make a case for a moral conscience? These simply folk, our ancestors, were all the more able to do so because they were close to the faith that had animated their forebearers' hazardous venture. Very often their childrens primer was the Bible, while the village elders were in evidence about the streets of the village, dispensing their beautiful shrouded wisdom of Scripture to any who would lisen. The good folk of Plimouth knew right from wrong and handed this discernment down to their scampering progeny.

Morality was not burdensome among the settlers in Nw England. It defined their way of life. One ought to remember that the Puritans and their successors to the settlements belieed in the doctrine of righteousness before God. They conceded their own sins before Him, most of the villagers, for there was between themn a homogeniety of blood, background and belief. God could bring to judgement those who defrauded their bretheren, a judgement that the Kings Star Court could reach. They, however, construed their King's maneuvers *viz-a-viz* the Townshend Acts and the Intolerable Acts to be the maneuvers of a tyrant, perhaps appointed by God but astray from His annointing and his precepts.

Would a Holy God annoint the King and all of British Parliament to wrong the devout and to try and imprison the pious and just?

Whenever they had acted outside of Gods laws, as expressed chiefly in the Ten Commandments and Christ's example to them, they could repent and be forgiven, but whenever they acted outside the *king's* law there was no redress. In this matter their personal hardhships had mde them a dauntless people. Neither the King nor the Pariliament frigntened them, even when they violated conscience and tricked or defrauded their London bretheren. Indeed, even as King George kept his heel on the necks of the Colonists, they condemned themselves as inqiuitous. They also knew that the justice of the Crown that transgressed her ancient *Magna Carta* of fair trial and due process, did not reflect the justice of the rightous God of the Hevrews and the Christians. The Townshend Acts ere intended, they firmly believed, to magnify the corruption of the British Crown and to keep them in subjection.

Until the Colonists through their Burgesses, their Committees of Correspondence, their forums and speeches, pamphlets and broadsides, should find a voice to object to the Crown's repressive measures, the singular acts 'of Colonists who at the risks of their lives sought their own fair-play measures, their own defenses of equity, were actions in which the choice to be legally wrong but morally right gave to their motives sway and power and a certain legitimacy of honor. In the aggregate they were mounting up and coalescing into public displays if condemnation in the bully pulpit and in the streets, demonstrations.

Brutish laws by mid-century were by now wearing the mask of deceit and fraud and bearing the standard of corruption and dishonor. As Britishers, the Colonists felt that they had been done in by their own government and to a great extent by their own people back in England. Their Declaration of Independence was their response to the Crown's outlawry, the king's coverups, as it were, for his actions. His Star Chamber, his secret tribunal of justice, stood ready to condemn, not the martyrs as of old for their God, but the insufferably rigthetous rabble who dared to rebuke the king. The laws to govern a people were one thing and ought to be oveyed. But the absolute authority to concoct regulatitons or reasons outside the pale of political comity and for the express purpoe of unjustly subjugating Englishmen was an immoral authority. The Colonists at last realized that that authority ought tos be disobeyed and so they took up arms and there thundered down the American Revolution.

Few will discredit individual liberty as a makeweight to a free society; but many are her headsmen when it comes to the toleration of wanton and immoral license.

Make of no man a pawn to obtain liberty for it cannot be bribed, purchased, negotiated or sentenced, lest it become something other than liberty. It *is* from the beginning.

The source of the contract that permits a man to use his liberties must have divine but mortal justice for its human conception. The contract is as fallible and yet as honest as the parties who write it.

Law and justice in America either furnish proof of God's grace or they are a great delusion of intelligent devices and accord, liable to self-destruct.

True liberty is not profligate or censorious, being neither a wanton device for personal aggrandizement nor a form of judgement to condemn non-conformers but a moral ideal and practicable way to live.

33. FROM TYRANNY TO LIBERTY

The Puritans Brought with them a clear understanding of their individual responsibilities—first to their God, then to their community, both for their *mutual* security and well-being and survival, and then to themselves. Theirs was a theosophy of life. And inextricable from their lifestyle, as we describe their manner of living, was the exercise of their Biblically-informed consciences as believers in the Christ of the Gospel of grace. Talmudic Law furnished grace and tolerance for Jews within the Gentile Community of Saints as bretheren of God's holy Word and and His providence.

They—all Anglicans who had so practiced in England-eschewed the High-Anglican Church as Popish and too ceremonial, in deference to the Calvinist tyle of worship, plain and unadorned. They had made a covenant with God and with the Colony governance by His Elect. They accepted meted-out punishment prescribed for the sinner's failure to follow Commonwealth religious observances among which was mandatory church attendance. Basic to their theosophy were the Ten Commandments of Exodus and the palliative precepts of the Beautiudes. For they did in fact consider themselves to be among the meek and lowly and greatly blessed by God. Of course there were always the devious and the rebellious, but for them there were the stocks and water-dipping and other means, publically, to determine moral guilt and to exact pennance. Public confession at town meetlings was frequently practiced to clease the soul and make aright with a neighbor, this contrition established long before for secular barristers had signaled any kind of authority in the early Colonies. The Pastor and/or the elders of the village settled land disputes, thefts, charges of unfair barter, cheating and other violations of the Ten Commandments, although a man's conscience was deemed a gift from God and, together with certain "tests", found to be suitable and pragmatically useful to adjudge guilt.

One's experience of the work of grace required confirmation; while among all who adhered to the Calvinist doctrines of unconditional election (salvation), limited atonement (for believers) and irresistable grace (for all mankind), there was the common belief that liberty guided the light of conscience, irrespective of any weakness of personal faith. None of these matters of faith, however, permitted the Colonists to embrace a corrupt monarchy or clergy which, to their minds, sang too much of the praises for Caesar and not enough of the Christ.

But the freedom of responsible moral choices came naturally, intuitively and by practice to the Colonists of the Bay Colony and of Plimouth. Governor John Winthrop of the latter settlement proclaimed that the colonial Covenant with God would be strict on the inhabitants thereof, under the penalty of exile for disobedience. Roger Williams and Anne Huchinson received this penalty of banishment. As for Williams, he denied that church attendance was proof of, and preserved, one's salvtion, proclaiming aloud that such a practice and injunction constituted *works* of righteousness rather than Luther's salvation by faith alone, *solo*. Anne was not long in joining him in his new colony of Providence, having endured ostracism by the devout. Williams promised religious liberty to all who would join him.

Life in the English settlements was arduous and frought with the danger of Indian attacks; death ny disease was a continual spectre. Yet such an existence expanded the Colonists' perspectives on duty and obedience to the laws of man and God and moral conscience in matters of self-discipline. Mixed in with these serious-minded concerns were reported visiions of the more devout—later to explode in the Salen witchcraft trials. The Colonists seemed to have a liking for civic debate, personal, informal and indigenous to the town-hall forum of local self-government that was to follow these green settlements. That propensity for self-government was to follow Americans all the way into present day society. Rancor and disaffection with their lot were considered a part of the human condition; there were ways to mend too much of this kind of zealotry: public exposure, shunning ostracism, and outright exile from the colony. They pralyed hat these measues would prove beneficial to the Penitent soul, an attitude that carries over to this very day in America's penal system—reformation of the criminal.

Villagers faithfully attended their community meetings. They organized quilting circles; for the men it was quoits, similar to horseshoes, woodchopping contests and turkey shoots. Farming discussions ny the men concerned their dependency upon God's providence, a tenet of Christianity that reinforced their dependence upon God and His goodness. Their British cousins were not so reliable in granting their blessings. Universally, these strange early Americans practiced their faith in all the ways and for material things of life on this earth. They did so without question, for Ithey were enjoying their Creator's provision for them.

They participated in town meeting forums, often held in the tavern, the largest meeting hall in the village. Although the Separatists and the Pilgrims all too often in the beginning came poorly equipped for the ardors of their adventure as axemen, carpenters, blacksmiths and weavers, they arrived with a sophisticated comprehnsion of the meaning of power and government corruption and human frailty. It was precisely this understanding which, in another one hundred and thirty years or so informed the making of the new Republic, initially by the Articles of Confederation and then in the post-Revolutionary writing of the Constitution.

From the very first the colonists believed in God and his justice as being intrinsic to a local colonial government established and maintained by; their obedience to its Mayflower Compact Covenant, of communal authority and ordinances under God. The work ethic began here—he who would not work should not eat. There was thus established early in time the efficacy of labor. The poisons of British feudal authority and Crown cruelty had tempered the fibrous wood of their character.

Population growth in England and overcrowded jails had prompted the king to allow colonization. Competition for world power against Spain had augmented, reinforced and enegrized this royal motive. For his part, the typical colonist believer and skept, alike, sought religious freedom from priest or intercessor or any remnants of the earlier royal vicarage of Christ that the Crown may have entertained such as the "divine right of the king." Anglicanismn in the colonies did not disappear completely. It simply was not motivational. If found expression in acts of penitence, whereas the Gospels proclaimed repentance and God's forgivenesss.

Yet in a larger perspectve on the religious comport of early colonial settlements, it was the light of conscience that showed the way, and it was, by the "fullness of the spirit" that lierty was accomplished and enjoyed—but not without error, inasmuch as all men were deemed imperfect sinners, stricken with depravity since the Fall in Eden. This religious *ethos* shaped our very system of government with its separation of powers and enumeration of restrictions and declaration of individual rights. A realistic understanding of human nature was, from the beginning, evident in American government.

The Colonial attitude of mind was not to dissociate one's self from one's kinsmen in England. It was only after another one hundred and fifty years of abuses and exploitation that the Colonist came to find in the Crown a hostile adversary and in English regulaions a millstone hung about his enterprising and industrouus neck. The British Parliatment's statutory Acts and Ordinances, apart from case law, may have been intended to correct colonial bad manners. The King's onerous burden of taxation without representation was, however, an attempt, while raising revenues, to impound Colonial religous faith under Royal contro thus making religious worship was dependent upon him as a form of neo-Popery. The Crown condemned Colonial dissatisfaction. These upstart ingrates were denying their glorlious Britsish heritage.

Punishment in Massachusetts Bay Colony and in Plimouth for wrongdoing was almost always a public spectacle. The Separatists shared a belief in the power of public disapproval and condemnation, much as is practiced in contemporary America when the press villifies a politicall candidate or pillories and condemns an incument in office, or a defector from liberal *dicta* if they think justice is betrayed. Having no media to influence his conscience, the colonist understood that particular inner liberty as a quality of his character makeup. The individual settler comprehended divine direction by way of the Lord's providence, a word so often in the puvlic consciousness that it was used to christen ships, towns and milkmaids. Providence was separated from secular fatalism by the religious source of the former. The Colonist grasped the fundamental Bivlical conept that man was gifted by God to know right from wrong, that he had free will, that some men were His Elect unto salvation, and that salvation of the soul was not by works but by grace alone "lest any man should boast. The Puritan lived in the light of the logic that there musrt be a God, proof of which was that if one thought about such purity of mind and his deliverance and had sufficient faith in the Scriptures which he read daily, then He must exist. In the secular idiom, one cannot think about a God unless he already exists in some tangible form. This was the root beginning of a pantheistic nature worship of Thoreau and the occultic supernaturalism of Emerson.

"Freedom under God" was not an athiestic lampoon, a governmen pejorative, a trifle of English churchmen, a semantic quagmire for liberal philosophers. The expression held a real meaning for the colonists of New England, it being useful in their day to day struggles to survive. In his humility—for whom could he stand proud before?~the settler knew that no king or Parliament had ever instructed him in fine moral discrimination. The origin of life's moral choices were British homes and the Holy Bible, origins that like fireflame carried their embers overseas into the Colonies. Sometimes certain ones of the faithful went to the extreme of banishsing the non-orthodox in the practice of the faith. Roger Williams' Providence was a *net-colony* to catch all believers in freedom of worlship. In his instance of revelation he expanded the concept of freedom from its narrow Calinist doctrine of God's elect to the more inclusive provision for other denominations, including Jews and Catholics. This ecumenicism was the first of its kind in America. It sustained the doctrine of "common grace" that was God's gift to all mankind and not just for the Calvinists.

Colonial understanding of basic liberties communicated into Philadelphia's Indendence Hall in 1787 when those fifty five delegates who drafted the second Constitution remembered the liberty, the struggle, the triumphant hope and the damning doubts as holy covenenters in a new land. They remembered through their speeches, their letters and their documents of state, the letters of *Correspondents* and the sermons on liberty that they had heard. Their anecdotes and trivia must have inspired Franklin's *Poor Richards Almamac* produced at his print shop nearbyto Philadelphia Hall.

They showed that they had fathomed the reasoning of the Commonealth liberty of Thomas Hoves, translated into States' rlights; the equal authority of all men to prohibit, indemnify, suppress and punish, their authority belonging to their equal "state of nature," philosophy of John Locke, his and Hobbes' ideas belonging to the Enlightenment. The Framers also showed that they understood well the minds and attitudes of men much as Cotton Mather, John Smith and John Winthrop with regards to civil obedience and productive labor. The beginning of 19th centlury capitalism established root in Merchant Colony investment in New England and, in Pennsylvania, by the King's land grant, Geolria by control and investments of trustees, Massashusetts as a producer of tobacco and indigo. The connection between property and its productive use had opened the way to an agrarian America and, evenually, to an industrial giant of the 19th century.

The Colonists were aware that education had for its chief purpose the instruction of the child to read so that he might read the Holy Word and the school primer that was loaded with pithy aphorisms of moral instruction. The Colonists were keen to invest in the child's education so tlhat he might also might learn simple math lin order to callculate the acreae of a plot of ground or clipher the value of a keg of nails. A child's education in moral rectitllude was to enable him to avoid the wiles of the devil and to lead a life of purity, sacrifice and obediencel, first to God then to the elders and one's parents. These doctrines of "the good life" instilled in the young the acceptance of accountability. Many of the earliest settlers, as gentlemen, had been too much inclined to lean on their family pedigrees. The thrust of learning was now pragmatic, theistic and disciplined.

The liberties of the Colonists were not to be taken lightly. Barring the King's revocation of their charters, as happened to Massachusetts, hotbed of troublemakers, they would enjoy the fullest freedom to say what they pleased, yea, even if against the King and Parliament. They would chose to be pleased by whatever mode of living best suited their needs and fancy, and those of the colony. A man's connection to his community was his life-line to existence. So it was that responsible government began in the colonies and with religious precepts of accountability to man and to God, and that liability that reflected the intrinsic worth of the man began on the local level. Meetings of the villagers and the final ordinaances of their Selectmen, as regards to drinking and foul language and labor on the Lord's sabbath, kept the peace and regulated daily intercourse. For citizens felt regimented by their own neighbors, who were not yet Countrymen, in contradistinction to royal oppression. For their very lifestyle inferred the integrity of absolute moral rigflit and wrong, scripturally mandated and self-imposed.

The first colonists little speculated so far into the future that they shaped their daily life to meet the exigencies and demands of some far off intercolonial government, at least not for another hundred and fifty years and the advent of their Provisional government under the First Continenal Congress of 1774. Then they would concede a larger unity of purpose in settlement living, a larger plan and vision of interdependency for their own security and welfare, in the face of the king's refusal to hear their continual petitions for redress of grievances.

They had grown apart from their British "cousins." They had begun to distinuish themselves as a merchantile people, middle-class artesans and shopkeepers, who were demanding recognition from their own King Georfe III. Out of their pragmatic self-interest came the buyers, traders, shippers and manufacturers, hewn in a large measure from the sophisticated minds and ways that mimiced London's merchants. The colonists had learned the basic lessons of supply and demand and of merchantile competition that were to become their trademark for all time. America is fundamentally a nation of merchants. All other endeavors also lead to the marketplace: finance, literature, science, education, government. In these early colonies there appeared that amalgamous beginning.of the American culture. Some gentlemen adapted, others returned to England. But all who stayed, like it or not, cut their respective grafts into communithy life on the logic of productivity. A strict reading of the United States Constitution will disclose this genius of America's might, not just her productivity for lthe marketplace, but her commersce in thought, in the arts, in education and inventions, her proliferation of and access to boundless opportunities for all men. Separated by water yet bound by Enlightenment ideas and British precdeent, these things came to be accepted as a matters of "destiny."

The word *liberty* came to have very pragmatic meanings for the colonists. They cherished their liberty to think about God and to worship Him, with this significant discrepancy: the New Enland God of the Puritans was not so much the God of wrath as He was the God of truth, a bellwether whose immediate divine precautions were worked into the utilitarian bent of the Yankee mentality. They were Proverbialists who believed that by adhering to personal virtue they were fulfilling their covenant with God for their "City on a hill", the New Jerusalem whose apotheosis was the application of liberty in the lives of these pioneer people.

If what worked was pragmatically good, why could not that good be made applicable to all of society and therefore affirm its moral goodness by the hand of God as a social virtue. The Great Awakening grew out of this idea. Thus there merged a salient "American character," in him who was a believer, confident of those paths he had pioneered, and ready to dispose charity toward all men. Liberty would find its paradigm not in a multiplcity of rigfhts and other cultures, but in laws to preserve the peace and happiness of all citizens, under the sovereignty not of a king but of a compassionate God. The truth of this dclaration is seen in our hopitals, child-labor laws, prison reforms, charities, work safety laws, those enlightened activities representing the Biblical precept that all men have a value because they were made in the image of God. That is a germinal idea in Americas history, a liberating idea which no tyrant could either inspire or produce, As the State gains in power over the people, this idea diminishes in power and importance until secular humanism snuffs it out. Strangers will then decide whose life has value.

Our nation's early settlers knew first-hand about the liberty to sow the land and reap the harvest and to enjoy the products of their labor. They comprehended without any bioethic markup the simple liberty to walk up and down in the vilalge streets without the king's representatives challenging their way; the liberty to find early tithing of grain beneficial;to the colony for widows and orphans; the liberty to fume against British merchantilism and dispute the heavy hand of the monarchy on their hard labors; the liberty to object to the King's proclamations skewed as they were by the Crown's self-interests, its prodigal ways and expensive indulgences.

The colonists, both the early settlers and later arrivals, yearned for the liberty to hear about hell and damnation and God's bountiful goodness without their having to genuflect before altar statuary or confess to the priest or pay for candles which they dearly needed in their homes for light. They appreciated the liberty to invent, improvise and concoct for the pleasure of creating a new and useful tool or item of comfort from the crude resources of their wilderness. They knew the liberty to sing with joy and to weep wih grief, attributing all events to God's providential will and not to the 'caprice of the Crown' or to the English nobility. The colonists accepted the liberty to criticize their own mistakes in self-government and to prepare for their own defense agaisnt the Indians and, in due course, against their own countrymen for offenses listed in the Declaration of Indiependence, the torch that ignited their Revolution. They treasured as belonging to their happiness the liberty to lay up a cornucopia of goods, amenities of life and artifacts both useful and oranmental which their labor had produced, these things held in thrift against poverty or famine, for they were basically a conservative people. They relished the satisfaction of giving honor where due or disdaining what deserved to be disdained as politial treachery against them, the choices being theirs. Indeed, they knew the liberty to chose whart deserved respect in man or animal, and to pay homage to right without the Parliament's interference ny threats, as with some new controlling Act. This comprehension of liberty was so for the first sone hundred and fifty five years of colonial existence in the New World.

Until the Quartering Act of 1768, when 4,000 British trooos were sent to oston to put down riots against repressive taxes, the colonists enjoyed the liberty tp live in their homes safe from sudden royal intruders. Amidst this turmoil and outrage, they accepted the right of choice either to return to England or to stay on and make the best of their new lives. They took for granted their liberty to gather in town meetings for political discussion and debate. The Committeee of Correspondence kept them informed of the predisposition and fears of colonists throughout the settlements. Broadsides and pamphelets, such as those by Thomas Paine, became a staple intellectual source of ideas and hidden fury. The colonists increasingly fulminated against the tyranny of the King. Custom officials and "lobsterback troops lived in jaopardy of their lives against colonial anger, Philosophically and technically, the Revolution had already begun, precedent to the Concord Lexington out break of actual warfare. Colonial liberties belongd to and were the expression of the precious freedom which the colonists had found in their New England home.

It cannot be denied that certain 12th century ideas had their genesis in the Chrsitian faith: God condemns false weights; He loves the world He made; He enfranchises the human race to exercise freedom, commanding only that they be accountable to Him. Money is important to God~it is mentioned many times in Scriptures—therefore thrift and good investments are important. Principles dealing with justice were imported from England; case law and legal preceeent, the presumption of innocence before trial, a jury composed of ones peers, no double jeopardy or cruel and unsual punishment: these ideas implicit and stated in our Constitution. They were ideas grounded in an understanding of human nature and in man's deepest yearnings for personal freedom. The wildernes experience of survival deepened their trust in themselves and gave rise to a self-reliance that is so markedly a part of the American character. Emersonian selfreliance combined with hatred for an oppressive tyrsant evolved into a doughty, enterprising, competetition with the Mother Country, a distrust of her magnificence and her capricious laws, and a growing flame for independence.

Personal liberty in colonial times was enormously simple of expression; it was embodied in the belief, reducable almost to empirical adage, that if enough of the people think a local law or community action is rigfht, then it must be right or, in the minds of the devout, righteous before God. Theirs wwas very close to a thiestic society; the lack of an overruling clergy and the absence of tribal dissention kept it from being so. Since the days of the Mayflower Compact, the individual colonist had to act responsibly toward his fellow villagers when—as the Calvinist belief mandated—he sinned. This axiom some have called "the tryanny of the majority", a not unusual idea since the notion of oppression, as such, was so keenly motivational one way or another in colonial life. After all, the King had his heel on their necks to work his wicked will on them. Thus the majority will of local opinion and personal conduct was a reaction against the conentrated power of lthe Crown. The darker side of this popular *sequitor* of reaction led to legalism in religion and a kind of village pharasaicalism in such realities as the "blue laws" for village conduct. As time went on, the Salen Witchcraft trials became an inevitable result of these religious ordinances of the townsmen's insulariies; whilest petty fueds and jealousies were violations of the conscience that only God could see, the which led to the unconscionble accusations one villager against another and the resultant hangings for witchcraft. These trials were shot through with perjury, venial ill-willl, insufferable jealousy and outright vengeful hatred of villager for another. The doctrine of God's casting the sinner into hell became the vehicle for for his unrepentance—often for a fictitious crime—led to his and her condemnation by the trial judges. Religious piety was seen only as a ruse of the woman who was hung for a witch.

The colonists of the pre-Reolutionary decades felt that the King was graudally throttling their initiative, their enterprise and their Englishman's right to strike a bargain, that is, to form a contract. Crown pressure was forcing the village black-smith, roper, cooper and fisher to participate in a form of extortion upon himself to the immense profit of the home country. His artesan's goods were worth more than he received in payment for them by London merchants. He was being forced to cheat himself in order to satisfy the Crown's interests. In a word, King and Parliament were exploiting a social and political Colonial minority. For pre-cisely the reason that the King's had granted Charters to his colonies—to recover what he had loat in Britain's war with France and to fatten his treasury for his personal induences—the colonists felt, and rightly so, that they were being unjustly used through these charters by the levying of taxes. It was that injustice that supplied the impetus, and indeed was a fundamental cause for, the American Revolution. Taxation in which they had taken no part was imperious and outra-geous in the view of the Colonists, especially when they were taxed on what they had created.

Under this kind of oppression, the surety of a constant God began to crumble before the exigencies of necessity and circumstances. Spirual ties to the village religious atmosphere of moral conduct weakened as the population grew and the church lost its Separatist power. Rapacious men, eager ro gain wealtth, assumed that conscience was the tool of the fool. Thus certain outlawed, shuned or exilic settlers began to engage in smuggling, chiefly in Spanish and Dutch veswels to nearvy Jamaica for rum and gold when either could be had. This illicit commerce was carried on under the noses of the Britlish admirallty, they who were Lords of the Seas. In this manner the oppressive taxes of the King were working their power to destroy colonial British affinities and to weaken the power of the Sepa-ratist body to redeem its presence in colonial villages. America's Declaration of Independence was in the making.

Grand larceny in America was not invented until the Boston Tea Party and its extortionate tax, and not until the governors of the Proprietary Colonies were made to submit to the Act of colonial Houses of Burgesses in order to receive their pay and retain their charters. This latter political action was, in fact, an early form of colonial self-government and was an historically precedent example of the principle of checks and balances in government. The House of Burgess, a colonial Congress, coul withhold thd pay of the British-appointed governor as a veto to oppose the enactment of a British-mandaged law through the governor.

Such checks were useful. The common citizens, who were still British subjects, knew that the sins of greed and deceit and exploitation, indigenous to the Crown, reflected to Man's total depravity. The Constitution they wrote in 1787 affirms the empirical insight that was theirs. Liberty therefore was not an illusory reaction to infamous laws by irresponsble Kings Chamber judges. It was the issue of colonial experience, and a vision for the rectitude of a new country in laws and in everyday life.

What was said to be an illusion of liberty was said to be so by the spoilers of liverty, the disenchanted deconstructionsts who would replace the alleged illusion with the actuality of their nondage to to self-interest. It was not any inherent weaknss of practiced liberty that fomented license for rebellion but, instread, was the abuse of the natural right of moral choice, predicated upon conscionable actions, that led to the grasp of power and to vengeance. Contemplating their possible losses through violence, rich merchants with the singular exception fo Morris and Hancock—and there were otherw—did not find revelolion attractive. They were accountable to the suppliers in London and to the properietors of their respective colonies. Liberty had become a repugant shibboletth of identity to those Britons who found insufferable the distant threats to their personal richess. After the Revolution they would attempt to seek indemnification for their losses, to collect a form of Crown insurance activated by the Amelricans revolution.

By the time war arrived in mid April of 1775, there were in existence thirteen colonies most of whose inhabitants were either against outright revolt or indifferent to it. And whether or not the war should touch him personally, as in an invasion of his lands and home, he was certain to experience a dramatic change in the manner of his living. The alignment of active participatants, the militia, in the cause of liberty with the majority of self-exiles and onlookers occasioned another axiom of the American expeience: that the indifference of a people to a great cause can be brought to heel when the pragamtics of the purse threaten hardship and compel solution. Peace loving was to be guided by enlightened self-interest, the morality of whcih was, and is, mercy and justice.

Until recent decades an old and corrupt Europe has looked to our moral leadership, for it is axiomatic that tyranny has no common cause with that volunteerism and compassoion that are the gifts of liberty. One may dispute that the City on a Hill has todlay any reality, but he cannot deny that the potential talents and means of the individual American can find their maximum expression in the unmatched opportunities envisioned ny her settlers and her Founders.

A people keep liberty alive not by submitting to the encroachments of civil bondage, the plethora of bureaus, but by rejecting the political emoluments to its survival, e.g.as the United Nations Heritage Sites.

Only the patriot in America knows the value of his liberty, since it has no worlth in the eyes of disdainful aliens and traitors.

Rioting is scoffed at nowadays, not to make it seem right but to conceal the deception of its anodyne, the rule of a mawkish liberty, as street marches for outlaw causes.

Few dilemmas demand more insight than the question of the parameters of the deeds of wicked men, who drop a curtain of the deceit of relativism to hide from the law.

If an unwise decision endangers moral choice, re-examine the misapplication of that liberty to chose, not its threatening options. For the effects must not contol the cause or the ends will then justify the means.

The death of liberty for one law-abiding citizen, as when he discards his trust in leadership, can ulimately lead to the oblivion of freedom for all law-abiding men and for this reason, that the" price of liberty is eternal vigilance."

34. AUTHORITY, LIBERTY AND RESPONSIBILITY

One of the fundamental axioms of liberty asserts that every person is born with a free-will capacity to make choices and to reason out his destiny. Another tenet states that he is gifted by his Creator with a conscience the capacity of which is to discriminate moral right from immoral wrong. These two axioms confront the apostles of evolutionary "natural selection," for having this capacity the child and the man alike are capavle of doing evil, of breaking the law, of acting in isobedience to the vested authority of laws both good and bad. These things the early settlers to America understood, but which modern man by his sophisticated reasoning continually denies with relativistic logic. He invents euphemistic substitutions to conceal the fraud behind his reasoning. His modern technoloy implements the fraud. Let some examples be citied: the Modern, we shall call him, poses himself as a victim of other men's wrongs by which psychological transfer of guilt he escapes any sense of moral misdeeds, hurtful action or moral responsivility on his part. He comes to believe in his Tightness before the law and therefore he has no need for God. The Modern betrays his lies by a multiplicity of devices to show others where he has been wronged, in schools adopting cheating for honesty, in government adopting brivery for honest support, in churches blaming his condition on God's wrath or chuch hypocrisy, in matters of common courtesy adopting the manners of barbararians to dispel any distrust of his own inferior upringing; and in the matters of public safety, eschewing the right to self-protection as somehow harmful to society at large, outlawing in the process any act of violence that returns violence as a means to survival. Thus the gun is fast becoming outlawed as a defense against brutal crime. Modern man is by these disingenuous means destroying himself and his personhood, the marks of civilization in his nature and the attributes which a loving God once bestowed upon him in our society. Colonial man survived by conscionable and toleravle ways of fgihting back, by lws and by guns and by reliance upon God. Modern man will not survive because he aspires to outlaw all of these and to deny in the process that he even has a soul that marks him as human, conceding to the evolutionists as he does that he, too, is only an animal. Any sane man knows that animals have instincts but they do not possess a sense of moral choice.

Concealments of his spurious "truths" are the ancient subterfuges sthat circumvent the law; they are the lies to his own bretheren and to representatives of a disdained authority being his chieftest means of moral escape. Satan has been called "the father of all lies." These subterfuges, in government, schools, churches, are the inventions of satanic escape from accountability. They often parade in the guise of "a fair chance" that is no more than a tolerance for immoral conduct. Poor men often remain poor because they elect that option. Criminals remain criminals because they, knowing the law, break it as a choice. Elected leaders make devious choices of irresponsible posturling because they place personal ambition over public welfare.

These detestble "flaws," shall we calll them, of human nature the Framers of our Constitution understood as veing inherent in all men,l from monk to missionary, from harlotto statesman. Therefore, their wisdom and their esxperience instructed them that laws ought to be the authority, explicitly written down, theocratically true as in early New England and deistically grounded as in more mature confederate America, and inferentially wise as in our Modern Republic. Man has the inordinate yet natural capacity to wrong mankind, to exploit "mans inhumanity to man," as Pope phrased the enmity. The principle of separation of powers embodies this understanding; the *separtion* principle was not intended to thwart cries for liberty—unlike the *hubris* of the French Revolutionaries who found most ancient regime laws except death by the guillotine contetemptible in their class-hating and barbaric Reign of Terror, The Framers placed limits upon the powers of each branchs of government for that reason of human corruptibility. They defined the rights of the citizens as *inalienable* and to be eternally protected by laws from an the follies of an oppressive, arrogant and magisterial Central government and from the ambitions of corrupt men seated therein.

This basic unerstanding by our Founders of man's weakness for wrong is a fact proved by centuries-old European conflicts for land, power and wealth, a warfare extending past the *Magna Carta* to the Englightenment document of the US Constitution. All of human history cries out against "man's inhumanity to man."

Within the context of modern governments, errant and questing humankind must always know (1) what comprises the authority that governs over him by his own choice and consent; (2) what are its legalistic terms of definition; (3) its limiting parameters of power and effective use-force; (4) its stated ways to implement its powers; (5) its juridical evidence found in ancient case law inherited from England and borrowed from Rome; (6) its evidence in legislature-enacted statutes for contemporary conflicts. (7) Man's proclivity is to disobey the law. incurring stipulated penalties for atoneent. (8) Preeminent are the fact and reality of class-division into landowner and tenant, into indigent and settler, into the enfranchised and non-enfranchised, and into those with elected and those with appointed powers. These discriminations are evidenced by the words and phrases, the postulations and injunctions, the forfeitures, compromises and prohibitions in the Constitution, from the beginning Preamble to the 26th Amendment.

The matter of the posession of power involves the person, ways and extent of authority, and the subjection, opposing power and protections of those who submit to that power, and, most important, their civic responsivilities. An irresponsible people lead to tyranny, ineluctably. Their weaknss sinvites tyranny. Being accountable to lthe entire body politic, the Nation as a whole, the people must accept the consequences for their actions, their voicesof assent, referenda, voices of oppossition and townhall consensus. It was this two way, this reiprocal, action which the Founders had in mind wlhn they constructed the Constitution: debate and disagrement within the law and never above it, as has occurred in all other revolutions is Western Civilization. The peasants stormed the bastile in the French Revolution of 1789 to seize aristocrats imprisoned there, but hey had no plan after the Reign of Terror. The Kerensky government in the Russian Revolution was not ready to govern after the Czar and his family were murdered and the property of rich Bourgoisielandowners was seized, in the name of the proletariat The closest thing to a success was the establishment of the Weimar Repulic in Germany after the amalgamation of feudal states of the German arons. The uniqueness of the American Revoution was that it established the validity and reality of self-government. The Americans had a plan. They had learned when they were still Colonists, that self-government demands compromises, adaptation and self-sacrifice to the integrity of not of a ruling class, but to the law. Indeed, the Articles of Confeeration that had governed them through the Revolution demonstrated that *representative government* was not an "artful dodge" of citizen responsibility but was the affirmation of moral good will and action for each of the citizens and was a reflection upon himself projected into *responsible* law.

If Man has the capacity to sin, to do wrong, as an evil and immoral act, or to break the law as an unethical transgression of a code of ethics, granting that he has the precognition of good and bad, whether one believes that the capacity is arrived at by evolutionary chance or was given by a Creator God, he will need **rules** by which to live that are apart from him yet involve him and ssurround and impregnate his life. They cannot be impovised to accommodate changing circumstances without dooming the future to directionless effort and social chaos. In America, there is no such reality as human rights achieved by demonstrations. The legislative process must be involved. Therefore, increasigly complex laws have evolved to control Man's natural depravlity and to reward his goodness. There is little evidence, if any, that his human nature has advanced toward a state of perfection over the past 2000 years, since Christ set both example and precept for living in harmony. This thesis of human decline in ethical and moral behavior is apart of the overall theory of human de-volution.

The authority of government is not in place to indict personal liberty; nor is goodness in liberty a denial of the need for government but is, in fact, an affirmation of the laws' working, pragmatic utility. Strict utilitarianism in government is a dangerous philosohy; its excesses are constistent with dictororial power. But an ethical utilitarianism does rescue pragmatism from purely personal motives and can, and does, keep big government from failling into disrepair when the immorality and misconduct of tis leaders tend toward chaos, rebellion and unremmedial self-interest. The usefulness of a law can then fequently assure the people of its Tightness, if not its righteousness before God. For example, the Constitutional protection of the 5th Amendement: No ciltizen "shall be compelled in any criminal case to be a witness against himself—is a moral statement that under the law protects the innocence of the accused, but before God denies the efficacy of the prohibition if a crime was in fact committed, The prohibition exhalts human judement yet gives credence to the divine examination of the conscience. The one is useful in promoting justice; the other implies a court of mercy. Both appear lin Constitutional law put there by our enlightened and pious Founders.

Utilitariansim and Egalitarianism are linked by their sharing the perspective: that the individual is not what he seems to be. Under the second philosophical point of view, he is an individual with the capacity for making conscionable choices. Under the first philosophical point of view, the individual is, instead, a "unit," or "entity," a "cipher," an "operative resource," a thing without person-hood. Americans have arrived at that state of depersonalization in which they have allowed themselves to be used by big business, big government and the world's epicenters of power, such as Washington DC and the United Nations. In their frustration, the citizenry are aware ot the beginning of this new Millinium that their responsible acts of rational choice have been compromised by their corrupt leaders and the power hungry of Europe, Asiaamd America. The personal liberties that they, we, have enjoyed since 1789 are, some of them, today put in the balance of amoral, unethical decisions by the United States Surpreme court and by large segments of American society. **Relativism** is eroding ther moral base of America's history. What is useful today, such as human "animals" for bioethical experimentation, is in no way egalitarian. What is uefiil today as computer-speak is, in fac, a degeneration of the language in order to simplify "communication," the thrust of which destroys all semblances of egalitarian diversity, a contradicory illusion, with a counterfeit semantic-linguistic unity. When students try to write a paper on, say, "the uses of images to promote a product on television," they are torn vetween what they know—called an illusion—and what they are expected to write, the counterfeit uni-moral language of relativistic teaching.

The common citizen's act of rational choice, as in seleting a job, chosing a wife, a place of residence, a candate for office, is an act that is fully compatable with a free society. His suffrage contains the dynamic of political power that moves the nation, and that is not imposed upon him without his consent. Our enormous American bureaucracy has totally lost sight of that concept, of committed citizen involvement—if, in fact, its minions of workers ever understood the irony of their partiipation to begin with. Although a State does not possess a conscience, its laws and its policy conduct must reflect the conscience of its millions of citizens; or else it is an oppressive State whose leaders are corrupt. Lately, on a natioanl sca;e, America's elected leaders have demonstrated the harmony possible between corrupt officers and the corrupt consciencs of their consititituents. No amout of rationalization can obscure that congruence corruption of some of the voters and corruption of certain politicians which derelection of ethics almost always appertains to shared parochial satisfactions. Political bribery called "pork," is of that kind. "Earmarking" funds for irrelevant projects in the Congressman's home state is outright bribery in which the rest of the country is made complicit.

While it is true that the conscience can be violated and corupted, it is equally true that an ethical and moral consensual by-vote government of laws is fundamental to our way of life. Life, liverty and the pursuit of happiness are what most Americans desire; therefore a moral cirtienry ought to give evidence through their use (or abuse) of a liberty that they condone in obedience to a a governmental authority that protects their ideals, protects and does not attempt to enforce them. The governmen cannot legislate or enforce morality, an idea often stated by ohers. Nor can the government replicate what is given by God—the *conscience,* doubt that as some will If right and wrong are seen to be envirionmental constructs and relativistic, then the entire body of our laws falls into rubble and dust and we are left with no government at all except a modicum of feelings toward one another. This horror scenario is coming about. This is not the place to itemize moral lapses in the American psyche. Suffice it to say, however, that technology has assumed the role of the priest in moral chocies, in quality of life decisions, in the giving and taking of a life, the accoauntaility for which did not ever belong to a stranger on the OB table. Make no mistake about it: the courts are already supporting *Man's inhumansity to Man,* without their defining any moral basis for doing so except a fallible decision as to "quality of life"—the satanic usurpation of God's will. Murder of the unborn, seizure of private property by the State for the benefit of another private citizen, destruction of the traditional family as the chief institute for training the young in moral conduct, and suppression of the conscience to speak out about religious faith:—these are other seizures of elective conscience that undergirds liberty of choice in America. Let the government continue in this role of pre-emption of conscience and in time America will become the melting pot not of diverse ethnicities but of "flexlible laws" and juridical incompetence and *Balkanized* neighborhoods that have become so for their self-protection.

Restraints put upon personal liberties are not only the laws of the land. Other restraints include social disapproval, community consensus, group admonition and non-acceptance, social outlawing stigmas, mockery and taunts, as by the liberal media, religious shunning and, lately, psychiatric counselling implied in situation-ethic movies and in "muckraking" journalisml. Each of these goads and pressures has a special mechanism for the codification of conduct by giving to that conduct the appearance of personal liberty of choice and action; yet the

which, those condemnations, actually quench the desire for life, liberty and the pursusit of happiness—to a greater or lesser degree. They often implythat the viewer must change his morals to be "cool," or in contact with reality. These modern day "stocks" clan, and often do, lead to the spiritual suicide of a person who did what he thought "was right." Television ha acted as a consellor for his moral lapses, which in fact are not his but are those of the vido's writer and producer.

In brief, what others do, their opinions, their actions can obliterate the fullest use of one's liberty of mind and movement—be politically correct, stay out of our Deep Souths neighorhoods, marriage sucks, theft of the White House furniture is *cool,* man, that aborted life is only a blob of tissues, do not interfere in a situation to save a life lest trial lawyer dogs devour you. Social disapprovals such as these are a form of inferentisal propagands, its modus, its insuinuation, its objective being ***person control.*** For tlhat reason alone, any kind of political correctness is an insidious instrument for the destruction of an environment of intellectual fredom in America. When that occurs, with the benediction of party-in-power politics, almost invariably the Democrats who espouse control as agenda, government drifts from consensual to oligarchical and in due course to utilitarian pragmatism . At that end of the activist spectrum lies anarchy, precedent to the conrols of a tyranny. For tyrants ***use*** their subjects to perform a social tasks that are useful to all of society, whether or not those tasks are ethical or moral. Thje president of Mexico i an example of a pragmatist dictator who uses his serfs for self-interest, keeping them in poverty and therefore in subjection to him and to the Catholic church.

Man's latest capacity to do wrong, if he is not confronted by the consequences of his action, necessitates more laws and then still more in order that there arise no circumstances in which his folly has not been interdicted. Were all men perfect the Golen Rule might suffice for most clashes and socio psychological dislocations. Our Nation's Founders who believed in God and His providence, His creation, His inalienable gifts to us and His wisdom were they who understood and asserted the natural depravity of humanity—even though they were Deists—wholly in contradistinction to Rousseau's philsophy of Man's natural goodness, the *Noble Savage* of history's silent romance.

In answer to the Colonial delegates to the Constitutional Covention in 1787, Madison urged upon them that they acceed to the call from the floor for a general bill of protection for the people, an added Bill of Rights to hedge about the citizenry from assaults and encroachments upon their rights by the Federal Government. The spirit of suspicion ran high in those months; for some even feared

Washington might desire to become another king. This contemplated Bill of Rights would conjure up, based on experience and manifest desires, all the possible infracions and potential dangers that were incipient in freedom, which would not voice any desire by the "one people" to disobey their Constitution but to insure that Centralized power would never transgress their "inalienable rights."

They had had enough of those unwonted and cruel excesses by George III of England and his Parliament—for indeed it was *his,* bought and owned by himself. And they knew the condition well of their own neighbors some of whom had not yet accepted the reality of the new nation but, instead, had hidden from view their undistsurbed loyalty to the the the king. Knowing men's minds, shrewd of insight and cognizant of the favors of the Crown to subvert colonial justice, Madison and his supporters reasoned that laws confining the government and loyalists to actions nearly harmless to the public weal would have to be enacted and passed eventually by all the colonies. The Bill of Rights, with its subsequent sixteen enacted Amendments, today stands as a testimony to America's acknowledgement of lthe human condtion, of its corruptiblity, incipient or actual, and also as a transliterated warning to other nations *of our people power.* The Founders who would keep the Colonists' liberation from Brsitish bondage permanent and trustworthy through the Fundamental Law of their new Republic.

Personal liberties enjoyed by those early Americans were not designed to indict the laws so that the Constitution would not self-destruct. Their lifestyle affirmed that their laws were protective, inspiring, teaching and honoring for all the people. Foreigners can point out, and have, to this Country's failures under the law; Europeans have in the past been quick to do just that in their readiness, at least in the 19th centsury, to see us as a moral people, defending against evil around the world. Yet nowadays they will often point to our inability to measure up to the Judeo-Christian expectations, for the New Jerusalem and to the delusory character of our respect for the fimdamentl laws of our own making and moral devising. We are at last charged with being naive, Puritanical and parasitic as if no longer worthy of emlation. And so it can be said that to an increasingly larger extent this proving to be true. Our compassion is called into question when we start brutal war gainst a people in Slovakia, when we murder the newborn, when we scandalize the White House, when we taunt, as it were, the "good people" in other contries by our high crime rate, our high incidents of divorce, suicide and drug use. Still, in all, we remain a great and a compassionate people, despite these derrogations and our own follies. We are still apostles of our written-down liberties that remain a confrontation before the dictators of the world.

It must be said, nonetheless, that in the carnage of the Civil War, and in the internal strife of former bloody strkes, urban combat, flamatory riots in the streets and union-mnagement brutalities, that we have not seen a total failure of our civil law to mitigate and to justify, or not, our people's conflicts. Instead, we have watched in operation the people's conscionable choices in the forms of resistance to these outrages and civil offenses, and we have always sought a common ground for agreement and cessation thereof. We are not failures under the color of liberty of personal choice of action. Instead, we can point to the tensile strength of freedom for adjustment under the aegis of liverty. The liberties imputed to us by our Maker and by our Bill of Rights are not unenforceable promises. To the contrary, freedom provides a maximum toleration of openness in American society, at once our joy and our vulnerability, as we live, unconsciously for the most part, to display and to use our personal liberties. Each of the rights mandated in that Bill, first enforced Decemver 15, 1791, becomes personal when matters of choice and conscience affect our lives. The 1960's Civil Rights movement proclaimed this truth.

The inalienable right of liberty manumits the slave from a morally irresponsible force of institutionalized power and its practitioners.

Thought policing is another stratagem of censorship; it is realized largely through people's dereliction of a duty to sustain liberty of conscience. The crusade against moral absolutes is the poison of the nation. Leadership cannot default to naked chance and unobstructed power without destroying liberty.

A right is neither a tolerance, a permission, an endorsement nor an edict. Like the liberty to reject a wrong, it is a legal proscription against a wrong, purely. It, therefore, as a right, is empty of content unless its claimant defines and affirms a corresponding accountability to the rest of society. Liberty is a power that activates the conscience. Activists do not engage in a right to march or to riot.

Freedom of choice involves the liberty to decide the good and the bad, the morality of an issue or the ethics of an act. The latter involves a sustanting decision, the former issues of probity, characterand integrity. A choice can be both moral and ethical yet not both immoral and ethical or both unethical an moral. The values work in harmony.

35. LIBERTY AND INDIVIDUALISM

A diversity of life styles, of taste in music, theatre, dress and enertainment, is a diversity that is posible only to society where free choice is encouraged and promoed and fostered by the majority of the people and is upheld and defendd by the laws. Any force such *aspoliitical correctness* that works to levl opinion and choice and to outlaw personal idoms of expression and other unique options not outlawed that result from the active conscience: that force is both dangerous and immoral. Public tastes change and in doing so reflect shifts in a transcendant political power clique within the leaderhship. Family values, consumer preferences, religous innovations, the radicaliztion of social roles and school expectations, all draw a certain amount of their survival energies and sustenance from the well-lobbied political enclaves in the State capitals of the Nation.

Favoritism in the Congress is an expresion of the Party and, if a majority caucus, an indication of Federal preferentces. It may appear that a questionable law cannot be made to bcome an absolute law—such as the wilderness-protection statues cannot, on the instant measure of mere opinion, be outlawed. However, the fact is that such a statute as the Multiple Use Statute appalicable to the nation's forests seems to some a tentative and a bad law; whilest that opinion is usually found in the application and not in the principle. This is axiomatic and is a restatement of the tenet that absolute values are inherent in moral choices. A people who disavows absolute values even when exercising their free choice will often deny the reality of conscionavle choice. They cannot plead the sanctity of consciene while at the same time reserving unto themselves the right to let the situation dictate the moral choice. *Situation ethics* mandate a-morality. Situational morality is a contradiction in terms and meaning, an oxymoron, since the code of absolute virtues and not the situation is the genesis of the moral action. A situation that usurps motivational conscience or a value system is never moral.

Liberty to chose and to evaluate are inseparable as is the freedom to enjoy a new experience and the personal development it may engender. The danger inherent in the *risk* of miscalculation, of misstep, of moral error ought not to deter one from the initial investment of his life. Were there not dangers inherent in the Colonies break with England—not with English laws, by the way, which some loyalists considered to be proof in fact, of the Revolution's immorality. In America, the individual has the freedom to be himself as a person and as an individual, provding that he offens not God if—and even if not—he is in the faith and he harms not his fellow beings, God's requirement by His common grace. Were not these two laws stated by Christ to reply to the lawyer who ashed

Him—which are the greatest of the laws. Love first God with all your passion and then thy neighvbor as thyself, came the answer.

Society is assured that such focused individuality of itself is nurtured by common consent and ideological consensus. People usually will accept one who is inoffensively eccentric. By the authority of its laws and inherent police-power society is the protector of the individual. Thus the outrage over gang wars. The question then often arises: what agency or what tradition of extraterrestrial power, gave birth to the individualism scorned by the Marxists, and to the personal liberties lauded by patriots? Renaissance Man, of course, who rediscovered his potential. Yet Man being the source of Man is a tautology. That cannot be denied or rebutted, at least according to the Secular Humanists. Therefore, he is by that circular reasoning a redundant entiry, capable of being cloned and subject to his own fallible reasoning and blinded to his true potential. He is who he is because he and no other power-entity tells him who he is.

Next, it may be said that tradition is the societal agency for the transmission of individualism in America which, attested to by the evidence of historical records from diaries, logs, manifests and letters from many sourcs, began in Colonial times. The Colonist thought of his, and of his family's, personal survival. He thought more individualistically than communally, though he felt compelled to bow to communal laws for the sake of self-survival. Order and productivity, self-sufficient and inventive manufacture existed in Jamestown after about 1608 when the colonly almost perished their first witer for their lack of survivql skills. It was chiefly because John Smith imposed the work ethic that the colony came around after that first hard winter and began to revive: "These who will not work shall not eat." Individual effort was a *moral imperative* imposed through the characxcter of a single strong man. Smith had marshalled the indivdualism latent in the people.

Yet and again, individualism is a risk whatever the enterprise. It is a remnant of pre-tribal patterns of living when "noble savages" were single hunters and food gatherers. We see these tribal virtues among the American Indians and, surprisingly, in the nuclear family in which the husband and father is the gatherer, the "breadwinner." The need and the duty are as old as mankind. This continuum of labor and enterprise is said to move in the direction of an evolutionary hypothesis that extends man's productivity over millennia of time—from individual to tribal community-although how the fittest came to rise above the unfit or who were the unfit and what they did lack are not always made clear by the classical evolutionists. Possibly there occurred a flaw in human initiative, a hesitation of self-defense for some, an aggressive and barbaric attack upon others. These manners of extinction being tentatively true, we surround these vestiges of our prehistoric ancestry with the complex civil laws of our culture that find pragmatic individualism useful, as creator, consumer, collaborator. Down through human history failure has been the precursor to invention.

An overstress on teamwork, however, is ultimately bound to emasculate creative initiative and to that the politization of the fine arts in deference to a bureaucratized science thatis amenable to control. Individualism goes into an eclipse phase when this happens. For that individualism of expression can no longer find any sanctuary in or affirmation by utilitarian science. This impassee is very much where Western Civilization is today. We are losing our capacity for individual self-expression in deference to our utility as *things* lacking personhood in a scientific world. Technological greatness, however, does not bestow humanness.

Are there not others reasons for this entrophic decline in the intrinsic value of the human being as reflected in major reversals of his personal fortunes and cultural wealth? Scientists have theorized that the trivbesman was the human result of communal living but that he met with reverses: huntingt became scarce, floods wiped out small villages, trivel leaders fought among themselves and dispersed their clans and diseases killed all but a few survivors. Another possibility exists to explain this reversal in human fortunes, and that is that individuasof fearless courage rebelled against communal restraints. They were outlawed or took flight as fugitives from the angry gods and like the ancient Hebrew scapegoat burdened with tribal sins was sent forth intol the desert, or, as an Zarathustral Anchorites or Odysseus figures, they became archytypical of today's individual. Annointed by the gods, they went forth thus to explore and to discover and through poetry to conmmunicate their adventures. These Archytypes remain to this day: dictators, devout practitioners of the faith, Mother Theresa, Luther, Ghandi, musicians Beethoven, Handel, Statesmen Washington, Lincoln, and so on, through adventurers Marco Polo and Columbus to warriors such as Npoleon and Ghengis Khan. The point is that these repreentatives of indivualism all owed their stature and existence to their practice of singular and absolute codes of action, virtue though a warrior's, and integrity of purpose. Their lives are the records of the passage of time and the power of committed genius.

To feel awe and to gain understanding were Man's earliest attainments. The individual was always the genesis of progress, the outlaw, as it were, the radical innovator, the rebel. Perhaps it is he and not the crminal who is the fittest to survive, although recent theoriticians say the criminal is the fittest who deserves to be iconocized. If the doctrine of virtue through conscince is correct and Mnkind is gifted with a natural capacity to discern right from wrong, and all of his other gifts to mankind by his archytypical genius are to be acknowleded as individual-ism at its greatest, bad or good, then the criminal and the human creator stand in antipodal relationship to each other as the fittest in human history. The crimial is simply a social mutation that the State is charged with eliminating; and only Christian compassion and rertributive justice stand in the way of a dark kind of preeminence. Raskolnikov, the student lawyer in Dostoievsky's **Crime and Pun-ishment** theorizes that some men, for him Napoleon, were above the law and should not be condemnd but, instead, emulated. On the other hand the individ-ualism of Christ presented new truths to the Roman world. He therefore by example and word, stood outside of Caesar's code of justice, the reason why He seemed dangerous to Rome. Both men were deemd by the ruling authorities to be outlaws. Both men were murdered. Thus do individualism and outlawry sometimes bear a resemblance.

If the average American's rights are inalienable and therefore irreducavle and unhangeable, then his personal liberty is an expression of his independent person-hood and of his capcity to make moral choices. Therby does he find his separate happiness in life's rich potential and in those labors which increade his sense of personhood. If he is the fittest of his ancient foreberers, he is so ironically with the help of the State, which in modern America contrivutes to the conrol of if not to the exorcism of his individualism. For medical purposes alone, the State is attempting to define and to fix for ethical promotion the individual's quality of life if it deems him to be helpless. Medicine becomes the elixir of happiness and the State the manufacturer *of entitlement goodness.*

Numerous modern societys benevolent institutions, social "fabrications" as it were, sprang up from the religion-based belief in the value of the indivdual human being, in contravention of some primitive religions and sacrificiall rites. For those who live in Western civilition this notion *of human value* has the origin in the Judeo-Christian religions. Prison reforms, hospitals, charitable organiza-tions for the poor, political enfranchisement and due-process justice grew out of the recogniton of Man's innate worth. This, notwithstanding that there is a code of commands in almost every ancient culure, from **Zorastersm** and the **Code of Hammurabi** of the Middle East to the **Buddhism** of the Orient, from Asia Minor's **Vedas** to Latin America's **Catholicism**, that suggests the Ten Com-mandments of mortal conduct and that acknowledes Man's passion for wrongdo-ing and his need for some kind of religious-philosophical control. Indvidualism in America can hardly be called a frontier phenomenon exclusively. The millions of years of Man's existence on this earth, if one accepts the evolution model, track the human race from the barbarian to the polished urbanite without any abatement to his moral insight or his capacity to survive.

The fittest takes on new definitions down through human history. And the liberty that we here in this Country today enjoy is simply the conquest of his barbaric nature by intellectual-spirtual enlightenment and his commitment to laws, religious in origin with Judeo-Christian predominating, that contend against that nature. As for Man's afttempts to extend his life span, the Ponce de Leon fountain of youth will be found, if at all, in modern day science and technology. When age is of less important than achievement, that is progress.

Always, it will be said, there must be some form of requisite authority, punishment and lawful constraint of that sinful human nature whether by physial force, laws of intent and action, or by social mores of direction and intimidation. By their presence these enablements support the concept of *inalienable,* as though from an impersonal and neutral distance. Trial judgements can be reversed based on those same laws by means of new decisions. By sociological definition an outgroup can become an in-group, a school, a transit line, a business can become integrated. Discovered evidence and perfection of the judicial process can effect this change wherein individualism from one sanctuary of liberty into amother, rules for the ageing become rules for the infirm and thence to rules for hospice care. Children move from day care into and through their different levels of maturation and schooling. These changes, all of them without exception, involve a requisite authority that protects as well as it controls. Yet in Western society freedom still survives, damaged by war, fratracide and all the other applications of tyranny but it survives nontheless. Our daily lives are the proof thereof. We are shielded from tyranny and depredation by the laws of liberty. That is our hope despite activist judges who find that protection obnoxios to their self-righteous sense of power.

Never in the history of nations, ancient or modern, has personal liberty been less circumscribed gods, fear, sacriices of htred, or punishmet than it is in our our enlightened society, all inequities notwithstanding. This happy condition will remain visible, if not inwardly, for so long as the State does not subvert the consciences of its citizenry hapless laws of demnd and usurpation against their best interestsl—unnecessary surveillance, for just one exqample, promiscuous recordnig of intimate details on a national data vase is another, the nationalization of the police is yet a third. These devices will in the end override he people's moral scruples. That is almost axiomatic with the State' tyranny, its oversight, intrusion and intimidating tyrannical power. Clamoring today for moral approval are the bioethicists who, as strangers to the helpless, have attempted and will continue to attempt to survey the fundamental moral values of human life by their assignments to a human life of "quality," "futility care," and "unnecessary social expense." This kind of moral subversion is the *reducto **absurdum*** of meaningless living,. Extermination as an act of comapassion to extinguishs pain in a suffering patient invites society to condone prescriptive murder, the firing squad is its political analogy, burning at the stake its religious parallel, lynching its legalistic example and social cleansing its bloody prelude. When the State assumes the magtisterial role of omiscient god, then the State must be resisted first by supplication ad then by violence-to preserve those inalienable rights.

A child's education may begin with cur= bing or blocking the wrong choices in his conduct. To ignore them is to invite habitual wrongdoing and eventauly criminal acts.

The proclivity to do wrong is built ito every society as evidenced by individual moral error. To do right always seems to be the harder course to follow, since it requires accountability. Strident clamor for "rights" usually infers that accountability is built into the right. Not so. That is a dishonest intel-intellectual presumption. The right to be embraced isusually the authorization to behave in a beneficial way. The clamor becomes riotous in the ansence of this imposed accountability.

One man's moral choice ought not to be another man's curse, and becomes so only if the value that undergirds the choice is im-mutblc-not as value but as a good choce.

The libertty of lthe citizen as an individual to decide a political issue cannot ve separated from his welfare or that of his society. To a attempt to do is is to invite the rebellion of riot, elixir madness or visionary utopianism.

36. LIBERTY AND THE ALIEN IN AMERICA

Alien immigrants in America are a nataural phenomenon in our streets. The onrivute their taxes to our economy when they are naturalized, even as they infuse the spirit of their diverse cultures and the inventions of their other ways of life. Many of them, however, or one reason or another refuse to vecome naturalized citizes. The question, therefore, arises: to what degree and in what ways ought our liberties to be extended to aliens who adamantly owe their allegiance, their love, their patronage, their personal histories to the culture and the government of thieir counties of orgin?

It is a tuism that liberty is not like a commodity that own no preconception, no attitudes, no loyalty to the consumer. It is not like tree whose fruit can be plucked with a minimum of labor by all who exist within our orders. In a few words, liberty is neither material nor consumable. Yet it exists on as a reality; were this not so unnaturalized aliens would hesitate to emrace her. The process of naturaliztion, in contrast to the surreptitious, illegal crossing of our borders, requires two things: commitment and effort. There is where those who reject America's spirit draw the line for themselves.

Liberty can neither be accepted nor rejected "for light and transient reasons," to borrow a phrase from our Declaration of Independence. Indeed, Liberty in its fullest meanings and expressions is not for every alien who manifests his desire to come to America as a refugee from religious or political persecution, those being the only llegitimate motives. Fully distant frrom the primary reasons, yet entwined with it, why illegal aliens mirate to America is to enjoy its freedom, our bountiful way of life nd the opportunities leading to them. To echew naturalization is simply to exploit the gift of liberty and the givers, millions of whom are alrealdy naturalized. They must pay for the costs of illegals' enjoyment of America's goods and services. Their tax rermittance, on tt;he whsole, is puny, since it is no secret that the largest share of their earnings are returned to Mexico and oher native origins. We are, in effect therefore permitting these illegal aliens to buy into America instad of to earn it by naturaliation. They, however, do not see the difference or if they do they reject it.

To submit by sentimental overtures and Pollyanish political apologies favoring amnesty and open border access to our country is to deny that the blooshed and the sweat of our forebearers was of little value or meaning, and that this nation simply sprang up in the 20th entury ready for international exploitation. To give way to this century's re-emergence of the last century gold rush fever is to threaten or despoit the existence of those who are already the possessors of wealth's benefits, they often having come here lately themselves. Indeed, those who rushs to occupy but not to commit feel at the outset of their illegal entry that they are entitled to the rights that citizenship confers—medical care, food, housing, work-as though rights come without responsibilities which being but half-comprehended or not at all, cannot be appropriated by the foreigner just like that! His entitlement begins with his citizenship; some candidates wait long years for that glorious "coming-out" day of taking the oath of allegiance.

One can use such words as *alien and foreigner* knowing full well that their connotation will arouse anger; but the fact of non-citizenshp in the absence of the oath of commitment fixes them for all time as aliens—despite Presidential amnesty for the politics of puffing up an ill-informed vote, as an act of liberation yet, in fact, is a corruption ofl the office of President. Nowhere in the Constitution is the President of the United States authorized to enfranchise 12 or more million illegal aliens to our country for whatever reason. That is not an act of grace; that is a disgraceful act of Presidential outlawry that makes the President complicit in the crime of illegal entry, in the nme of a foolish compassion that puts some 280 million Americans at risk.

The loyalty of the illegal aliens is therefore questionable; amnesty requires no surrender of former loyalties, no severance of political bonds to their mother countries. Therefore, to grant them as modified aliens all the privileges of citizenship with none of the accepted responsibilities—to learn about out history, our Constitution, and to learn English—gives away the farm. This give-away of citizenship by amnesty for six million illegals (1999), now 12 lor more millions-illegals is called compassion. In reality it is sentimental foolishness. It is but a replication of the that social ignorance which the aliens experienced in their own countries, an ignorance that tolerated bloodshed and military dicatorships. Only in America does our sanctuary give such protection for counterfeit "citizens," the amnestied aliens, the thousands of Mexico's felons included.

One of the liberties that the illegal may be said to possess is that of movement, although that can be fettered as in the instance of the criminal whom the FBI ferrets out, in which case he is returned home. Perhaps ... hopefully. The illegal is acknowledged to possess freedom of conscience, though the values which it adjudges are almost invariably those he has been reared with. It is a lamentable empirical observation that where his mores clash with those in the American surroundings, he will expect the American to make the greatest changes, uncognizant that he is a guest and not the host. True it is, also, that the illegal has the liberty to speak out, but that is conditional and he knows not from whence that freedom comes. As a non-citizen he can and does join political groups and far too often trumpets with arrogance against the policies of our government. Basking in Americas freedom of expression, the illegal alien all too often will engage in those tactics of disruption, disobedience, disdain and deliberate cultureal alienation which he was accustomed to in his own country. While he has a job at sub-standard wages, he remains quiet. But wait until he feels the assumd righteousness of his cause when he should feel put upon! Millions of American nincompoops, stripped of their sovereignty and heritage, will consider **him** the true patriot! What a joke that will be!

He teaches his alien cultural superiority to his children as well, failing as he does so to instruct them in their Constitutional liberties, the which he has not taken time, or made the effort, to learn. The illegal alien, made volatile by a sense of injury, becomes a loose cannon without any tiedowns, all flame and iron at the barracade as his own history dictates. His tether is the *chain of green* sent back to his home country. These undocumented aliens are the importers of incipient violence and panderers to the functionl illiteracy amongst themselves. Only when we remove our borders and deny our sovreignty will they be mollified. The poor we will always have us us. Why do we need more?

Everyone coming to our shores is enounters certain laws regardiang non-citizens, laws administered by the Immigration and Naturalition Service, and laws governing movement on our streets, monetary exchange and consumer taxation. However, neither priest nor clergyman, politician, governor nor judge is authorized by Constitutional law or by statute to extend political power to the unnaturalied alien. Untill he disengages from his allegiance to his own country and pledges it to this Country,to the U.S.A., he remains an alien in name and in presence. No euphemism of forgivness can change that without making the naturalization process nugatory. Presidential amnesty for the illegals by one President and now, in contemplation, by another are acts of forgivness for the illegality of entry and residency. Assent to amnesty makes the politician(s) complicit in the crime of those who unlawfully cross our borders. Period. Amnesty does not, nor can it, confer citizenship on the alien in the manner that it is conferred upon those who take the oath of allegiance to America, and who have demonstrated their willingness to surrender up their former allegiance, doctrines of civil conduct, habits of thought about American freedom and opportunity generated in third-world climates; showing their desire to conform to America's laws for responsivle integration with the host communities. This amalgamation cannot be lawfully passed without creating a "Balkanization" of new alien communities.

Personal liberty for the illegal alien is hedged round by conditions which command the duties of commitment, loyalty, obedience. In their absence it is difficult to conclude that he can, ought to and will enjoy full liberty of choice. For if "iinformation is power," how can he share in that power without accessing its venues by the use of English? He cannot chose a job withsout authorization by the INS, without citizenship. He is otherwise a maverick worker who must be paid in cash 1st the checks of an employer divulge his secret of illegality to the INS. His ethnic friends and relatives may take him in, but he cannot vote without qualification, that is to say, without citizenship. He therefore is tempted to vote by fraudulent registration and is encouraged by corrupt politicisns to do so . LInthismanner he will absorb America into his own culture. He cannot own land, except unethically, under our laws, until another person unlawfully sells it to him and conceals the identity of the illegal-allien purchaser.

Furthermore, he cannot run for political office because he is not enfranchised. He may protest in street violence and in our free assemblies, if he dares to speak out, yet his protests are inevitably ethno-centric because he doe not thiink like a native-born Americlan. He wants what he wants at the expense of his host country. And if corrupt politicians promise him his pie-in-the-sky, he will vote for them without any comprehension of our laws, little appreciation for ljustice, no fwnuinw gratitude for his new freedoms—except the freedom of lthe marketplace to make money. He cannnot lawfully approve of the authority over him; he can only do so unlawfully.

Illegal aliens are prone to commit acts of anarchy and depredation of vandalism out of contempt for the community of the law avbiding citizens. Clinging to that allegiance to their mother country, they come as tolerated guests only and, to the degree that they make themselves obnoxious, as imposters and invaders, these aliens who chose to remain and to enjoy the "inalienable rights guaranteed in the Declaration document and upheld and enforced by the Constitution, ought to work on the demands of citizenship, the rights of which are not co-extensive with their former ethnic loyalties "at lhome." The liberty for all, and for the particular illegal alien, resides in the temporary suffrance granted to him by America, his host country. He and his kind have necer had it so good; but they have forgotten or have never known, that contemporary America is the result of our history of blood sweat and tears, and that amnesty overlooks, indeed negates and condemns, and attempts to obliterate, the great sorrow endured by this nation with the sacxrifices of her fathers and sons in wars abroad for other nations, for alien nations ...

The illegal alien, when he arrives is indulged and the with gratuities such as former waves of immigrants and the American pioneers never, ever enjoyed. Yet he is the essence of discontent. He is given wealth care and shelter and put under our miiltary prorection, and as soon as he can he puts his children in our schools. With each child, born an American citizen, he hoped to tap into our social security system, our Federally-supported child care and our system of justice, depending thus on the proxy power of his child citizen, each one of whom is come into this world by the obstetric care in our hospitals. He presumes, this lillegal alien, that America owes these benefits to him. To add insult to injury, he often feels that he must be liked and cannot fathom why he is not, calling such resistance *racism* in mimicry of the liberal mantra and the liberal mothpieces of socialist reform.

This is the modern illegal immigrant, the true alien, the contemporary foreigner who has made his and her way across our borders illegally in trucks, packing cases and car trunks Thr morality of our people commands compassion; it does not mandate a brotherhood with outlawry, it never has and never will. Othrwwise, why have a penal system or a sovereignty of law under which all citizens must live?

The choice of the autocrat is autonomous with himself; he is the anarchist in disguise. The choice of the republican is synonymous with th people; he is their represenatative-apparent. The chocie of the State is antimoniian; the State stands athwart the peoples moral judgement by demanding faith—in him—alone. Yet cynicism pre vails—globalism, low voter turnout, rising crime, corporate disloyalty.

The choice of the law is by the authority of the citizens. That choice of the individual^ just act coincides with liberty in the fundamental moral meaning of a just regime

Freedom is often a misnomer for liberty. The one provides the absense of all restrints, but instinct or social disapproval. The former appeals to the great number of Americans who leave a liberal bureaucrat to think out heir destiny. Thus can a demagogue speak callously of freedom. Liberty appeals to the individual who must decide upon a course of action that is his alone. His responsibility is a moral choice of right or wrong, and involves the ethics of honesty and duty.

"Liberation ethics" is so strictly utilitarian as to exploit children's attraction to false authority-figures and popular icons. Thus, rewriting American history accomplishes nothing of lasting value except to reinforce ignorance, first of students and then of the teacher.

A person's conscience is valueless when it affirms a choice based on harm or no harm alone; For then its possessor survives as the dogma of pain or no pain. That is so exclusionary as to be. an illussory choice thus becomes mere antidote and opiante.

37. LIBERTY AND THE BLACK MAN IN AMERICA

Liberty to the American slave meant that he could live in his dirt floor cabin, put his hands out for a year's clothing, one pair of shoes, an allotment of food usually consisting of pork, to which he added what "colard greens" he could grow in his garden patch. His liberty lay in a constant fear that if he did not pick enough cotton to fill his tow sack he could be whipped. His liberty was his to doubt his personal value as a man that included his love for his family, often removed from him by evil force of sale, in itself a kind of emasculation. His liberty was of the imagination to rest his hope in heaven, which vision he wove into his spirituals that embody African rhythms and the moods of his ancestral heritage. His liberty consisted of release through the hidden and subvtle lamentations, from the field outcries to him in the Mississipin Delta to the conscious liberating improvisations of the blues, embodying as they still do a tribal beat, the sophisticated "improvs" introduced into his songs and dances and, later, into his human vocalized jazz, all of a spontaneous music that remains uniquely his.

His liberty dwelt in a not uncommon love for certain members of the plantation family, the sons of the white master, perhaps illicitly the wife of the master, or the black plantation child he had fathered. He ws hostile and passive, joyous and subdued, bewildered and yet fearful when he gained emancipation. Want would humble him; release would empwer him,opportunity would momentarily overawe him: these things even while the plantation system of the South's cotton economy continued on as before, the black man's entrapment and his master still. "Jim Crow" laws and the enforcement of "separate but equal" chained blacks to the past.

The black man's liberty consisted in his yearning to be free, daring to take the few avenues offered to freedom and manumission, the underground railroad, a naked flight northward through the then-existent woods. Even when he succeeded in crossisng the Mason-Dixon line, the North begruded him his liberty through flight. His liberty was spectral, since always before him rose up the phantom of his ignorance. His liberty, when he finally lay his hands upon it to claim it was tempered by experience under bondage. He was the one who had been harmed, captive and enchained both physically and immorally, though not spiritually. Liberty for him was never a question of authority not to injure anoher person, the justice of forebearance. His liberty was conditioned by the fear that he would be beaten or whipped if he transgressed he parochial rules of plantation life, a heritage that has ever since—an perhaps until the Civil Rights Movement successes-made him suspicious of the white man's beneficent authority. Whenever wrongfully injured, he has come to expect nothing more, no better resolution to injury than retaliation or submission or lynching.

After the Civil War the hawk Rules of the Reconstruction became the rules of the white man's society and government agencies. A mule and an acre of ground was the white man's solution to his former servitude. The black man's slave transgressions, however slight or uninteneded 'or implied in the situation, had taught him that his own use of liberty was not his to enjoy to the **full** exrtent of that the white man enjoyed his—the extent of the law. But that he must always factor in color and its history of servitude. In the very process sof learning what liberty means under the Constitution, he has carried the burden of biglotry, exclusionism, murder by lyching and voting disenfranchisement. He has been made the catalyst of ambitious politcians and the scapegoat for other singular crimes, on the presumption not of innocence but of guilt, always to the embarrassment and shame of those white men, many of then Southerners, who sympathized with and loved his humanness.

The fact that the black man in America has endured abuse for so long yet kept his compassion is one of the astonishing accomplishments of his people; bitter hatred for the white man is not endemic, it is indvidual. His patriotism is ardent and unquestionable. He fought bravely in the Civil War, as he has so fought in all the wars since. He searches and will continue to do so to realize and to enjoy the fullness of the spirit of liberty and its venues for expression within his community-and outside his community—where and when he feels creatively free to contribute to our Republic. Whereas he created a Harlem Renaissance in the arts in the 1920;s, he has today engendered and propelled his own Renaissance in learning. When he denies that, retrogressing into the past, he acts irresponsibly, for in so doing he denies what he has already given to America. He must continue to be the black man of Amercia who projects hope and joy for the future of both whites and blacks.

Because he remains visibly black and because white men remain visibly white, there will arise ill-will and at times vitriolic clashes. For it is not in the human heart, the human will and the intentionality of the soul to forgive because men by nature have been born with the inclination to do evil. So, liberty for both races, both humanities, must be hedged about by strong laws and their enforcement, not to the point of alienation, a delicate and tedious boundry, but to the extent of furnishsing reassurance that liberty through justice is at leastossible no matter how different each race in appearance and, indeed, in consideration of their likenesses and affinities and mutually-shared responses to the responsibilities of citizenship. They must share their heritage of common values whose basis is not money but the Christian mandate to love one's neighor as himself, in manner of God's forgiveness. The black man qualifies as our neighbor before the Asian, the Latin or the Indo-European despite their large immigrant presence in this country.

Cognates of liberty—such as *liberating* and *liber alsim,* can be misleading if not kept within the etymological confines of the base word *liber,* transmuted into liberty to *free up, allow to create,* to *think and to be conscionable and right without restraints* except by man's conscience, his character and the precepts of the law.

It is not liberating to blacks and whites to resurrect the hatreds or to the recite past offenses which nurtured hatred. Reparations cannot be sufficiently selective so as to capture ancient offenders or to reward the carprices of skin color—or, for that matter, to reconstruct time as the unltimate referee. Can racist entities be liberated from their hatred without recourse to laws already on the books? The obvious answer must be no; since the ancient memories remain and the stories of inflicted pain, of harsh and cruel treatment ... and of compassion continue to be passed down from generaiton to generaiton. Injuries suffered in the past time of slavery are not the memories of personal reminiscence; instead, they are memories historically communicated which pale as auguries before the achievements of the black man in America. One may as well ask for compensation to be paid to all the descendants of those white famillies, both North and South, who lost fathers and sons in the War Between the States. They sacrificed for the cause of the black man's liberty and the preservation of the union, in ways perhaps we shall In nrver fully undetstand. I would likewise deny reparations to them. Injustice becomes more intensely enflamced by the constant recitation of injury. II there be a debt owed to one side, it ought equally to be owed to the other for any claim to justice to be lain in equity. *Remembering* is a precaution to the future, not a revival of the past. And so it should be.

The cleansing away of old hatred is not a semantical problem or a silencing of the voice of affliction or, indeed, a **cause celebre** to steal from contemporary generations for the purpose of fattening activist lawyers and clergymen. These are the enemy, not the blacks they claim so stoutly to remember and "defend." The two races share moral values today, that is no empty notion or sentimental urgency emboldened to demontrtate white man's irresponsible response to the institution of slavery. That should be a given. Yet that sharing exercise in political recogntion and representative empowerment has prodced a kind of camaderie betweens the races folly visible in institutionalized interaction, a fact affirmed abroad today. Naturally any signs of hatred between blacks and whites in America is always on stage before the watching world. Yet what hypocrites they! The British, the Indians, the French, the Vietnamese, the Germans, the Jews, the Hispanics-all have only within the last century begun to clean their own houses. Curently, 12 million Hispanics have illegally entered theUnited States from a corrupt Mexico. What do they claim based on foreknowledge—chiefly money and ways to earn it. Most are not willing to learn about America and could care less about her future. So be it and yetdo they not stand in ignorane of our history?

Our own "race problem," still virulent in some small Southern towns, is least visible and often virtually non-existent when the races share hardships or when, under other circumstances, they combine against a common enemy as they have in the military service of America, or in common religious worship. Tolerance grows alike between individluals first, and then between whole racial groups. Until the 1960s, however, and Martin Luther King's leadership of passive resistance, in the cause of racial equality, the 360-year old memory of slavery and the recitation of that fact failed to inspire in blacks—or in whites—expected feelings of total liberaiton. Slavery had left its residue of bitterness and racial hatred. A great harm was done that still requires, I fear, another hundred years to rectify in the name of justice. It is only because of laws which now gird about the "racial equality movement"—satatutory acts as well as amendment provisions in the U.S. Constitution and precedent case rulings—that there has emerged the slow recogniion of racial equality in many areas of American life. It is an indispensable mistake of moral choice and a misinterpretation of "inalienable rights" not to demand full equity for blacks in the marketplace ... and so this has come about. Whilest blacks and whites must not be unqual before the law, and admittedly are different and unique in their abilities and achivements, blacks, like whites, want to enjoy the full panopoly of their god-given gifts. It is the particular arrogance of white men that they ascribe to God racial favoritism. With Him, however, there is no favoritism toward any race. By God's divine choice, the sons of Noah were racially different!

Blacks will continue tor resolve the question of experiential insight versus blind obedience to the historicity of slavery; of philosophical liberty over and against controlled conduct and fettered creative invention. Their finest achivements have come by working innovatively with materials at hand: cotton, the peanut, wood, crafts, as well as social insight tried political judgement, etc. Sports and music, of couse, are among their talents. In this context is implied liberty of the imagination, of inventive thought, of astute congnition and good jugement ... as well as liberty of movement. Among the greats in the black American community are: Supreme Court Justice Thurgood Marshall, Harriet Tubbs, Oliver

Brown, Rosa Parks, W. B. DuBois, Crispus Attucks, Martin Luther King, Jr., George Washington Carver, Frederick Douglass … and the greats in music, theatre and sports. These are the steller achievers in the long and somber drama of lament and pain and courage of the black man's emancipation in America. Because the white man does not, since he choses not to, understand fully his black compatriot, even as in a like manner he calls the Oriental "inscrutable," both races will need to enlarge their vision beyond peace-marches and the Civil Rights Movement as "happenings" in history. If the black man in America fails to realize his dream of full equality, the white man will fail to show forth the dream of his Nation's Founers. Their dream-unity based in racial harmony unity cannot be broken and must find common grounds for sharing America's great advantages and opportunities. This is the morality of the Civil Rights Movment and of the doctrine of *love*.

Liberty is still the means by which blacks "overcome" their own reactions to bigotry. Only faith and not laws of government can purify the heart of hatred, not neigborliness, not intermarriage, not eulogies, tributes and marches, *ad infinitum*. Those changes are *just* that change and do not deceive the inner being of thoughts, attitudes and feelings, the soul of a man.

The black man will never realize his freedom perfectly, nor will the white man his from out of his former citidel of self proclaimed dominance. Liberty does and will continue to define parameters in terms of the extent and manifestation of his personal freedom today; consequently it is a futile exercise in circular logic to try to resurrect old hatreds for the purpose of dissecting their mindset, and with a view to abetting the needs and clamor of the plight of the black man in present-day America—with money. A corpse will reveal only what was basic to the living organiasm. Its ambitions are silent; its dreams are removed by death; its capacities are confined to the grave. The corpse, the historicity of slavery, is fact and form ornly.

Liberty to the black man is tangily real, and yet he will probably always carry about with it, inside his soul, the shadow of his predecessors' enslavement. The question arises: how long will race-hatred memories last *if untended* before they cease to be a curse and become, instead, a triumph of individual blacks whose lives are beatiuful and confident and secure within the context and realities of liberty? The ultimate triumph for black man—and white too—is in his victory over himself and his cirumstances. And that laurel crown is gained by the anxious use of his inalienable rights, his liberty to be his very best in whatever world he inhabits. The vision of these glorious words, is true. Mounted on his gray mule, the noble black man can be just as victorious as the white archytype mounted on his white stallion. In either case the man's victory is singular, individual an ought to command admiration. He is better than the alien, the immigrant of the hour, the newcomes and certainly the iillegal alien. He has given much more; in war he has given all. The black man in America is from the beginning in 1619 a patriot, the essential American, the victor over circumstances. For if our Founders were correct in their certificaiton of rights as "inalienable," the the black man's citizenship is retroactive to 1776. He has experienced liberty from both sides of the 1863 line of captivity.

> Almost every painful relationship involves in some way the transgression of a moral value.

> The removal of the Ten Comandments from any public presence, especially from the schools, has preceded the expunging of morality and ethics from choices that tempt the conscience. Cheating has become the choice of losers.

> Guilt cannot be charged by means of analgous reasoning. Each instance must bear its own weight of moral discrimination.

> To deprive a man of his natural rights, it is only necessary to render him impotent in their defense.

> But what constitutes deprivation must stand the test of is verbalization, otherwise mere brutality triumphs.

38. LIBERTY AND THE TYRANNY OF EXIT POLLS

Public opinion in America is very much like a political leader **en absentia;** it is like a disembodid **icon** that plays the part of a living person, since a corporate body is a person in a legal sense. And the reference to corporate America endows this union of personhood with commercial significance. All one needs to do is to repeat numerical poll figures and then to ancticipate a shift in the "conventional wisdom" of the public, such "wisdom" being synonymous in all respects merely an expression of the public will, or, let us say, of that portion of the pollsters wish to claim as public, thereby making themelves prophets of the outcome. *Leading* is a favorite buzz word of the media hype. "Leading polls indicate" that Senator X will win by a large majority. This news hype is an attempt a *cop a plea* in an issue at hand, to to scoop competitor papers and media with a forecast. Such hype journalism is virtually meaningless, for it has no substance in fact other than numbers, the arithemetic of the dead, the de-personalization of the voters that makes of their free-will a mechanical fiction. Thus does media hype depersonalize the voting will of a free people by reducing it to mathematics while the campaigners legitimie their crusade by relying on the poll as an institution that legitimizes the choice of the people ... instead of affirming that it is an index only, and only that.

Censorship By means of Biased selection occurs in these election-time exit polls. They are mistakenly used to inspire confidence in the judgement of the public in Eastern districts, generally, and indeed at voting time millions of Americans, chiefly in the Mid-West and in the far West, will accept the exit poll results as just that: wisdom useful for making lazy, uninformed, undecided choices in the country's leadership. The 2000 presidential election showed a change in the wind, a widespread resentment of such fraudulent media leadership. *Caveat emptor* can apply to election polls as well as to a manufactured product. Such polls are the head of the dog that would wag the tail, a politico-economic power base in the Eastern "beltway" that would control the voting will of the entire United States of America. This is the illusion of power possessed by the Eastern elite.

Such a fiction consensus announced by sypathetic scions of the media is grossly misleading and is often inaccurate. Instances could be cited of this power-grab, one of the most famous being the preumptuous announcemnt in an Eastern newspaper that DEWEY WINS over Harry Truman. The principal reason that pollsters retain preliminary voter counts and exude such *blah-blah* over them is, of course, that their huckstering makes money for them and is good copy as well. Big names in the media industry assume the role of the side-show barkers. This kindof hawking of the vote is the old American push and shove to market a product, but it is dangerous when apolied to the voting process in our Republic. The use of the political forecast, which enjoyes 1st Amendment protection, is immensely useful when put into the hands of a candidate's campaign manager. And it is profitable whenever a corporation or an agency of the government, or a moveement's religious leaders, or an agenda lobbyist schmes to control the public's choice of a serious political candidate. In short, exit poll predictions are fraudulent news that tends to subvert our most important electorial tool—the vote of the people.

The utilitarian value to polling, which is a fictitious consensus since the consensus is inevitably skewed, has as its principal function promotion for money. Not just promotion, but cynical exploitation of voter doubt and poll-taking inefficiencies. There are no valid reasons that can legitimize this type of corruption.

To tlhe extent that it tends to oppress newcomer voters to the voting privilege, it belies the ethics of fairnesss and integrity; its Media practitioners deserve to be roundly censured. The same corrupt predictions also tend to ignore deviations from party loyalty, changes of mind at the last minute, the diversity of opinion in the selection process by millions of late voters. Media predictions therefore become a kind of media tyrantny. Who would dare to oppose statistics except statisticians. The genrus of this national cheat? Indeed, who in his right mind would dare to oppose the computer printout? Reducing the people's will to mathematics is do deny to them the humanity of free choice and to attempt to *arrange* the outcome of an election. Such Eastern editors make an effort to play God, having reduced Him to an irrelevant bystander or elmininated Him totally in the voting equation. That was not the way our Framers intended the people to manage their elections.

The tyranny of the exit poll is therefore a reality in America, anD the media have made it so. Such Blatant forscasting before the poling places are closed across the rest of the country is despotic, and anathema to the liberty of choice and conscience practiced and enjoyed by a free people. Yet Americans have continued to allow statistical polls to become the master of leadership selection at voting time, tenuously precluding choices of good men and women of high moral and ethical standards and statesmen-like qualities. This is intimidation by statisticts! Disaster will come upon us if we continue to ignore the calamitous runes of the pollsters. And yet Amerilcans seem bent on the worship of impressive and imprisoning numbers as such, merenumbers, the essence of our inherent pragmatism, the proof of our devotion to a system of government, the fallacy of a spurious kind of enlightenment, and the crruption ofthe public's willby the insistence on the mechanics of its operation with mathematics. This I call the mechanization of American liberty in America's self-disenfranchisement of political opinion by a blatant and aggresive liberal Media. Oddly, they continue to think of themselves as middle-America, promoters of main-stream politcal opinion.

The liberty to enjoy basic human rights is attacked more otten than are individual rights, since to destroy the environment of that liberty is to cripple the free expression of those personal rights that are basic to a free people.

By creating an atmosphere of conformity, the liberal media dampen the fires of creative innovation. This is the concept of media-Priest control of a society.

Alhough the will of a people may not necessarily be for their own good, it must even so, submit to the tests of experience in a democratic society. An administration can be largely immoral, passing laws for the benefit of political tenure. Yet the people will survive to elect another.

To seize the property of a citizen with a bench warrant naming the item to be seized and a probable cause for the action, this in the owners absence; or to attempt to enter and make a search and seizure without a proper search warrant is a tyrannical abuse of federal and police power The same can be said for the use of *discoveries* or seizures made under the authority of that power or, indeed, of eminent domain that transfers a piece of land from individual citizen to another, for the mutual profit of the broker and the buyer a-gainst the seller's will.

To take into custody a miner upon complaint by an adult of child abuse or endangerfment yet unsupported by any material evidence constitutes a felonious abduction regardless of the credentials presented. This is a criminal act done under color of law-enforcement.

It is a patent immoral hypocrisy and a travesty of justice to prosecute one who causes the death of an unborn child yet touches not those doctors who destroy life in the womb in the name of *woman's choice,* a socially-acceptable homicide.

39. INSANITY PLEA-SCIENCE TO DEFEAT THE LAW

The unsuccessful assassin of President Reagain entered a plea of not guilty by reason of insanity. He was thereupon committed to a hospital for the crimianlly insane both for his own protection and for treatment. His Counsel argued that *not guilty,* though it has not the same connotation as *innocent,* is reasonable grounds for keeping his client from long-term encarceration. That, of course, proved not to be the outcome in that and similar cases for, once cured, the sentence is imposed based upon the evidence and the arraigned one *guilty as charged* goes to prison. The plea of **not guilty by reason of insanity** is a semantic deception, an attempt to trick the reason with words, to borrow time and to mitigate the sentence by an appeal to compassion. When the court, in this instance, inferred that a would-be murderer who failed in his attemp to kill another man is "not guilty" what other state of accountaility remains but *innocent of the charge* regardless of the cause for avoiding the consequences?

The accused cannot be both guilty and not guilty at the same time, and medicine cannot empty the act of its inherent criminality. The sophists of the case would have the people to believe otherwise, tlhat the result, the gunshot, an injured man, another endangered did not actually stem from the criminal's abortive murder; but that he became somehow disconnected from his criminal act by virtue of the court's permission for him to do so, and by and the defenses plea. Experience tells us that a criminal can be found not guilty on the one hand, but not totally innocent on the other. Where the act of murder, successful or not, is as blatant and so visible, as it was, are we to believe that extenuating circumstances consist of a hidden agenda, that a secret inability to consummate the deed compels all nature to be turned on its head and to accommodate the killer for the benefit not of society but of the killer's psyche, his unannounced mental state of mind, his incipient testing of our gullability and our readiness to forgive? That is the essential underpinning of the plea in such cases.

This pleading way for the removal of a felon from society is one feature of the whole process of descriminalization of heinous crimes. But to dsecriminalize an attacker's actions for their having issued from moral innocence and being without prejudicial motive or crimianl intent is depravity on the part of the court. Such a train of logic is a fraud against society and a deceit practiced by the judge whose ruling and disposition of the case supporst the verdict of not guilty, in the face of non-esculpatory yet tainting evidence.

The example of the attempted assassination of the President is made to appear excusable, while coterminous with treason, rape, obstruction of justice and murder without cause, yet presumptively second degree murder. "By reason of insanity" is to "cop a plea," to plea bargain without any moral conscience for the insanity settlement. In this graphic instance the correct, and the moral, judgement should have been "guilty but insane" The burden, and the stigma, the taint *of guilt,* if you will, ought to have remained. For such a culprist can emerge, if not at he conclusion of a trial then at the end of his hospital incarceration cleansed morally as "innocent when in fact he lis still guilty but freed for lack of" convincing evidence." The only, the sole, intrusion of evidence in the trial which liberates, which separates him from culpability for the crime, is medical—or *jury tampered—evidence.* A judge cannot forgive.

The capacity to make a moral choice is not a reaction against social opinion, social mores, although American society is increasinly overriding the traditional voice of morality found in the Judean Ten Commandments and precepts in the

Pauline letters, particularly lin the Book of Romans. The capacity to make moral choices, an activity of human conscience, ought also not to rely on any scientific system of causality. The Behaviorists and proponents of Scientific Empiricism are impotent to declare a man's actions as either noral or immoral. Science per se does not and cannot assign a morality status to a human enterprise or acts. It can only deal with causes and effects, with actions and results. It is the intelligence informed by the conscience as arbiter—and not enlightened medical knowledge imputing derangement—that assigns the parameters of moral or immoral to the act, especially as an act of attempted homicide that puts at jeopardy the valued life of another person. This is not to say that medical insight and treatment have no place in criminal law; but that they ought not to define the nature of the crime an circumscribe the consequences of that crime. Would it not be just as plausible to say that lthe incapacity of an assassin to know right from wrong is, or was, not the result of a "sick mind," but was the absence of his esposure to comprehensible absolute values concerning the value of life and the harm to society of premeditated murder? It is a dead conscience, unable to make moral judgements, that is in fact the sick part of a man's soul.

Perhaps in other cases the arch-crimianl, the murderer, the assassin, the serial killer, is deranged. We as a people cannot ever know that for certain and must, as it were, fly by instrument, conjecturing, hypothecizing, taking "official" word for the meaning and significance of the court's ruling judgement. This, however, is not a perversion of right reason. Instead, such autonomous speculation is the rational acceptance of the bounds of one's personal liberty and the consequences that issue from its application or misapplication.

In the area of attempted homicide, the Court permitted a heinous act, in which one man was permanntly crippled (Brady) to achieve the status of a misdemeanor in the name of human compassion. Such colossal sentimentality is one of the flaws not of our system of justice in America, with its doctrines of presumed innocence, due-process, right to a jury trial, confronation by the accuser, right to remain silent, and double-jeopardy. Instead, such sentimentality belongs to liberal judges who presuppose the remedial purpose and function of the court is to mitigate the crime with a doctrine of non-culpability by reason of … or, in a word, to strike down the retributive nature of the ordinary punishment and, in its place, make the "treatmnen" of a crime a procedure that will rehabilitate the criminal. Such procedural treatment converts the law into a process of socialization, a school for the retraining of the killer's behavior in more acceptable ways compatile with civilized society. Why then should there even be a charge of guilty? Rather let it be that tlhe criminal's behavior was pathologically maladjust-

sed and go from thee. The court becomes a school for the indoctrination of self-conrol It thus appears that the criminal courts have morphed into existence to become the repositories of reforming magistrates and paramedical team players, as if right and wrong were in the last analysis illusory and chemical.

With reference again to the attempted assassination of the President, what if the word "innocent" were fixed in the mind of the cirminal so that to snuff out a man's life meant little or nothing to him personally? That is so often the case; few killers ever plead guilty in order to appear as innocent in their ploy. But then the motive is fundmental to the act despite all appearances of innocence. The people know this, therefore, when the court asks society to set side its reasoning, its over judgement. To ignore their common sense, they the people are told in effect to ignore the crime and to regard the crimianl as nol guilty, perhaps even innocent, because the judge orders it to be so by his rejection of certain pieces of critical evidence said evidence either irrelevant or gotten illegally. To justify the defense plea and the admonition of the judge, the jurors are being asked to disbelieve what, in the above event, they have already accepted the witness to. They are beiing prompted to turn off our cognative thought processes, their witnessing of *exltra-legal* opinion of the case, their understanding of *immoral,* evil conduct, and to subscribe to the ridiculous sophistry that for the reasosn of the criminal's fantasy, they should accept his irrational *innocence* judgement as the vemtral truth of a plausible an acceeptable, a lawful defense. We are urged o consider killer as though he were not even a participant in his own crime, since to place him at the scene yet fail to charge him as guilty lifts from him the burden of guilt and makes the fantasy the jury's.

The judge, in such cases, asks the jurors by his ruling to ignore the immoral anarchy of the criminal act and to accept his, the judge's, belief system, conceived in the liberty of his imagination, which states that a crime without a wrong (therefore with an innocent) intention, even though ruthless in the attempt, is not a fit subject for prosecution or for the challenge of culpability that might be raised. He givs the criminal a pass. By thus protecting the criminal in this manner, the judge endangers our lives and the lives of the helpless ones in similar circumstances. He has deemed an attempt at murder to be an *impropriety,* and for that he as an officer of the court is, himself, culpable.

The immorality of a crime is not erased by an act of the human will or by a stroke of the pen—unless to commit murder is an evil act that is contrary to and unsupportive of the absolute value of a human life. The judgement of guilty by a jury must always be delivered first, and then the criminal removed for medical treatment, if that is the case. Insanity as a valid plea cannort, nor will it, expunge the nature of the crime or obliterate the human and sociological consequences of that crime. The moral choice that led to the crime, even when not informed by conscience or by reason can never alter the seriousness of the crime or alter its character as criminal, either in the record or in reality.

Liberty is not the property of the government. It belongs to the people. When tlhe federal agency of the bureaucracy uses its enforcement power without representative authorization, it become a government *ad hoc.*

A police state begins with the unchallenged abuses of police power, no matter how sincere the pleas of police benevolence. It is immoral of men of characrter to say nothing.

It can be imputed to be an excessive use of police force whem they will-fully and with cognition violate an arrestee's rights. He becomes not one who is disenfranchized but is simply a victim of police brutality.

You cannot extrapolate from the guilt of one man to condemn another. Conspiracy theory ought to remain just that—theory, This leap of faith disregards the protections of due-process, substituting, instead, street anarchy and trial by media.

40. INALIENABLE RIGHTS AS GIFT AND DUTY BY LAW

Once this propossition is sput forth the ancillary quesrtion becomes: which, or what, laws will supply the better motivation to the citizen for him to pursue those rights? The answer to that question ought to be kept simple, not simplistic, since thereby do the majority of the people in a democracy apprehend what is theirs by birthright and, as to the immigrants, theirs by adoption, providing, of of course, that they swear allegiance to their adopted country of the United States.

Those laws which give strength of purpose to liberrated choice within the parameters of those laws, whether local ordinaances of statutory legislation, are those which insure that the citizen can utilize all his native talents to the maxi-mum of his own intelligence and wisdom. That is, the laws ought to permit him as well as to encourage him to conduct his affairs and to create his personal vision almost as though there were no laws hindering his development as an idnividual. This is the pragmatism native to America that was evident to the earliest Colonial assembly at Plimouth, where issues were often decided to affect the best result and the most equitable one for the villagers. The common laws, for the infractions thereof, yielded to religious provervialisms, and were based on those provervialisms which, in rsuth, were the amalgam of experience with religious commands and ordinances based on English case law. Thus, our earliest society was a moral society, precisely as the Founders envisioned. Acts that were civilly wrong were in fact also morally wrong or reprehensible.

But as for the making of new village ordinances, a pragmatic, utilitarianan procedure was often used by means of town meetings in which the villagers reached a concensus by voice vote. Thus it has come down to us in these times that the legialatures of he states will enact laws that have been proosed by the people through the *referendum,* which is the democratic *popular vote* of the peoples will.

This freedom to act that citizens have come to take for granted in committed to the laissez failre doctrine that grew out of the Enlightenment under which influence the citizen, by use of his enligtened reason, could resolve his own problem with very little of any interference from a central government. In Coonial times tlhat was the Burgesses, composed of village elders and Crown appointees, who were also villagers.

Th biblical origins of many laws faded before the pressures and demands of political consciousness, as did moral reasoning. The increased autonomous, crown-disengaged reasoning also reflected the lessining of Calvinist influnce. Today in America trial-and-error pramatism in our government occurs on all levels where laws are enacted, executed and adjudged. Indeed, outside the courts 1 laws "already on the books" are expounded, examined, circumvented and forgotten. The legislation of new laws, many of which are wasteful or redundant or motivated by greed, is an ever-changing process, Americans having insight into their own ways and wants to make new laws in their best self-interests—if they are not defrauded by the over-reaching ambitions of th press lords or scammed by the wheeling-and-dealing lobbyists in the halls of "Congress. It is a sad commentary on our times that if there ever was a group who had set themselves up as elitists and above the reproach of the common mans, is the liberal members of the Congress. In essence, they have squandered the peoples wealth without a conscience, and have adulterated the moral strength we inherited from our past.

The chief product of Congressional largesse has been their excesses and those of the liberal media working in concert to redistribute the wealth of the people, not that of the rich. They have leveled bureaucratic attacks against the Amerlicna work ethic and the doctrine of profit; these insinuations and mesalliances of faith have been allowed to thrive, providing the power of liberalism remains supreme. In this process of ethical deterioration-chiefly the work ethic—the bureaucrats have foisted upon the people clever stratagems to initiate and to convince as the *right thing,* a subtle propaganda that steals the political power from the people where it rightfully belongs. Bureaucrats and their *old-boy* politician consortiums and caucus groups in Washsinton have for decades played on the people's ears about the morrow, jobs, housng, etc., manipulating them into believing that they are incompetent to solve their own problems without the help of power brokers. The lamentable result of this political deception is that the politicans have often enacted laws that are unfriendly to the spirit of the people. Elitist politicians long in office have become the corrupt masters, manipulators for the vote *par excellence,* while the people struggle as servants to the government bureaucrats.

Civil liberties, in the matter of proposing law, requesting it, contesting it, utilizizig it, are involved in each of these distinct processes. Each proposal, enactment, elimination of a personal right by an ominous governmnt, is the eradication of a moral right of conscience. Universal gambling, prostitution, euthanasia are choices that affect th entire citizenry. Indeed, the poisonous *ober dictum* of political correctness, enforced by the thought-police on America's campuses and work places, has made progress in the popularization of those evils. Attacks on the police and the good judgment of the common cirtizens have begun to erode and to efface that code of moral law inhrent in our history. The impact of such centralized corruption occurs when the spirit of a community is perverted by prostituion and when drugs require policing and hospitalization, and when gambling brings racketeering and police control and gun elimnination, and when enthanasila validates the idea that life is of little value wihout a doctors endorsement whilest death is then more expedient and less costly, as the bioethicists and hospital committees will presume to demand.

The morality of enacted laws should reflect the morality of the people; or if they do not then evil laws will create within the people themselves a yeaning for a tyrannical power to guide them and protect them from harm, as from terrorists. If, however, the laws are moral laws, with their inherent wisdom guiding the nation's affairs, eschewisng evil and embracing *Right,* such laws will be consonant with the people's happiness our Founders intended. Then civic harmony that results from such moral examples to the rest of the world will allow for, nay encourage, embellish and engender growth in all areas of our Republic.

And an apt general appreciation for in dividual effort and personal excellence will be the fruit thereof. Bad laws and wicked politicians consign the people to mediocrity. The best way in a Republican democracy for the people to match moral laws with stable human values is for the people to exercise their liberties of conscience, rational judgement, moral discernment between right and wrong, all of which leead to the informed duty to preserve those laws as a sacred inheritance. Civil rights and political integrity are inseparable in a well-regulated society. They inpose the personal duty to practice the ways of a moral and equitable justice. To live responsibly in a dmocracy is not easy and requuires constant vigillance in the defense of right. To be judgemental is to exercise moral convicrtion.

A right is made secure when a tyrannical power over it is despoiled of its power.

Liberty of conscience is an illusion only to the morally blind.

The liberty to make a moral choice is beyond the pale of the dedicated criminal.

A man who feels that the enactments of the goverment have liberated his conscience has indebted himself to the winds of chance and caprice.

Override your instinctive knowledge of wrong and you expose yourself to self-pity and eventually to self-abasement.

It is not the absolute nature of God's commandments thart vexes many people. Instead they are vexed by presumed pro-hibtions against the right to do wrong-absolute freedom, anarchy.

Absolute what is the word but the stability of certainty amid chaos and uncertainty? Yet how willingly some chose the latter!

To say of a man's act that it has moral value is to ascribe to it great worth in human affairs conducive to happiness.

To say of a moral absolute that it condemns, judges and tyrannizes it to plead the case for absolute utility in human behavior. Has not a person thereby substituted one absolute for another?

Relativism issues from the stigma that attaches to convictions.

Whereas absolute values appear conducive to rigidity of behavior, in actuality they liberate the individual to make the most of his natural abilities with out the rigidity of conformity, the true absolutism.

It is not the Commandments of a sovereign God that man objects to, in the main, but rather to the oppressive uncertainty as to his personal worth in the absence of God, a worth he feels compelled to prove before the world.

Make no man a prisoner of your conscience for he hath his own to deal with.

41. LIBERTY AND THE HERO IN AMERICA

Some rather wise persons have asserted that a people given the inalienable rights Americans enjoy under their Constitution lack the wisdom to govern themselves without inviting down upon their heads: anarchy, intercene warfare, permanent revolution, incipient "Balkanaization," a political "homelessness" of *belonging*, and social chaos. Such a curse can come only from those who are ambitious to hold the means to power; while their austere superior regard for those around them can only arouse resentment, unmerited awe and eventually rebellion. In Colonial times the Loyalists believed in this Divinely annointed curse—the King can do no wrong—aided by the British lionized Crown. The non-signers of the Declaration of Independence were of a like mind, finding revbellion unlawful, odious and insulting to the Monarch. There were, however, degrees of strength and weakness of conviction among the signers who were yet all of one accord. These British citizens among the general populace who defected after either years of hostilities had begun to share opprobrium against the "renegades" and the forecast of a dismal faislure in the War for Freedom. But those who, in addition to their faithful compatriots, pledged their sacred honor, their lives and their fortunes to the cause of liberty were justified bythe historical events that followed the 1789 adoption of the Constitution. There is in all true conviction the essential of faith both in men and in God; many of the signers were, in fact, Deists. There is in the all true and covenented commitment a regency of the soul that lacks any grain of cowardice and would perpetuate a vision that could, and did, astound the world.

The question then extant especially before the Revolution, was—why should a free people be incapable of governing themselves, providing that they enjoy a courageous and moral leadership, men and women of character, of statesmanlike abilities, purposes and perspectives; and providing that the lesser public servants will not indeed cannonize themseles but will, instead, look cautiously to the will ofl the people for their just promptings to govern. The answer for over two hundred years has been that they are truly so capable.

Politics: *impotence* is not a product of natural inability, or of genetic absence of character or of intelligence. That weakness, which is a civil cowardice, is most often due to the lack of suitable models of moraliuty as well as to the lack of an inherent moral strenglth of characrter lin the leaders. These models are useful for emulation of their virtues, affording to their followers instances of resolved moral dilemmas and the right conduct that invitatably follow.

One of America's shortcomings today is not her lack of historical heroes; it is her failure to eulogize and to make exemplary those she already has. Not all heroes need to be or should be athletes or astronauts or peacemakers, although figures in those venues are heroized by millions in the land today. Definitively, the hero is always a product of the folk culture. Otherwise the revered image is not that of a hero but of a chosen one, a selectman, a figment of human capricxe, publicity and mindless circumstances, and often of money and political patronage and media puffing. Myths are invented to srround the true hero; alibis are concocted to justify the eminence of the false one. A counterfeit hero is usually popularized, as a propaganda piece, foir the exclusive purpose of promoting some transient cause or agenda. A true hero stands alone, in and above history and the yen for accolades or the lust for power.

A true hero will inspire other individuals to perform great deeds, to rise above themselves and above their contemporaries in some outstanding enterprise or venture. A true hero is sufficient to lead for all times. The genuine hero does snot emerge by the empty cannonization of a figurehead or by popular sports entertainment accolades, or by an eccentric, religious or pagan, racial idolatry. For these forms of eulogy and deification are not lasting and though momentarily exciting they rarely inspire, rarely invade a person's life, rarely "convert"—to the extent of translating a person's slife into one of unusual achievement and characer and quality. Christ, Washington, Lincoln, Ghandi, King were among such men.

A hero, furthermore, is not made so by an adoring public who love his image, style or his adornments (house, car, jewelry), or who covet his bankroll and the attention of a proselyting media. These subtle voiceless and spoken powers have all too often raise up lmen~and women—who later prove unworethy of the acclaimn, worthiness or ultimaely the *impramatur* of centuries of respect and awe and leadership for their virtues and characrer. Such false accolades are subversive of true heroism anf even act to destroy or neutralize true heroism by the process of political conformity. But, inevitably, a worthy hero transcends the fragile and volatile issues of his times to rise in stature above the commonplace idolatries of his day. The "popular" hero can become the silent spokesman for all times—as a moral and ethical precursory example.

A genuine hero in a nation of responsivble liberty is the expression incarnate of human liberty of action, that is: liberty of choice, of achievement beneficial to all mankind, of orginality and creativity of purpose in his life, and of conscionable deeds. These are some of the traits that ought to belong to the folk hero, he who shares the virtues of the common people. He often is, by the application of those personal advantages, a successful adventurer into realms yet unknown to other men. We then must sinclude Admiral Wm. Byrd and Lewis land Clark. The folk hero, by his using his freediom in a positive and wise way, finds new paths to walk. Thus by doing so he gives to other men a vision and a sense of their potential usefulness to mankind and their greatness in history. He exerts a liberating influence that frees the imagination to soar with the eagle. Not infrequently, but parenthetically, he intertains in these soaring flights into discovery.

Ancient Greco-Roman heroes were tyspically mythological gods and demi-gods, prototypically similar to the human species. They were arbiters and judges over men and demanded pacification not by jealous mimicry but by abject appeasement. The jealousy of the gods was well-known. Attempts at mimicry were mawkish, comedic and sarical; efforts at appeasement often proved to be tragical and sacrificial as in *Oedipus Rex* and the *Oreestes Triology* of Aeschylus. The point is: that in America today, the liberal leaders of the "godly" Establishment expect mawkish mimicry by the people and yet call the people's faithful support *sacrificial,* detesting as they do so the grassroots voices of the common people. The "old-guard" in American goverment supposes a godhood that is not theirs to claim, except by rote, infinite tenure, and by estrangement and alienation from the people. Certain sly, deceitful aphorisms are used to cast the people into a more familiar mold: such as: poll-figures, consummers, contributors, ciphers, units, six-pack Joes, 21st century Americans—all reinventions by the gods *of political correctness* and social promotion agendas. Are Americans not citizens, with all the time-honored connotations that that word conjures up? The Liberals in America would de-humanize the voters in order to make them amenable to control by the constant citation of percentages, numbers, consumer tags, and "official surveys."

In the diaorama of gods and men in American life, the dangerous attempt is been made to *exorcise* from the books and from the people's consciousness the historical figures of our history, most of whom are potential heroes to the young, thereby rewriting America's past including the establishsment of her inalienable rights for all. Are Americans a nation of fools to accept this *historical re-visionism,* as if to embue our native heroes with hero status somehow falsifies our democratic faith in America? And as if to deny citizenship to illegal alien invaders somehow denegrates our heritage of limmigrant formation. Is the acceptance of such bold *anarchy* a confirmation of our cherished freedoms? I think not. The end result is the destruction of patriotism and nationalistic fervor. Just one example: The Supreme Court's power of *Judicial Review,* and Washington's first Chief

Justice John Marshal, who initiated Judicial Review, are both excluded from major School Textsbooks on American history. Why? To prepare the ignorant and the young minds for Executive tyranny and Congressional exclusionism and, eventually, to make straight the way for demagogues who clhampion political correctness, read *conformity*.

Therefore, should wealthy baseball players replace historical figures as the true heroes of American history? Does our true folk history begun with the works of sports and entertainment moguls because the ignorance of the young can no loner be breeched by teachers and books? How apathetic! How arrogant! How blind1 A people who have lost touch with their history is vulnerable before the tyranny of corrupt leaders, as we have experienced. In the vacuum left by the forceful removal from halls of honor of true leaders, by the insolence of misinformed teachers and textbook publishers, and by the arrogant intrusion of self-appointed guardians of our liberties, such as the ACLU, we shall reach out to world heroes and embrace their alien ideologies for our own, thinking in doing so that we have thus broadened and reinforced our own values and liberties. Then, if that should happen we are done for as a people and as a nation. Our rich heritage of heroes has been sold for a "mess of pottage." When the bearers of that history are gone, who will know the difference or even bother to care? I have sketched the face of the hero who has lived and is still livng, in our history of personal liberties which the rest of the world has never known.

> **Reason may not be consistent with a moral choice when the ends are either wealth or power, A grab for power is often irrational.**

> **Reason used to justify corruption is persuasive before men of no morals or of weak conscience.**

> **Wealth gotten honestly is oft in defiance of reason. That is the risk factor. Wealth gotten easily is oft dissipated esasily.**

> **Understanding the differences between right and wrong and not reason alone, ought to dictate a moral choice by virtue ol the wisdom of the understanding.**

> **A people who allow the benfits of the Welfare State to control their lives have surrenered up to an impersonal bureacracy their capacity to make fundamental moral choices.**

Morality is not like wig to be put on for special occasions in order to impress others. It is the heart and substance of a man's life, his basic integrity that counts most.

A moral value, as honesty, is not like a commod ity—exchangeable. If it is not in place in a man's early years, then nothing short of a religous conversion can implant it within him;

To tell the truth is far less taxing than are efforts to appear to tell the truth by lying.

42. IS IT A MORAL CHOICE TO LEGALIZE LIBERTY?

Personal responsibility and liberty are positions imputed to the people by their lawmakers under the law. Indeed, it cannot be gainsaid that certain 17th century ideas have their origin in the Christian faith, not just in the Enlightenment. God condemns false weights; through common grace. He loves the world He made. He enfranchises the human race to exercise freedom of will, that is, choice, demanding that they be accoutable to Him. The marriage contract is still sacred, the Ten Comandments were, and ought to be, in foil force and effect. Slander, theft and murder are outlaw activities. Compassion for widows and orphans was and still is practiced by benevolent societies. A lying and deceitful tongue in Colonial New England meant the stocks. A suit in tort for malicious defamation is still possible under the law, as is a suit in trover to recover stolen, misappropiated or converted, goods belonging to another man.

There was, however, a third influence that profoundly affected that institutionalized liberty in America:—the wilderness experience, based as it was on the protection of self-interests for naked survival against the Indians, against the elements of nature, against semi-starvation and disease (cholera) and against human predators. Americca has thrived and grown great because her liberties are the fullest expression of that self-interest productivity at work, commerce and invention and grand enterprise have utilized them as instruments of competition. Production efficiency and creature comvort are the natural upshot of such competition.

Personal liberty in Colonial times was by contrast to today's blaze relativisms of choice was enormously simple and was embodief in the belief, reducef ble to the succinct adage: that "if the people think its right, it is right." This axiom which some defectors have called the "tyranny of the majority," was a reaction against the concentrated power of the Crown. Such a *sequitor* lead toward legalism in religious conduct and pharasaicalism in secular laws and village conduct. Witchcraft tlrials and those blue laws were, later, the concomitant results of such social rigidity and spiritual confrontation among English settlers. The Colonists felt, furthermore, that the King was gradually choking out initiative, enterprise and the Englishman's right of contract, forcing the village blacksmith, the roper, the cooper to commit fraud by dealing extra-legally with British merchants at home, to the immense profit of tradsesmen, shippers and merchandizers of the goods, despite vigorously enforced trade laws …

British monopolistic trade practices were a form of extortion and compliance an act of participation. Because the village artesan's goods were worth more than the compensation he received for them, he was being made to cheat himself to satisfy the Crown's greed. He was veing exploited as America's first social and political minority in the interests of th larger British sociely. The British bully was omnipresent in early; New Engvland.

It was the colonist who could survive at his trade that oftentimes practiced the art of smuggling, and when found out was exised and brouht disgrace upon the village. Though useful in the years of the Revolution to bring Frencxh guns into the Colonies, in the earliest of days, rebels in contraand invited God's curse upon the poor sinner.

What, then, was the nature of that severe Christian morality lthat distinguished it from pagan experiental antimonianism, that is, faith without law? And from the utilitarian concept that all religious law served a god and was functionally related to everyday life? That severe morality can be identified as a kind of non-secular righteousness, a foreshadowing of the partial secularization of the Colonies when commerce would dampen the relgious ardor of many early New Englanders. The shift in thinking would move from a biblical "rightgeousness" in colonilal life to a secular appliation of tenets of compassion, industry and mercy, with the foundiing of hospitals, prisons, public schools and social relforms for the suffering and needy. America's institutions of compassion were the reaction against British instituted cruelty, drawing and quartering for simple theft of a pair of shoes, shipvboard flogging on British merchantmen for minor seaman infractions, the poor house for needy, hanging for violations of the King's laws, like smuggling. Men's natural mercy would result in the elimination of social ills, lin responseto which moral absolute laws, as human governors would then no longer be necessary. We live in that dispensation today. The Puritan work ethic would work its designs and advantages. The Christian faith in the providence of God would give strength to new visions of colonial independence. And the materialism of colonial trade would supply the bread an means, if not the gold, for futlure separation from England. The musketmen of the Revolution were, most of them, quite poor.

Nowadays, obedience to the law is rationl behavior that conforms to the law. The result of reason is the self-assurance that liberty of conscience, though perhaps illusory, will seem to exist and to be demonstrated—this in the avsence of religious faith and withsout any need for immutable lmoral laws to dictate a fixity of moral choices. Pragmatisms thus governed much of America's development and was the instrument of Yankee inventiveness. On the oher hand, "Trust in your gut feeling," first rather than in your conscxience became the credo for today's quasi-religious society in America. The patent result of this thinking, widespread as it is, has lead to an almost universal scheme among Americans that hypotheses a *situation ethics* to solve all moral dilemmas. That philosophy, alone, often dictates answers to questions of moral choice. Juries increasingly today vote against tangible evidence in order to satisfy *gut feelings* about the accused! Every man has a right to be right based on his own feelings. That lis the New-World "morality." The New World will bring maximum freedom with minimum respsonsibility, in other words, the corruption of America's glorious hisltory and her stabilizi8g instlitution such as marriage and the family and schools are and will lose their relevance to greatrer society.

Can a man act morally by adheence only to the utilitarian leadership of the Country, tlhe dialectical materialism inherent in State mandated welfare? To anser that question, it is necessary to point out the truism that the law is not the predecssor to morality. Although a man may follow the law, he at the same time may not e moral in his conduct. For example, a man may be legally married but his abuse and violence within the marriage is immoral. Or, a man may own a black panther for a pet, but if he mistreafs the animal by keeping it confined and fails to feed and to care for it, he acts with immoral cruelty. Again, a mother may give birth to a drug-addicted or diseased child, but her immoral, her wlicked and inexcuseable conduct during the pregnancy is immoral and therefore wrong. For it has endangered and maimed the new infant.

By his assigning the priority of morality over the law, a Man arrives at the cardinal purpose of liberty and that is as a guarantor and guardian of his conduct with its propensity for evil. He cannot do oherwise lest he throw himelf into a quandry as sto his basic human nature. He gropes, he searches even today, and yet he does not know hmself, not unless he acknowledges his linkage of his uniqueness and to believe in a power greater than himself. Where he undertakes this quest without moral values, he denies his real worth as a human being. He settles for the narcissistic counterfeit man of shifting standards, empty of conscience, subject to self-pity in his godless night and remorse only for what he cannot possess. Much of America's merchantile success involved the vein of self-pity … or material lack, for injustice and for personal failures.

Liberty's power of persuasion toward realization—this is called a *vision*—and its wisdom in moral discernment react to oppressive ideologies and cruel despotism because of that inner linkage of man to his Creator. There is no other way to express that power adequately, such as a capricious causaity in human affairs, a nihilism of belief and thought overlain by personal will do not explain it. When absent, mere will-power cannot defend against terrorism, for terroristic fears and to an *unknown fate* without conscionable direction in life. Reliance on will alone conributes to modern Man's dilemma of uncertainty for the future. No moral compass directed and undergird by liberty, no certainty of venture or choice can only give rise to anarchy in human affairs or to the desperation of defeatism.

Terrorism is today a bi-product of Modern Man's denial of his self-worth as a created being of intrinsic value, not as an evolutionary result of blind chance and inexpllicable purpose. Liberty is the ultimate target of all terrorism, religious and secular. The Inquisition, the barbarisms of the Huns, the hordes of Vandals that marked early forms of terror, as Ethnic Cleansing in Bosnia, Hitler's "final soslution" before WWII and the shadow of atomic warfare mark today's terrorism against Mankind. Despite the thunder of violent and naked terror-threats in today's world, it remains a truth of Man's spiritual history that he was made in God's image, an image which presupposes godly standards of conduct and value, howsoever attenuated. Atheism is self-destructive because, in attempting to justify his soul without God, he destroys his spiritual nature and thus corrupts his being with an empty self-adoration. He makes the science of his personhood his idol. He is his own ultimate harm.

Meantime, it remains more than problematic that the law's protection of *victims* of crimianl acts will always lag behind Man's ingenuity in contriving harm to himself and to others. This axiom is, in truth, a demonstration that morality and immorality are precedent to the law, justifying the law and undergirding liberty as the lodestar and "inalienable" gift of rights to free men wherever sought in bondage.

One should realize that is not the good to another or to society that prompts us to call an action "moral." The morality of the act is "discovered" and is reinforced by reason and does not necessarily come from one's religious faith, though that is often the case. Moral conduct is rational, although it always dictates the effect and controls tlhe result. But the morality of an act consists in this: that death in the sense of dehumanization and of attrition of integrity involves motives that reach beyond oneself or others. They are motives that extend beyond the mere mores and active traditions visible in one's immediate surroundings. That death which is precipitated by an immoral act, death to the conscience, death to the finer sensibilities, deaths to the basic human feelings of all men with will inevitably affect greater society. In short, cruelty is catching. A man's moral wrong does not germinate in a social vacuum of rational acts or an emptiness of the conscience. A moral wrong can never create new hope or life because it signifies those deaths mentioned herein. To expunge the conscience is to expunge love and compassion and civil conduct.

The immoral act, no matter how insignificant, will prove or will demostrate a high degree of selfishness. There can be no other standard for the secular measurement of moral purpose, since one's obedience of disobedience of a particular law ceases when he wrongfully acts is completed, but the morality continues to exist as a *raison d etre* of human perception of conduct. The death stigma adheres to memory of the moral wrong., perhaps hidden but without that punishment by society that attempts unsuccessful to redress either the stigma or the injury to another person. The immorality of the act thus continues on as if it had a life of its own, aided by tlhe media, a wrong given perpetual action by human memory even as the immoral act has ceased in point of time. Therefore, the conequences of the deed rise up to confront, like Hamlet's father's ghost, not only the mere absence of conformity to the law, but the law itself. The law must perforce subsume the moral value which gave rise to the immoral act, be it a misdemeanor, a crime, a social disgrace or a calummy against another person. For it was the corruption of a moral precept which gave rise to the wrong in the first place. Though "conscience doth make cowards of us all," it also prompts us to achieve the courageous goal.

From these considerations one can see that the moral basis of a particular law cannot be exorcised by a politically ambitious person without his converting the law into mere pragmatic hypothesis controllable ny political manipulation. Nor does breaking the law create the illusion that somehow the law no longer exists by virtue of the breech thereof or by the arrogant assumption that a peronal violation extinguishes the exisrtence or the efficiency of the law that was broken. Criminals young and old tend to think in theis manner of logic, that their violation somelhow extinguishes the law as it was intended for another man

Same-sex marriage, political bribery and euthanasia are, alike, lacking in lmoral virtue. Moral conduct is not predicated upon a personal restructurinng of human values or upon radical social eperimentation, as our illustrious US Supreme Court has in its liberal mindset tended to think. A human behavior that violates or contravines established laws—and to a lesser degree, rules and regula-tions-marks a precedent that ought not to be followed by political or social cus-tom. We are this day attemptin to customize illegal alien entries into this Count}y and we find it hard to accommodate lawful custom to the act of break-ing the border law. Precedents ought always to be subject to formal challenge or informal suspicion. For no amount of semantical restructuring of the dimensions of semiotic meaning can alter value-judgements of the conduct of law break-ing—that is, not without one's commiting an act of intellectual dishonesty.

If the person who acts morally doth put himself into a situation of real risk, of palpable danger to himself to the end of helping or of saving others from suffer-ing and death, such as Dr. Jonas Salk who discovered the fficacy of penicillin by firsrt testing it on himlself, then his action is undeniably moral and commndable. It is scientifically logical though uncaring of personal safety.

Anyone in making a choice between means and ends is at liberty to chose to obey the law, whether or not it is moral lw. But he ought, when he can, to sever his thinking from mere obeisance to the law, mere rote shamanism, mere obesquious aceptance of the law, without any consideration of its social effects. For only God's law is absolute, Mans isl fallible, is suvjelct to change and must always proide for the spirit of compliance. When he does that, the individual has expressed his liberty to consult his conscience as to the right or the wrong of his actions. This rational act is the statement, unvoiced, that he has not allowed his feelings to be his arbiter and guide. For we today live in times when feelings, *per se,* constitute the omnipresent authority over our actions, and pridefully so. Who can argue with anoher man's feelings—his reason, yes, his judgement, yes, his assumptions, yes.

But not his feelings—? "My gut feeling is," "live with gusto," "only one time around!" "get in touch with your feelings," "anything goes just so long as you don't hurt another," "Im okay, you're okay," "How do you feel anout this … election, that issue?" And on and on do we Americans drift withs the current of our feelings reinfored by the banalities of television and the mediocre presupposi-tions of an amoral liberal media. We would almost rather thrsow away our democracy rather than abandon our precious feelings. Much of todlay's raw noise about racism has its basis lin feelings rather than in logic.

It should be pellucidly clear liberty cannot esist in a State that penalises moral conduct for the obvious reason that immoral laws and personal moral conduct are at loggerheads. Our founers realized that truth. Laws ought not to rest on faulty choices as to the moral right or wrong which they will induce ot propagate. The dilalectical materialism of communism is nased on a morally erronious perception of human worth; that man is a mere complex assemvlage ofl molecules, withsout a soul and no higher than the animals, of which he is one. Violence in America today, both its perception nd its causes are the direct result of vengefiilness, ofl taking revenge out on a thing or another person. It is therefore barbaric, to say the least and is, indeed, propelled by feelings and directed by a state of wcikenness, of evil, of sin. Revengeful violence is but a replication of the anient justice of stoning condemneld by society for having broken what then was onsidred the law; there was no forgiveness, no trial of the facts, no arbitration of the causes, no preclusion of innocence, all amounting to the compassionate reserve promulgated by the infusion of Chrsitanity into social relationslhips. Choice governed ny a moral conscience liberartles humanl activity, feelings alone tyrannize. And though the law will at times command the conscience to rectify the will, always fallible, we cannot lose that conscionable moral perspective withsout losing our persosnal lierties and evne our democractic freeodm. The authority of the conscience is the fundamental cause for the laws and every writ and script and *debentur* that belongs to Western Civilliation. The spiritual *nimesis* of punishment and social contract are interlocking ideas, lthey are inseparable dista.

It is immoral to stand in judgement of another mans act of conscience; for how can one 1 possibly know what agony of doubt he has gone through to reach his moral objective?

The liberty of a free people is feared by tyrants.

It is beltter to have spoken in defense of liberty and erred in the assumptions than not to have spoken at all.

Those who have never defended liberty on the battlefield place a lesser value on it than those who have.

Liberty is to the French always foremost the absence of a king and only secondarily, the presence of a conscionable code of conduct. Thus he raps the American for being too moral uemlocratic egaltarianism rules out the need for a conscience. Fraternity is, at best, the confirmation of natrionalistic pride.

Republican equality inevitably tends toward the expedient in government. Only our Electoral system and our various veto powers hold this impulse in check. Committes, in turn, frustrate that veto power. Political stalemate, however, is impossible because of the driving power of the American economy. Absent that power, Socialism takes over.

43. LIBERTY, ACCOUNTABILITY AND PUNISHMENT

It is an anomaly in a society known for its personal freedoms that a citizen who habitually breaks the law feels least accountable to others for doing so. This is the case because the criminal says that he is "not guilty" and should assume no responsibility for his crime. In fact, he often convinces himself of his innocence by pointing out the Tightness of his actions. This is the law of self-justification in action that belongs with hearsay, old-wives tales, second opinions and perjury.

Where does this denial of accountability come from? From Eve's denial of sin against God? From Adam's pathetic complicity? From the paternalistic family, the self-esteem sndrome, the "no-fault" protectionism of insurance companies, marriage counsellors or a-moral judges? In the face of evidence the lie is always always obvious even if sometimes not visibly demonstrated. One cannot invade the conscience of the malfeasor or the felon to determine if a sense of guilt was there before the act, or even after the act that is defined as malevolent, unconscionable or devious outlawry. Indeed, the word *outlaw* defines its content. In all cases the fear of punishment leads to the denial of culpability, the law-breaker like a school child ready to point his or her finger at another person as scapegoat. Self-justification most often motivates the denial, the criminal armors himself with his silence or his alibi or his fictitious defense. He habitually draws upon facts in a haphazard but selective way to give a semblance of truth to his story.

Removal of the punishment would not, in the long view, reduce the numbers or alter the nature of the crimes committed on Americas streets. Muggers would go on mugging, robbers robbing, rapists raping. Only they would do so with a greater sense of freedom and anarchistic resolve. Some forms of punishment are a mere hobble on the desperate natures of men. An increase, however, in the severity of the pnishment can, and does, sometimes act as a deterrent—but obwiously not in every case, mainly because the penalties of imprisonment and fines are scaled down by lenient judges, plea bargainng, immunity witnesses, political commutation, and the myriad of technicalities that clever defense lawyers raise to defeat the plaintiffs cause of action. Fraud in the courtroom is frequently the name of the game for the defense, whilest a jury's emotions can, and often do, persuade the jurors singly to unconsciously lie.

Accountability for a crims is so closly linked to liberty of action that it is taken for granted until challenged to the degfree in which it factors into motives. Rights!—the strident clamor is for rightls! A man can be motivated to kill a shop-keeper, injure a stranger, damag a neighbor or his propertty, or main his own child, indeed, urged to cripple an animal or to destroy an imagined enemy. Yet he will plead that he was at liberty to do the wicked deed because he had a right to do so. He may even admit to the acti, although that is not the usual case, and at the same time he may rationalize that he is not accountable because he was drunk or on drugs or suffered from a deficient diet, or that he was at a different place at the ltime of the crime. He is therefore necessarily innocent. Family, friends and mother will attempt to reassure the Court of their "boy's" innocence, of the sincerity of the love between the killer and his dead love. All of this garbage makes entertaining newsprint and TV time, but is not justice. The insanity plea is most interesting. Who out there can say what madness is, but the audience out there will accept ga-ga what the Defense Consel tells the court lit lis, and will call in a specialist to affirm his decision. "Reasonable doubt" wears many faces.

To the criminal mental makeup, *accountability* is a condition of the mind, a variable, not an absolute, and he or she thinks that it is **intention** alone that confirms the lawless result of the criminal act. Without the proper deliberate intention, there can be no murder, no rape or robbery. *Accident* is no excuse. Thus much has been made of "stalking," of the improvised spur-of-the-moment crime, the robbery and slaying for a six-pack, as if the triviality of the goal lessened the enormity of the crime. It's as if the crimianl has the option to accept or to reject the results of his violence. Whereas the very admission or denial is an imputation of criminality incipient in the evidence of the case, proof is another matter. Anarchist that he is, the crimianl presupposes that he is the master of his own rules of misconduct, an oxymoron of meanining and that he puts the stamp of his own values upon what he does. That much is true, yet the irony is that society has granted to him this liberety of intention in full knowledge that, as still a free citizen, he has not only the capacity but the *right* to damage other members of that toleratring society. Feelings have triumphed over moral value—a judgement in the accountability phase of much ofl the criminal behavior in America today.

Still, society protects itself while searching for the causitive agent, the malfeasor of a crime. Inasmuch as the accountability of an alleged perpetrator remains moot until evidence can prove the charge, what then do we say about the perversion of liberty ind the commission of the crime? Is the broken law like an unspoken writ, ready to be affixed to the culprit if he or she can be found? Is liberty severable from its possessor? I hink not, at least not at the outset when the crime is discovered. The freedom of one to make responsbile choices has been temporarily eclipsed, lost sight of, in the crime and its corruption, having become entangled with motive and obfuscated by society's conjectures vi-a-viz the media. For the crime remains in the subjective possession, the memory, of the criminal who,when he is discovered and proved guilty, is caused to surrender up his previous citizens liberty the potential of which he can no longer exercxise during his punishlment. He exchanges an inalienavble right for society's retribution and its preservation of the inalienable right of its innocent members. That portion of freedom that was his as a citizen is returned to the general fund of social order, like a returned loan, and the balance of equitable justice is restored in the peace that follows the crime. By ever so little, the crimes that are left unsolved and the criminals who are released before their terms are up do in fact reduce that fund of moral stremgth tat belongs to the liberty of the people. If this were not so, no amount of crime or numbers of criminals could ever corrupt a society. In a word, crime corrupts freedom.

It is that reduction that gives rise to terror, apprehension and social insecurity among the people. By this line of reasoning it becomes apprenl that crime, especially unsolved crimes, weaken the people's moral fibre, quench their resolve to fight crime, perpetuate opprobrium against the police—a form of moral suicide since they represent the sustenance of personal liberty. In the end it is the people themselvces who self-destruct when and if they fail to confront the crimes in their communitlies with matched resistance and moral strengfth. The truth is not that the cops are a moral police force, though they reflect society's moral values. Instead, they are a morall social construct that represents the basic right of self-defense.

At a glance one can discern the connection between conformity to moral law and the legal agencies of enforlcement and prosecution that insure against any mounting damage by out awry to the State. It is the fear of that damage that the despot—and free-wheeling outlaw is a despot-contemplates. He perceives that the more innovative, courageous and ambitious members of society, once they gain legitimate power, can destroy his own *self-imposed* **jehad** *of death to Ithe nation.* It escapes him, usually, that the strength of resistance can ever be the issue of combative moral fervor; and yet it was so in the American Revolution, the Civil War, WWI and WWII. That is the terrotist's particular blindness. If, howeve, that ruling class should become an oligarchy or a dictatorship, as in the Germany of 1933, the individual who is loyal to the this absolute State submits his conscience and his librety of mind to the manifests of the ruling clique and their ideology. Like the prisoner who goes to jail, he exchanges his liberties for security and can no longer acquiesce that he was or was not accountable. This is the double-mindedness of the life-time prisoner. He is often schizoid. His silence is mute testijmony to the extinguishing of his citizen rgihts, on which restsed his right of plea. Parole is only a tlemporaryl restoration of that right. The long-term prisoner will often conclude that his surroundings are an atificial environment that ils made to seem a "cruel and unusual punishment" for him. But its very artlificiality makes the criiminal's conformity to prison "goodness" possible.

One might guess that they whos are falsely imprisoned as a miscarriage of justice are less than one percent of the total prison population. That could be proved, despite today's bent toward the gathering of DNA evidence. The State has removed from the prisoner, by extinguising his sense of society's acceptance, any former attitude of accountability. As already noted, it is that attitude that infers the rightful power of a man to make personal choices. His inner soul and physical person now must anwer to the supreme law of the State ... or of the County ... where he is held captive. The NKVD and sthe Gestapo imposed this metamorphosis upon cilizens who were aware of the protections of liberty that had surrounded them at some time earlier in their lives.

Once the citizen surrenders his liverties, his accontability for his actions answers to the demands of the victim and of society's retribution. That retribution reposes in solitary prison confinement, his time of incarceration, his labor in the "nig house." Instead of its being reformed, his seared conscience is directed toward a mineless obedience to the State. And so it must be if he is to surlvive in his new environment. By this regimen society protects itself from the immoral conduct of the criminal who has rejected the law instead of accepting the lighter burdrn of individual moral responsibility. The law by itself was of insufficient strength to deter him, even though he may have undersrtood the consequences for his criminal conduct. The rewards for his crime were at the time of its commission, too tantalizing for him to resist.

Punishment under justice is always moral in the power of law-enforcement. If not, then the punishment for crime can be only naked revenge, an assertion all too frequently adopted by liberals in these times. Their absurd compassion imputes exoneration to the murderer, the trator, the saboteur, in short, to those who put themseles above the law. For willful *good* cannot be elicited from a philosophy of Nihilism. The good for society, if it comes not from a sense of accountaility by its members or the pnishment that society imposes on its crimianl defiants, must issue from a value system that requires *goodness* as a civic responsibility and duty. The law of torts reflects this perspective and power.

There is an insecurity in the risk of moral choice, for the world abhors absolute standards and contends to destroy them.

Morality is the strength and life of a nartion. Without it, amid the genesis of chaos an civil strife, its absence can be clearly discerned. Then why

was it not installed in the opening assaults on societal integrity in the 1960's?

intent, dissidents against th *status-quo* conspire to desroy what allows them to give voice to their rebellion—freedom of speech. They are the epitome of intolerance who condone rabid solutions yet silence adversarlies under color of tolerance.

The man enslavced vy an alien philosoph will ve stusng by lthe vciper of lits negations. Ironically, he will look tol them for the source of this per sonal identity.

Remember that it is not the human rights that are at fault lin the injustices within a society uf the human beings who practice them in selfish ways.

A man's self-identify is the product of his self-acceptance, his errors, his virtues, his prom ises,lhis capacities; and of his signularity, his uniqueness before a Creator God. Yet so long As he refuses to repeant of his worngs he hides from a part of himself. God need not leven be consulted since that part of him is his soul.

44. LIBERTY TO KILL-COMPASSION Vs THE CONSCIENCE

The doctor-patient fiduciary relationship that secures medical information from third-party scrutiny is today under attack hy hospital committees of patient case-review and medica-insurance carriers who, tragically with increasing frequency, "pull the plug" to terminate a patient's life, ease an elerly person out of this world with dignity at the recommendation and request of a stranger known as a *bioethicist*. More often than not, the bioethicist is non-medically qualfied to render such a draconian judgement as to life's worth or the advisability of ending it due to the absence of ilts happiness-value. Sort of like judgeing over-ripe fruit or a fixer-upper house, eh? This curious stranger-of-death is the successor to that growing numefr of doctors who, in complete violation of their Hypporatic oath, decide that the *quality of life* of a terminally-ill patient no longer merits the use of life-saving technology, expense to the relatives or to society in general; and that were it not for the administration of death by starvation or dehydration or, indeed, the lethal injection of a powerful lnarcotic to induce coma, the patient would suffer prolonged agony while depriving other patients of the doctor's attention. How precious! Those pale-riders are increasing in number, and boards of case-review examiners are coming to rely increasingly on their own judgement. *Candidates* for that kind of terminal "care" are also not infrequently those who are chronically depressed and so find living too painful to endure. There are doctors in swelling numbers, like Dr. Kerkorian, *Doctor of Death,* who exempt themselves from laws of homicide assuming the oversight of such patients with a terminal "care," in the case of infants, with dehydration. In the case of adults—both the terminally ill and the electlive suicides—that 'care" consisrts of a drug overdose or the removal of the respirator and deliberate starvation. "Safeguards" such as family consulation or multi-doctor conferfences or even hospice care—the most humane and compassionate treatment—do not guarantee the procedure of death-dealing as an honest one. The doctor(s) involved, the bioethicist, sometimes a family member anxious to be quit of the financial burden, will smply rationalize away the guilt of murder of his own kin. Quite often the deceased's insurance money comes in hands by pay off the physician and the estate lawyer. The State of Oregon presently endorses this cozy arrangement.

But factors of cost, blame-sharing and the waste to the rest of socety in personnel hours and hospital technology, including lab work are, in the eyes of sociey, tricked out as *compassion.* These terminal cases but a few of which reach public attention have the inpact of desensitizing the ignorant layman, the young and those who have never watched one of their own loved ones dying. So long as the bioethicist—now a specialty, a sort of secular Priest yet more of a hangman—approves of the doctor's opinion and, in numerous cases, makes the decision himself or hersel to end a life, the notion of medical malpractice does not seem to arise. The bioethicist priest has given asolution to the doctor. Surely medical murder of this stripe must constitute some sort of conspiracy with patient involvement, the patient not infrequently acquiescing to the final act in order to escape the horrible pain and suffering. The patient then in a legal sense becomes the victim to this policy of death-with-dignity, makilng his death suicide not murder.

The law does not authorize the doctor to take a life irrespective of his Hippocraticoath. It is society that authorizes him unknowingly, whilest thinking that he is practicing his oath and attempting to extend the life of a patient. There is a dark deception in all of this. For his contetion that he is helping the terminally ill or the severely handicapped infant is nothing but a plea to commit murder. The entire procedure is unethical administratively and morally corrupt medically, for it exploits a medical situation with the pronouncing of a verdict upon the value of human life. It is in the doctor's power to overwhelm the next of kin with a dread prognosis. It is in the power of the Court to stay his hand. It is in the power of the closest relative to veto both agencies. It is in the power of God to shut down all venues to survival.

If society in time consents to the reversal of the role of the doctor-healer to reliever-killer, for whatever the reason, this schizoid conduct will by professional association tend to indict many good doctors for immoral conduct and, ultimately, to mediocratize the medical profession. Quackery will have become an accepted reality.

Perhaps more insidioius to the moral health of the nation will be the callousing of society to accept doctor-assisted death-by-choice reasoned as love. Reason will then rush to the aid of hysteria, fear, calamity to do its evil work as subversive stratagems of "remedy" in supoort of liquidation. The neo-Nazi mindset now enters upon the scene, the *politics of death,* and Americans will have surrenered another inalienable right, the right to life, into the fallible hands of mortals mediating the necessary death of another person/s loved one.

Can the Good Samarlitan argument of lawful emergency care extend so far as to embrace this new mode of "emergency," for so it will appear to outsiders who are unfamiliar with the patient's case? The combination of physician and mortitian, animated by the bioethicist" practitioner," will prove to be a real challenge to conspiratorial reason when the press reports the Dr. Jekyll and Mr. Hyde procedure. The deliverer of health has become the pepetrator of death. The grim; irony is that the doctor does, and will conintinue to, believe in his mission of mercy on which he so fondly and dispassioantely extinguishes a life in the name of life. There is a satanic aura and cogency of deception in this whole gruesome business.

What are we then to do? How do we spell out the liberty of life-death choice, of rational decision, of moral conscience so that the ultimate *sentence to murder* becomes comprehensible to Western society that for two thousand years has believed in the value and the sanctity of human life? America herself is gradually coming to condone this mode of medical practice, like putting a wounded animal down out of compassion. Indeed, that is one source of much of the dispassionate misery: that science, reflectling upon human beings as mere animals of a higher order and therefore without souls, need feel no remorse over *mercy killing.*

The answer to the question posed is simple: absent any lawful authorization before the indicated circumstances of premeditated murder, sociey ought to allow the doctor to complete his hideous mission and then compel him to face the legal consequences of his actions. The reason for this solution is quite honestly in the nature of a logical entrapment for the killing, i.e.to make of lthe murdering doctor an example to all. One doctor has indeed avowed that he would in fact announce each termination murder for the PR value and the education of a dull and unresponsive public and then proceed to administer treatment, the justification for which he finds in his self-righteous condemnation of America's heartless system of justicable-medical justice. He has lamented that his victim is being focred against his or her ill to live. Has geriatric medicine and hospice care been wrong all along by closing their ears to pleas of uselessness voiced by aged and dying patienta? Indeed, will society at last condone euthanasia based on Bioethicist reasoning?

If we shape the justice of our society to conform to the predelections and will of the physician bent upon the exrterminatioin of one life, augmented by Political dialectics, then we can bend to the will of an imposter with armies for slaughter and a despot intent upon killing any and all at will, to put the leper, the starving, the crippled, the diseased and the insane out of their misery, in a lword, to cleanse society of its human discards. Who will then be allowed to practice his evil science and craft on a hospital ward in th dead of night? It will be just such a man as the evil angel of death who will administer the final solution to the powerless. Remember that phrase: *the powerless,* for they like the newborn murdered on his birthday will be exterminated on their decision day, the decision to die finalized by strangers and misinformed onlookers, including the liberal media who continue to impugn God in the public forum. What do those calibrated fools know about human life from their bench and laboratory?

These zealots who favor population control might at some future date catapault this lawless behavior into law. But law without any control over the doctor's ambition, the patient's will, the mortification of the flesh or the pretension to a mercy that no longer exists. With a sentimental compassion more akin to imbecility, this poisonous god of merlcy might, ultimately come into full power to put a fright into the elderly, the suffering, the suicidal who are powerless. There it is again, that phrase: *the powerless,* from infants to the diseased, to the aged. There is a liberty of choice for the patient that finds its expression in his request for death; yet, correspondingly, there exists a liberty of conscience possessed by society's members that condemns that suicide as an insult to the its moral integrity and to its very survival, even as doctor and patient alike deny that harm will in fact result froml abortion, mercy killing or euthanasia.

More and mor in America we are watching the slow erosion of the centuries-old value that made the life of a person either sacred, or at least secure from injury, and his to possess permanently until death. What we are seeing are attempts to change the role of the healer to that of a messiah, from that of the supporter of life to that of the giver and taker of life. Euthanasia, if practiciced covertly nowadays, not many years hence it will "ome out of the closet." The immoral act is to cause the death of the patient which, within the framework of the philosophy of growing numbers of physicians, is adviseable and is a tolerable release from pronged pain and hopelessness. Indeed, from mercy killing one could draw the analogy that euthanasia and hospice "elimination" are a recurrence of Medieval burning at the stake, in the extant case for the doctor's privileged philosophy of life's worth. Yet those victims involve self-immolation to reduce medical costs and population numbers, rather than a religious cleansing of at the fiery staeke justified by God, not by the government. The life that is ended by deliberate annihilation is valued as a plague upon society in costs, grief, trouvle and consumption ... and danger in the imbecility of old age. The doctor becomes satan's acomplice as the destroyer of choice and therefore anti-God.

Doctor-assisted death is a form of suicide regardless of whether or not pain or worthlessness gives rise to the request. Yet the science of killing replaces the morality of preservation under termination circumstances. The death, indeeed, may not appear to be harmful to the victim, but his and his doctor's liberty to chose must necesarily involve the compelling interest of society, the State, against whom such a preocedure creates a general acceptamce, by example, of human worthlessness. The science of remedial medicine supervenes in the liberty of moral choice and, in fact, begins a precedent for medical care.

One may, indeed, ask what means liberty of personal choice of if one has an inherent right to commit suicide or to request his physician to put him out of his pain, real or imagined? Liberty as a code for living derives meaning from the sanctity of life, but that value does not bestow upon its possessor the license to kill either himself or another human being. Since Ihe is not the giver of life, he cannot be the taker of life. Central to the question of freedom to commit suicide withsout opposiion is the quiery:—at what point does harm to another cease to be crimninally actionable and morally reprehensible, and become, instead, humane and compassionate? Or to phrase the speculation another way:—should it be a crime for a terminally-ill patient to commit suicide and to effect this remorseless endinng involve his docor—or any specialist in death, as a nurse or a mortition or, indeed, an estate lawyer? Would not death by the hand of a hired assassin be just as "moral"? Certainly there are those in this country today who wish to bring about this mournful stratagen through "enlightened" legislation. They are asking that question, hoping that the liberal courts will give then the woeful authority to proceed on this calamitous and infamous course. It is very likely that a liberal Supreme Court will in the future "legislate" into existence interpretive law that protects the *privacy of death,* just as it has "legislated" into oblivion the life and rights of the unborn infant up to the very threshhold of separate personhood, that is, in late-term abortion.

Once society permits euthansia and mercy killing it establihes the precedent for other acts of compassionate killing, abortion in America being one such irresponsible conspiracy between the assenting Supreme Court and the practicing physycian. Fewer than 2-percent of abortions are performed to save the life of the mother; all others are elctive for the convenience of the mother, sometimes of the father. The Romans threw away female babies because they could not become soldiers and constituted a drain on the economy of the Empire. The Eskimos set their old and inform adrift on a floe of ice to let them starve to death. In our country, starvation is practiced as a means of ending life, of either a malformed infant or a brain-dead/heart-dead person. Which determines the death-sentence at thle hospital is controversial. In the last centurys the Nazis practiced homicidal euthansia and genocide with their "enlightened medical experiments for the good of medicine and the Third Reich. The Aztecs of Mexico practiced ritual live sacrifices to their sun god, which carried with them the kind of shamanic annointment and social acceptance that euthanasia in America is heading toward. The Priest, the Rabbi, the minister will all be there at graveside to entone thanks to God for his goodness in giving release from pain to the deeased. In the United States, the *novelty* of removsal of the unwanted from society, whether by suicide or by society itself, has come to the fore politically. And we are constrained increasingly to fix our approval on this wicked and barbaric custom once practiced among pagan, animistic peoples of the world. Ought we to adopt their customs of pre-Christian polytheism? And why not, if the ACLU wants God removed from the people's consciousness and the athiests consent.

It is altogether right that society for the time being has overruled (visible) euthanasia, since it is society speaking in their own defense who make this judgement. Suicide, being a physical injury to just one person, might in due time include others in society, since to continue to tamper with population control and numbers quotas, with genetic engineering, food consumption, medical-care scarcity, and for another reasons of convenience leads to the devaluation of human worth. Again, once the precedent is established, only a Solomon can predict what evil reasons for the termintion of life will occur in this country, in Amerian society. Human sacrifice will wear the mantle of sacred honor, a pious acceptance of death for the reason of compassion. Keep the hospital beds rotating! Push out the old, fill those beds with young illegal immgirants who can still work. Could that be the distant cry of the mercy killers? If so, then we as a people have replaced compassion with a conscionless extermination, piously cleansed by the State-read "killled"—of the helpless and unwanted lives among us. This medical abuse of liberty can and will destroy America.

> Liberty must be lived to be fully understood. It is not enough to theorize about its benel its and advantages. For as we see nowadays to change the name of a thing changes its meaning e. g marriage, privacy, truth....

> A people, a nation, unaccustomed to our democratic freedoms repudiates them as mindless, directionless and impractical. They are used to having been told what to do by the reasoning of those whose power rests on the people's vassalage. Mexico is an example.

> Cultivate in a man the love for freedom if you would court his affection or marshal his loyalty and you remove the blinders to his capacities.

> Conscience does not derive from religious ordination, from precepts whose violation hobbles and imprisons the reason. Its source is the divine Author of creation. Its capcity is to make ethical and moral judgements. It has no content but is an instrument for the evalua tion of right and wrong.

> The appliation of conscience to assess and evaluate moral and ethical conduct is the simple means to foster political comity and social happiness. Therefore, violence in the streets is anathema to conscience and betrays its enslavement to personal immorality, a street mob has no conscience. Take care.

> A man will find his true nature among his loyalties, for they are but the facets of his master, who is either God or the prince of this present darkness.

> The practice of honesty im all matters, as much as is humanly possible, gives life to the spirit. If a man is honest about his motives it is usually difficult for him to double-deal with his neighbors.

> Trilable evidence confirms the whole tlruth. Left to doubt without proof, truth will often assume tlhe sound and appearance of half-truth.

> Make no man the prisoner of your conscience, for he hath his own god to deal with and to answer to.

The lack of self-esteem is much talked-about these days. Self pity is often its true name. Lack of self-confidence is another.-For personal esteem is passivce until it succeeds at excellence. Esteem thus earned banishes self-; pity.

If Man velongs to God amd separatges from Him, who then will afflirm his true manhood identilty? The State? His peers? Events of his own or of others making? Himself? His father? Or perhaps his dog.

If God is a man's mirror-judge, no-God—or atheism—shatters the glass, confounding and losing the man in the fragments of his shattered being. Conscience is his only means to restoration. For the Remorseful man that means involves confrontation sand repentance not to the State but to God.

45. LIBERTY AND RELIGIOUS TOLERANCE

Religious intolerance belongs to the disciples of its itany of pious exclusivity, to a monotheism of politics, to the cleansing from alternative faiths by a dictatorship regime. Evidence of spectral invasion of the Established rights, the spurious allegations of "think tank" Elitists of social impurity, i.e. political incorrectness, lead to the eradication of unacceptable speech, ideas and actions from public vuew. Such prohibitions are a chimerical secular form of righteousness that tends to impugn free thought as dangerous to a people's welfare. We will have no other gods vefore us: is the hue and cry of the Elitists. We will command your heart, we shall order your thoughts, we must censure from your speechand writings what transgresses our nobility of mind and our sacredness of attitude and, above all else, the correctness of *our* judgements. In short, the PC police wish to tyrannize over tlhe thinking of America's politcians and the students at our major Universities by theiir absurd, nefarious, banile, empty and undiscerning critical thinking, so called, and of human relations.

The search land destroy mission of such intolerance has its own crede of a denial of values other than its own. Political correctness intolerance is system of thinking that is losed to outsiders while lit pretends sa catholicity of opinion that is conditional upon the abandonment of traditional Judeo-Christian values. It, th PC creed, is a moral-ethical scam, a dishonest attempt to corrupt young minds into thinking that either their parents or history books or moral leaders or, God help tlhem, the Scriptures are all wrong and that *they* are the righteous Ones, the Chosen Correct Few of this modern politically correct age.

Historically, religious intolerance has proclaimed that its faith is in conflict with the proofs an hypotheses of science. When secular challenges are bought into doctrinal arguments, a false piety will affect a tolerance for disbelievers that borders on covert malice. Perhaps the most formidible exclusivity is the denial by certain cults that free men have the right to be moved to awe by the universe, discovering its laws and mysteries. And that they have the right to discern error without fearing other men's condemnation. Religious intolerance, like political correctness, proclaims heresys as its private preserve for meting out justice, deigning to share the judgement of fallible men with the judgement of God.

The people of this Nation, departing from their Colonial roots in English Establishmentarianism and the Salem wlitchraft trials, have experienced no religious persecutions Ike those in Europe in lthe Middle Ages. But we have not yet fully rid ourselves ofl the kind of veneomed spite and malice aforethought that prodced the Salem Witchcraft trials. That tenor of passion is still among us tody, that religious intolerance that finds the secular expression in the absolute denial to believers of their right to openly express tenets of their faith on public land.

The Jeffersonism "Wall of separation" is not docrinal or ideological; it is territorial, therefore, it is basically barbaric in lits inquisitorial zeal. The fear of the secular humanists is not of the conmingling of Church and State; the fear of religious invaders' intent upon infesting the exclusive domain of secuslar humanism and invoking their faith upon the humble and ignorant inhabitants thereof. These Hlumanists, contrary to common thought, do not fear the imposition of traditionalism upon the people where, incidentally, it is already well in evidence. They fear that power which religious expression, proclaimed openly and on public land, gives to the people In doing so that people-power threatens the Humanists' domain of control and the legitimacy of their cause, to wit, that Man and not God is always right and ought always to be obeyed. Theirs is a religion and they have as much as said so in their *"Humanist Manifesto."*

Religion is not State doctrine. Faith is not a political advantage. Worship is not ritlual endorsement by the State. The Roman cross does not overlie the Goverment seal of the United States. The ACLU's destructive removal of the cross from the California Seal only promotes a lie about her history of the Mission era. Religious observances are no more repugnant to a secular society than are a pagan silence and a spiriual emptliness that must be filled. To be reminded of the Gospels is no more offensive to a morally sensitive people than it is to be reminded of murder, riots, corruption in Government, war and the pestilences of human relationships. Therefore, this so called salubrious and enlightened pandering to litigants-against-religious-'VjccommodaftW' is not the protection of First Amendment Rights. It is the destruction of the ***accommodation principle.***

The tolerant accommodation of religion by the State is not tantamount to an "establishment" proclamation. The grant of trespass rights by the State for the purpose of religious observance is certainly not church incorporation in any sense of the words. The observance by the State of its property usage is not unilateral to the atheists. The open display of religious messages, creches, symbols and music on public property is not State participation in the content thereof by its silence, concession or submission.

Nor does the rejection of any and all symbols conducive to a belief in a partic-ular faith, religion or creed signify neutrality of opinion, but, linstead, tlhat elim-ination identifies like the pathologist does cancer a dangerous intolerance for whomever differs from the Humanist's platform. That platform is largely politi-cal in nature, yet is not of the people. Such atheistic idolatry if allowed to con-tinue without opposition or discussion can desrtroyl the moral strengths and spiritual health of the entire nation, for then we should come to accept the athe-ism of the fully secularized State, as in Soviet Russisa where the bible was vanned and churches buned and the folk made to wsorship inl the forests as religious exiles.

The modern State tends to promote and to foster a *theism* that is religiously non-existent, by not allowing private or institutional dissenters to encroach upon its domain of "tolerance." Why; should a bunch of parasitic lawyers make State=relligion decisions for the rest of society? Threreby, with encroachment does the State create in an altmospnere of hostility toward all religion, an exclu-sivity that is clearly at odds with the documets of America's founding fathers. That some persons say they do not believe in God, or a god, is an absurd argu-ment for the removal of religions icons and the denliel to others of a forum for their religious expression.

The real question is: whose god or what god? Atheists have their creed as to the godly, herefore it is specious hypocrisy that the former, the atheists, shoudl be allowed to prevail agalinst the Raditionalists and always under the guise of neu-trality. Liberty could never have taken root on America shores had gold, skins, spices, timber and for the king been the only causal motives for the migration from Europe. Those incentives, the motivations, are much too weak to have ger-minated any kind of lasting colony except one for adventurers and suppliers who wosuld have stayed. A people's religious faith had to be a part of the mix in order to make setlement the integrity of the New World colonial venture. The tenets of Calvinism ruled out heresy and non-belief, at the other extreme. Therefore, again, the **accommodation principle** of the Constitution came into play and is just as valid today as it was in 1789. The *cleansing* factions of **political correctness** in America ignore or deny or ignore that principle.

It was not the intention of the Country's founders that a dissenting clique, organization or demagogue should deny to the people the right to express their faith by festivals and religious observnces, and by symbols, biblical scenes anf public utterances of faith in God. Yet the Humanists wouldl banish altogether such practices on State-owned property and by doing so they practice the system, manner and philosophy of Nihilism. Neitzche said that *God is dead'*, and he inferred that there is no god who exists that is worthy of worship except Man himself. In this territorial purgation there is an ominous threat to all religions in America, and to their worshippers who, as the hostility of pagan Humanism gatlhers strength, will be intimidated to replace their Christ and their God with the States liberal social servilce agencies and activist courts, self-seeking organizations like the ACLU, and demagogues in the Congress who abjure all religion. This widespread liberal omission of religious faith and practice is a form of self-censoship. Its acceptance constitutes the blatant denial of 1st-Amendment rights. The omitted news stories that do not obscure the truth about events appear in the conservative press. That media *truth wAfiree speech,* affirmed and guaranteed by the Constitution, are compatibles.

It thus appears with clarity that we are fast developing in this Nation a society which is foreign to the humanitarian intent and interests of the Founders' Constitutional system of checks and balances. For which branch,if it is ideologically liberal, will contend against the Supreme Court's rules against the equal sharing of ieological forums and the beneficial influence of prayer in schools and the posting of the Ten Comandments? To engage in Fundamentalist outcry is an act of outlawry. To propose public appeal to an Omniscient God of our forefathers is traitorous to the cause of Human Beings, whatever that may be. The bifurcation of Secuular Humanism applauds abortion but comforts those *afflicted* by the outspoken faith of others!

Having surrenered up all thought and intention for religious worship, publically, to the total absence of the identity of "Liberty," privately, believers are in effect disenfranchised from a vote that would put a religious conservative politician into office. A recent election has seemed to disprove that assertion. Only time will tell if the cabal citadels of excusivistic special intrerests can be breeched and diminished in their considerably formidible power over the voters.

In the matter of religious freedom we are headed toward a general purgation of openly expressed faith in all walks of life that is manufactured and controlled by an oligarcy of atheistic dissenters, moguls in the media and tenured liberal profressors in the universities. Many of then gave vent to their rant and free rein to their promiscuity in the liberal 1960's. Now in control, they wish "those damned conservatives would just go away." Today's paganizing of America comes in the main from these think-tank Elitists, billeted permanently in the above-mentioned venues and linked by inseparable ideological bonds to the so-called Eastern Establishment where, indeed, many of them reside. They possess the intelligence yet they lack the wisdom to lead. Wisdom cannot be manufac-tured out of whole cloth. It must be humble. It must transcend the times. It must be bound to faith in an omniscient God. None of these precepts apply to the Sec-ular Humnists, for they are indissoluably wedded to their own naricissistic indul-gences. Even if they are only animals, as they assert, they have accorded to themselves the blessings of wisdom that are denied to the other primates. Appar-emtly monkeys and chimpanzees did not need wisdom but man did, for his sur-vival. How solicitous of fair play is mother nature!

Society is the poorer for the absence of an expression of Man's humility before a sovereign God, a reality that helped to inspore the 1 st Amendment *estalishment* doctrline. "Establishment of religion" is not synonymous with "separate totality and exclusivity." The political pragmatisms of the former are not proof of the ideological validity of the latter. The Establishment doctrine does not prohibit the free expression of religious ideas in the marketplace and counsel chambers. The doctrine provides for an atmosphere of **tolerance rather than hostility.**

For its part, the Congress has become a den of confilscatory thieves who would profit by the review of the Ten Commandments. The establishment clause provides for tolerance by a government that is friendly toward religions, not hos-tile, the First Amendment never having been designed to stand as a stone wall that would forever drive believers underground in order to profess and express their religious belief and, be it noted, to preserve an inherent sacredness to our liberties and *inalienable* rights. Be aware that a changeable government cannot issue or be the source of rights that are inalienable. It takes God to do so. Modern day Chrstians have a bond with those who hid in the cartaombs and worshipped in the Russian forests.

It cannot be legally argued, except by hearsay, that the use of public propertty for religious displays compromises the State's neutrality, for the reason that the tax dollars could be and oftren are used to support partisan demonstrations of a seular nature that are repugnant to religion—as are parades of pagan drummers and of the special interest groups, the homosesuals, the abortionists, the same-sex family advocates, the free-speech obscenity-mouthers and the neo-Nazis, etc. But the State's "neutralityy" is not actually compromised for the State is not alloweed by law to take sides on issues of religion, involving as it does the *inalienable* right of God-emulation and God-benificence. One oes not neuralize what never had a polarity to begin with. Therefore even the word "accomodation" implies a power to grant, which the Constitution denies to the Federal government. Silence and inactivity are honest but inert and ineffectilve answers to articulated opposition and Stare intolerance of religous expression. The powers possessed by the government are delegated, not implicit, powers. And none among them inferentially singles out State-power over religious belief. That is the legislative creation of a liberal High Court.

Many times down through Western history the defeat of moral truth has seemed to demonstrate its falsity. There will always be the ignorant and the powerful who will attempt to defeat what is proved to be true in later years. The Greek and Roman civilizations fell becuse of their internal moral decay. Wars, extravagance and invasions only hastened the process. The museum of Man's history is replete with examples that show that gullible ignorance is the foe of proven moral laws. Religious displays of one kind or noher, founded upon the moral teachings of Christ, Muhammed, and the Ancient Prophets of the Talmud, do not threaten the continued existences of the State-that is, not until America's molock liberal judges began to demand the extermination of religious precepts from all public arenas. The threat is of *their* making, not of the Holy Laws' pleading.

We accept the right of ignorant men to applaud science yet deny to the religious men the rational open expression of their own faith among the society of non-believers. Very few actually wish to proselytize although that ils the Christian calling. Common observartion indicates that the reverse is championed by the moral rebels. Ought the establishsment, the liberal *status quo* doctrine, to tolerate atheism at the expense of at least a deistic philsoophy? In that case, there is no equal forum for expression available . Yet in the neglect, if not the elimination of the Judeo-Christilan ethos, the Easrern transcendental meditation of Hinduism is practiced on the premises of the people-owned Pentagon and Satanlism is recognized as a legitimate "faith" in the armed forces. The wives of presidents engage in astrology, spiritism and occultic empowerment, treading spiritually on the history of Dolly Madison and other stalwart and devoted women in our illustrious hisltory.

Indeed, do American taxpayer dollars make beyond-the-grave guidance acceptable in the Whiite House—or should they? Why must public school children hear only one choice of belief system, when *values-clarification* has all but wiped out traditional values. Why ought we to wonder at school violence? Also, their young minds are exposed to the closed system of Evolution, a theoretical corpus of largely speculation and theoretical hypotheses. The Medievalistic United States Supreame Court has commanded that all school instruction must abide by the infallible model of the Evollutionlists ... But the Court's evidence is constructive, not concrete; yet increasing numbers of geophysicists and palentologists and related scientsists are finding new evidence every year in support the "fanciful, mythical" Biblical account of Creation. The children are denied the option to hear this Second Model, being compelled instead to investigate the closed ystem of Evolution and to accept much of what is speculation.

Such legalistic intolerance puts to silence the scientist, explorer, philosopher and legislator who steps beyond State-mandated Nhihilism to speculate about the God of the universe. Conditional possibilities ought not to be expunged from tlhe exchange of ideas. We as a nation have survived on this premise. In fact, Utopian fantasies have never come from religion in practical government. They have always been the progeny of socio-political Utopians who, out of a senescent or patholigical frustration, deliberately feigned escape from a too arduous world. They then have repudiated freedom as dangerous, tyrannical, oppressive and elitist. To this group *ot **annihilationists,*** I coin a word, belong the anti-religion disciples who today would substitute for adherence to moral values their computerized ethical choices based on electronic result-analysis projections! If taken seriously, such mechanized value selections can only further dehumnize the people and their beliefs and further alienate tlhem from their 217 year old traditions of faith, leaving them clever, spiritually-empty electronic innovtions disguised as Truth.

Unethical practices in Government, supported by consensual acceptance by the populace, will eventually destroy democracy.

It is an act of moral cowardice and irreponsi-bility to commit a crime because "others are doing it."

He who takes solace in the wrong doing of others for the sake of concience contributes to his moral collapse.

Bribery is the heart of corruption in government.

The fall of our Nation into moral degeneracy, indlifference to her fsuture and the general acceptability of crimes large and small, inside and outside of government, travesties her hitory.

The alien who wishes to pluck the good things from America without the commitment of loyalty to her laws and to the honor of her history is a fraudelent presence on her soil, a trespasser and a mock citizen.

If social conscience determines moral values, then all America needs for her moral collapse and the deterioration of her felicitous ways of life is for demagogues and the morally perverse to lead the way. Those bent upon acquiring power are usually the best clandidates.

The false plea of innocence is of no avail in the ears of an honest judge.

Honesty is the genesis of all other virtues.

46 . EVOLUTION OR CREATION-CHANCE OR DESIGN—MINDLESSNESS OR RATIONAL CHOICE-LAW OR THE EXPEDIENCY OF EVOLUITIONARY ADAPTION

These options appear to consist of antipodal opposition, alternatives in the great orgnum of life both animate and inanimate. Evolutionary science, much of which is sheer speculation and unproved hypotheses, posit that changes in *homo sapiens* lie on a straight line from amoebae-like life, swimming around in primordial seas, to the simian animals of the great apes, orangutangs, chimpanzees and the like, and from there to intelligent modern man—all wilthout cataclysmic interruption or the rejection of evolutionary mutations! These changes are breathtaking but unproved. There exist identifiable gaps betwen the species which could be filled by mutated forms of intermediate ape-man. Yet scientists have discovered that a species automatically cancels out any true mutation as harmful to that species. Let the matter lie there. One must, instead, accept them by a leap of faith and continue the anthropological digs. All else is speculation.

Man, noble creature that he is, has also evolved socially from rudimentary primordial man with smple instincts for survival to today's upright specimen, *homo erectus,* as the specimen is called, the inheritor of capricious cognition and phenomenal mental powers. In short, he has evolved from a state of existence where he survived by means of his natural barbarism to a state where he relies often on lhis civilized and refined attributes for survival. One of the earliest evollutionay brain-storms was his capacity for making useful tools.

Who are we to doubt the philosophers of evolution not the least of whom are the nine Justices of the United Sates Supreme Court, they who attuned to factual evidence benignly accept hearsay speculation as credible evidence in support of a theory. Fools! Are we so stupid as not to perceive that dislocation of logic? The evolutionists posit that Man has evolved socially, a fact, they say that accounts for his reforms in law, medicine, education and political enlightenment. They would dissociate these changes from any religious creed. Yet we can only watch with dismay as wars erupt, ancient fratracidal hates flare up, and the plethora of laws engineered to direct and to control "civilized man" fails to change his inner being and his soul, as only a living God can do. Instead, his cruelty toward his own kind has never lightened in over 4000 years, but rather has found new engines for its application and new excuses for the use thereof.

Survival discord and savagery are still withl us in this modern age; only the weaponry has become more sophisticated,. Even that is no longer controllable. Man's social evolution is therefore, a myth, a hopeless fragment of the true potential since he was made in the image of his Creator. Man's improvement in his tools and skills, it is said, is one the evolutionist's main arguments for the ape-to-man succession. If that is true, why has his relationship to nature, the origin for their theory, entrophied. For he today wishes to encapsulate himself in his artificial environment. Is this envoronment—that is today fully mechaniaed and electronically designed for Man's passive participation—superior to the world wherein he used hand tools? His pride would lead him to afflirm that superiority yet his general unhappiness and discord belie any satisfaction with that superiority.

What then about Man's capacity for self-control and civilized consideration for his fellow men on this planet? Few are the changes we have witnessed over the past 2000 years in man's felt need to embrace his fellow man. The major shifts in sentiment toward civic and individual compassion and harmony have been brought about not by any essential improvement in his moral perception of the situational needs of others, although disasters and civil calamities have urged upon him certain remedical actions uch as humane aid, military protection, many basic freedoms we enjoy and sanctions against discrimination. Or, has he improved his environment but not his natlural drives, impulses and motivations?

We have developed as common grace the capacitousness of a benevolence that sees all men as human, if not as children made in the image of God, His clreatures. Yet paradoxically we are failing in charity and forgivness toward our enemies because we have rejected the source of those virtues, the eternal God who is said by the Nihilists to be dead. That Christian influence, however, has done more than our legalcy of the Enlightenment to bring into existence schools, hospitals, prisons reform, civil rights and organizations for the needs, etc. All of evolutionaryl change could not have brought about these things if left alone to *continuous*—*as* compared to ***cataclysmic***—evolution, its devices for mutation, its preinciples of cyclical modification, the laws of entrophy of energy, gravity and light, and its mysterious instincts for adaptation. There is a soul and morality ot human kindness that is human yet divine. Evolution, to be a valid theory must include societal as well as physiological adapatation, yet the world has not grown any more civilized than it was in the time of Augustis Caesar. Only the outward forms of conquest and oppression have changed, tyranny has remained unchanged.

The influence of the Christian ethos upon advances in man's social mans nature is not a factor that agnostics are willing to concede simply because they can find no scientific bais for the civilizing changes in human nature. They fail to explain why or how the immutable laws of the physical universe do not also change in sympathetlic synchronization with human perfection—the basic illusion of the self-made reeneration in morals and chimerical life styles. Evolution has failed him in his *Brave New World.* (Huxley)

The disconcerting fact is that human societies have always known cruelty and barbarism, reardless of the high state of their cultures. A few hundred years ago, or less, the Englidh drew and quartered a man for stealing a loaf of read or a pair of shoes. The guillotine was not designed to destroy the aristocracy so uch as it was invented to snuff out the reality of peasant inertial and class envy and to substitute human blood for the blood of bulls and rams, a sacrificial retribution, common in the time of Moses. The culturally-developed societes of ancient Egypt and China were no less ferocious iutheir contempt for and extertmination of human life. Our particular varieties today are abortion, onset euthanasia and mercy-killing.

It is justice tempered with compassion that is a mere 2000 lyears old. Christ taught forgivenes, not an eye for an eye. If Man was made in the image of God, as the Creationists believe, his liberty cannot be a product of natural selection because that is the narrow, illusory "liberty" of brute suvival and the phiulosophy of Neitche's nihilsim. If Man was not made in the image of God, then the sruvival of the fittest through natural selection is proof only that contemporary man is the most adaptanle while not necessarily the fittest in ways other than biological. There are today signs that the physical stamina and native intellectual acumen alre deteriorating or, in fact, that we are getting dumber and dumber. We search in vain for minds that will illuminate the human condition, finding him or her, as we do so, among the adumbrations of our obsessive obsession with entertainmetnt.

The consistent and sustained image of Man is, of course, the god-image, our capacitousness being no different from what it was a millnia ago. It follows, therefore, that modern man is fittest because of his sophisitated efforts to conquer his essential lonelines and the plea of terror to rescue his privacy froms further siezure by his government which he has created. In this arena of loneliness and fear, he has developed culturally by reason of his comquests of the natural world rather than having evolved mutationally from sub-species of primates. Indeed, he lhas become like the Chritian who avows that he lives in the world yet is not of it. Unbelieving Man has created, and is attempting to create, his heaven on this planet, for that is all that he has to sustain him, to feed his hopes alnd mock at evil.

Conscious intelligence, not random choice, has commanded design selection in archytypical form-function changes of *homo sapiens* that, in turn, have given rise to cultural changes. The fittest is illusory, the "most adaptive" fits the reality; and that is evidence that purpose instead of combative chance has controlled chang. This conceptualization of purpose turns attention toward God and away from mutative, random selection, away from instinct as the prime-mover of human conduct. For instinct is the trailt that is allowed to govern expressions of hedonism in contemporarsy America. He who would be his own god idolozes himself or herself. Yet a free—will governed by unconscionable moral choices mitigates that loneliness and fear. There is an inner peace that comes with doing the right thing.

> **Honor ought to be a binding force between two persons. Honor is accorded. When it is unilateral only, any oath to perform is usually transient and potentially fraudulent.**

> **Conscience always requires that the retribution for a crime be just. When compromised, conscience becomes servant to falsehood**

> **Just laws gird a nation with strength. When the courts trifle with laws, forbidding punishment, and substitute *correction* for the criminal, the people are no loner secure due to recidivism among good-behavior parolees.**

> **Liberty will last in a nation only so long as her people continue to find it to their disadvantage to abuse it.**

47. CREATIVE FREEDOM UNDER POLITICAL RULE

When there ils within a democratic people enjoyment of the internationally apprehended freedom of choice, there is almost always an improvement in the conditions that nourish and support ones' persoinal life as well as in the general welfare nd happiness of society. The single inviolate proviso is that the citizens are permitted, nay encouraged, to keep, enjoy and maintain that liberty by vote, by practice, by petition, by referendum and by debate.

Under a government of tyranny a freedom of choice hardly exists at all. Any deviation from the party line, any variation induced by the latest propaganda, any threat to change the system are all expressions of opposition and resistance that are met with force or threats of force and are branded as seditious if not treasonable. Sabotage of Hitler's empty demands for WWI reparations were so treated that good Germans did not dare to oppose his meteoric rise. Reparations for the "ancestors of slaves" in this country have fallen afoul of the identical accusations. White opposition is unconscionable an black repudiation is treasonable.

If that state of imprisonment of a person's freedom of choice is an illusion, although the *tyrant* invariably, unalterably lies about havling included basic human rights—afflirrming what I have just said about the international yen for freedom—this deception before the world becomes a device *par excellence* for touting those rights as his laws. Paradoxically, however, he grants to the people their right to feel their need for preserving personal liberties, while he asserts that their civil liberties are secure and in place. This illusion becomes so ingrained by the propaganda of lies that they believe in wartime suppression as a doctrine of their culural salvation. This was Chairman Mao's ruthless exception. Their unquestioning faith in a system of tyranny is to find, rockhardened and irrevocable, as if meted out by a god, that whenever old personal liberties are questioned by radical dissent groups, they are told that *certain liberties* must at times be curtailed for the good of the people and the cause of *the war*. Therefore, the tenor and atmosphere of wartime are everywnere tne evidence in a dctatorship whose *modus operand!* is war. Right by force of arms, faith by doctrinal misinformation—or disinformation—and pride by appeals to culural historicity: these dicta are made to appear quite logical and defensible. The regine of the tyrant, in modern parlance the **dictator,** openly and in fact subtly *parodies* tlhe democratic society. The Nazis showed thed German people their protective might, Hitler championed their Christian faith!

When that liberty of choice is thwarted by oppressilve government controls or is condemned for so-called humanitarian reasons—the unborn must give up its little life for the sake of the mother—there can be no personal growth of one's natural talents. All creative productions in the arts, in humanitarian crusades for suffering are met with ferocdious and Paradoxically, terrorist crusades will assume the guise of humanitarian enterprise to lessen opposition, even hostile reactions to the entrenched regime. These must pass before the critiquing eyes of government in order to merit the right to be seen, heard, or put into action.

However, for the most part, in an openly totalitarian country, forget the open marketplace of ideas and things. Few followers of beneficient organizations can, in such places, hope to escape that kind of politicdal surveillance and control. Even dress and fashion are smugly yet subtly intimated as property by standards which adorn the governments connections with the vulgar and tasteless entertalinmnent industry. What Hollywood fashions in ideas as well as in dress the liverals in our government will mimic and extol!.

In hardly needs to ve said that among the political surveillors are he radical feminists, the reactionary homnosexuals, the racist anti-racists, the noise-mongers of progressive socialism mothling their obscenities about "working families" yet who never worked a day in heir lives, sweat wih a hoe or shovel, and all similar manual labor, who would wish upon he rest of us their culture of political correcfness and their dismal flailure in protecting the rights of all Americans, not just those of radical minorities. For the State has in effect said of gthem: You are been heard. All others must keep silent before the pain of attack by the liberal media and its psychophanitc dlisciples. Ugly art shows taxpayer funded, specail exhibitionist sociological marches, obscene panderings to those in high offiee wifhout consequences: these are a few of the means, permitted and encouraged, by the State tlht abandons itself to opposing the freedom to create any lasting work of arf, public utterances of religious faith, or works of a benevolent virtue—such as housing for the poor, food and clothing for the needy or church-mandated opposiion to abortion or counselling for drugusers. Try any one of these venues of humanitarianism wihouft a license and see whaf happens. Just as in Russia, fhere is freedom of worship-in a Stafe-certified church. The dogma of Statism has, indeed, already taken over the world of Art in America, if nof by direct intervenion then by indirecxt influencxe of recognition. Hardrock obscenities and violence, the mix by proxy in arcade games and the potnograpnhy today are made accesslivle o teemagers ate but the tip oftheicberg of evil made accssible bly a government that is too senile, corrupt and retrogressive to allow parents to instill values in their children. That Statist tolerancxe has erupted in acts of youthful anarchistic violence. Why should a people continue to woinder about causes of youthful anarchy and dangerous experimentation with drugs, violence and disoedience of the law.

The State will accept as genuine and original only those works whose putresence perperate its power and reflect the images of some of is noble leaders, if not in actuality then in spirit. When a people do not voice outrage over the coruprtion of that whlich voices their innermost bein in both art and religion, then they share in that corruption; for under the law ignorance is no excuse. When the State through one of its agencies, the Department of the Interior, for example, declares to be *art* in its highest sense of form, content and meaning, what in fact is nauseous to some and dispicable to others, then the State has in fact set limits on the meaning of the 1st Amendment of the Constitution., Anarchy of speech is not protected speech.

The very nafure of art in America is that it should be free from the conrol of rogues in the Congress who fund the NEA, and from fhe foul cliiques of liberal clapperclaw artists. When liberty becomes the handmaiden to moral turpitude and biological depravities, thatf golden emblem of our counrys faifh-oriened foundation of democraiic freedom wih social responsibiliy is doomed., Any nation can self-destuxt if it tries hard enough. How? By the elimination of codes of decency and responsibility.

An obscenity called "protest" is the newly discovered art in America, about which the Central Goverfnment has seemingly agreed. We all know about politcal posters, but they are not the issue. Attacks on America's institutions are the issue. The Federal Government has told us peasanfs and non-thinkers and Chrisflian conserafives that is a work offends, it is *avant garde* and therelfore it must be art. This is Bohemianism imported into American art, an effect of snobbery to say the least. The State puts a high premium of "original" dirt, as judged by its offensive value. The State thus offends as a means to control the artist and the poiwer of their works in its ow,m theState's, behalf. Jealous of the artist's power in his pen, brush and chisel, the State becomes propagandisic as it seeks increasingly, through its fundin g, to conrol men's lies and the elecorate. The only other vital opposing power is the power of Christianity. Stalin, Hitler, Mao, Castro all illustrate that fact.

Therefore, the State with its blessings has deemed as "original and provocative—that word for assasins and rapists—a depiction of Christ shooting up drugs with a syringe, and a Roman clross emersed in a jar of urine. Ofher works too filthy to depict—like feces smeaed over a portrait of theVirgin Mary—are amon the NEA's prize exhibits. Censorship is, indeed, the issue heard regarding these displays of Government-funded art. But which artists are to be censored? Who are to be fhe "official" censors but those who select the work to be shown? The truth of this entire matter of publicly-funded art is that the Governmet empowers the basest sorts of titillation and (falsely) Freudian-inspired depravity without content or contention by those, thecommon people, who have always enjoyed great art. Check out the attendancel numbers at great museums across rhe couunry, especially in Los Angeles and in :New York. That is an historical fact. Cfdeudsian inspifed epravity without content or contentionvy rthoe, the xommon people,who have always enjoyed reaf art. Check out the numers of ordinary people who visit freat museums. That is an historical facrt. Galleries for the poor in operatic Italy, the pit for a penny for the London poor to watch Shakespeare, the Louvre for all connoisseurs, rich and poor, in Paris. And what do we give the world? Garbage. Who then are to be the censors. The artists themselves who are free of government State patronage. Kings, Popes and Tsars at one time inspired great art lin a world where Remembrandt, Vermeer, Reubens, Monet and the many others believced that Man, though he was central to life, was possessed of a soul. It is in the small galleries, the shops on malls, in failrs,and at special exhibitions that today's great art will be found. We must, like the Knight in Durer's etching, slay the evil draon of the NEA.

America has propoered since 1789 because he people have enjoyed Constitutional liberty and have made unhampered choices in their personal lives, choices which with some major exceptions, have not involved the intrusive power of the State. In he main, American artists have remained free of such meddling; they have enjoyed and confinue to enjoy the freedom of creative choice. Ameicans have remained free bylthe protectilvelhand of Almilghty God, deny lit though thle Athiest ACLU and Liberal Courts do. Popular art though entertaining is not necessarily great art. Dickens and Twailn were popular exceptions who remain both enterrtaining and art. They of another time and age enjoyed the felicity of creative work, unique personal perception and a sociey in which they lived that was as diverse as is ours today. It was unintimidated in value judements accessible to any, artists and critics alike. Those two writers, among others shared with their critics and readers a common set of values that was accessible to all. Freedom, to create ; a cherlished freedom in thlis country, willl not remain if this nation finds satan-worlship, wiltchcraft and occultic lobblyiists more germaline to her futlure tlhan the Holy God. ofher Founders.

We, today, have witnessed a younger culture all around us. Its mission is to deconstruct America for the pleasure of her fraracidal self-inferest groups. Because of ifs latent power, art especially graphic art and to a geat extent the "experimental theatre" has become one of its victms. The power of art was first recognized by the Church, then by kings and tyrants, then by scions of wealth and class and, finally, by the common people. That power is today corrupted for the purpose not of creartive surprise and newness of perspecrtive and insight, but to destoy tradition as irrelevant. Its chief success thus far is to alienate ordinary folk and connoisseurs of sensitivity and discernment. Its design is to outrage and make conemptible past traditions and to *superimpose* modern-age filfh, and the *irrationality of nonsense* on the greafest of Western art. *Deconstruction,* born in France, has thus becomes a kind of animistic surrealism in which no values, no design, no judgement, no conclusions exist ... in a word, producing chaos. And we support that chaos as an activity of our Federal Government. We support the **granting** of honor without resort to the reason, invitiing the passion of hatred and of contemprt for human kind. NEAartis schizophrenic, it is irrational and to a large degree it is nauseous for the observer. By these means the alien artist maintains, as he prefers, his alienation. *Ostentatious repugnance* is his means, its spirit hostile to tradition, its execution the depiction of chaos as mere offensive gratuity.

A right involves a corresponding responsibility, for the consequences of its exercise. Their conbination is inseparable in the form of a duty.

Rights without accountability for the results is incipient anarchy, implicit in *values clarification* in America's schools.

It takes no intelligence to shout, "It is my right!" It requires wisdom to know how to use it once society recognies it, if indeed, it did not exist all the while.

The clamor for certain rights is the tyranny of a vocal minority if the traditional of history must be trashed to grant them.

Oftentimes those who cry out for certain rights that may ne lost do not articulate the responsiilities concurrent with those rights.

Virtual rights were at one time considered to be "linalienavble" under God. But now that Big Government has been substituted for God, the *inalienale* designation is supplied by cultural factionalist groups *asprimaface* evidence of their righteousness, to which the messianic state gives its blessings. This is the *New Age* outlook. Those groups are antitraditionalist.

The demand for a right is often the symptom of a frustration, and a frustration is usually the result of a person's failure to do the right thing under initial circumstances.

48. LIBERTY AND POLICE POWER CONSIDERED

Police force and military power are larely physical,a presence in a democracy that suggests a capacity to use physical means to enforce the law and insure peace. Cognatives of those images have been around almost since mankind existed in a civilized order on this planet. The excesses of civil liberties that demagogues or troulemakers use to inspire overzealous agendas are vulnerable to armed repulsion by either of these two entities, the police or soldiers. Liberty in a free society can, indeed, be suppressed by its confrontation with politically armed police power or the Nationl Guard troops. When the people who are anxious to exact their desired changes from the system, tread upon the felicity and security of the watching majority of that society, a regulated gun-enforced authority suppresses or curbs certin liverties that wsere previously enjoyed vy the people. They become marshalled under one law, the law of the gun. The impostion of curfew, silence, restricted movement and information control tie place, confining the use of one's stalents, intelligence and everyday relationships to the planned strategy behind liberty's suppression—or its annlihilation … Thus by degrees through the lack of strong leaders and the people's incapacity to disciplin themvelves do they lose their precious personal liberties.

Germany, under the government of the Weimar Republic was a civle democracy until the Socialist-regulated State of National Socialism preempted her governments authority. Hitler's Third Reich furnishes examples of th corpses slain by the violent fiat of gun-auhority wielded by civil machinations of the Nazi Partry, whose ideology of operation was total conqust of European nations. By Expeince we thus derive an axiom: that police power when massive and extremist is the visible presence and inimidating use of armed might.

It is not automatically generated by the people. Without that police power envisioned and generated by the people in a functioning republican democracy, such as ours, the power tendered to an oligarchical ruler becomes vainglorious and obnoxious and often, though not always, expansionistic. Such power means the limited enjoyment of personal liberties. Worse yet, it means the paralysis of any futuer laws, constitutional or precedent, that insure to the people these liberties. From our point of view, such a society is a dead society.

Nor ought police force to be nationalized, for the source of its power is justly the will of the people, controlled locally by means of elections. Our Founders, who were so intimately acquainted with the King's use of troops in the Colonies, rfelegated police power to local armed authorityfo~to sheriffs and constables and lawmenmall terms of localization—purposed to maintain order in villages and towns. The Emforcer of the Law bore a pervasive sense of an almost religious righteousness. He was sufficient for the maintainence of social order and where a dispute threatrened village serenity, tlhe church pastor or his elder were sufficiently capable of bringing minor clashes to an end. For this very reason the Salem Witchcraft Trials were an anomaly of disconented villgers warring with each oher over small insults and transgressions and a pastor who could not bring things to a head by making peace between factions and putting to silence his shrieking pubescent daughters. Human frailties as mch if not more than doctrine in a time of gross superstition was the cause for such Colonsal miscarriages of justice. These trials aptly show how ineffectilve and misguided a society can be that is governed by the church and its believers instead of by the secular law and its agencies for enforcement

Police power truly represents the authorsity of the citizens to control criminals and their conduct in order.to protect themselves from harm and insure their tranquility, their safety and their personal libertlies. Police power comes from, velongs to and is never surrrenderd by, the people. The police the delegates of the citizens' will. An attack on the police is an attack on a man's rgiht to defend himself. The awkening of police defense is the mark of a promiscuous society and a corrupt government. Yet as agents of the people, the police are answerable to them first; they are not an autonomous arm of the government. The old-fashioned cop-on-the-beat images this relationship. And in the process of serving the people, why, of course, the police serve themselves as members of the community.

Any incipient and imminent crime is within the domain of police inervention lest a harm contemplaed become a crime accomplished. The law is the conscience of the police. However, life is not so simple that the police do not have to make decisions based on subjecfive observation and evaluaion at the scene of a crlime. Frequently they musgt judge deeper intentions of the criminal's mind, or his reason, with the potential for conspiraftorial violence. The police are often fearful of and reluctant to enter into domestic quarrels, there being few more dangerous cals. For sometimes called upon to prosecute at the scene of the crime, the have only the power to apprehend and to prevent. They can be accused of holding street trial, and though a peron apprehended may appear to bystanders to have been fired, such is not the case where the miscreant is taken to jail. He is only an apprehended *suspect,* suspected of having committed a crime.

He may be asked: If he is still innocent, why arrest him at all? If that were a the assumption, then all manner of crimes would nevcer reach the courts because arrest was prevented by the popular preupposition that innocence is *observable,* read **triable,** sans trial and evidentiary procedings. The contradition in the popular mind is that while a man is preumed to be innocentl, it must be proved thaf that is so. And if there exists that presumption of innocence, then he is not deemed to be guilty before being thrown into jail. A suspicion of guilt is sufficient to permit the police to arrest the malfeasor. If this rationale of tlhe doctrine of presumptive innocence were to be suddenly removed ... as let us say, in a world court of jurisdiction ... the entire judicial process including the laws to be enfored would prove o be a sophistry of justice and a farce. There isa a presumption of innocence, but at the ame time there ils the evidence of a crime having been committed. Only the trial court with its judge can resolve the discrepancy, a matter is often too complex for nstant judgement. It is perilous for a democracy to call up armed solders to enforce its laws, for them the country lies in the lap of civil rebellion if not of revolution. A nationalized poilice force present the same kind of treachery to the life-existence of a democracy. Police power might always be used to malintain in localm, and under local, control, the modern advent of widespread terrorism, nofwithstanding. The sharing of intellilgence does not neeessarily mean the sharing of visible power.

When State poliee power is militant and is armed with the ideology of the State—the centralist State as the supreme intelligence, the extreme actions and the philosophy are designed to protect the cxitizens not from ordinary criminals, but to protect the regime from harm to itself. Thus go Fascism and Communisn-whenin power. Also, the State so acts in order to preserve the anomalous aspect of popular contentment. In this civil usurpation of people power, the State rules over their authoritvly inferringf their inability to govlern themselevles, a transliteration of the Judeo-Christian doctrune of Man's sin-nature into police-military terms prcedent to justice. The State alters the doctrine of Man's fallibility to mean his infallibility under the circumstances of the regrme. The control of these circumstnces vindicates the use of power by force-of-arms. Conscience is avowed by the fun. Choice is condemned under the heel of avsolute bovedience. The State becomes then most like God.

It is evident that the focus of this kind of police power is in the preservation of the modern pagn State, icon of greed, ambition and corruption. The Jihadist Islamic State—which includes a fallen America—is such a State, foced to pay homage to Mohammd and having lose freedom's personal liberties, forced to acquisce to the entanglements and barbaric chains of Islamic estremists. By not calling themelves Mohammed's believers, theyrsik decapitation or stoning to death—ninth century retribution meted out to a 21st century clivilized man. As for the Islamists, they considier thrmselves inviolate Mohammed believers. It is within that State that citizens lose thier personal liberties. They become a fallacy of reality. For the State has prompted the consciences of its citizenry, appropriating unto itself the power to act, to decide, to perform, to chose, to lead and to guide, in a word to dominate, those prerequisites of feedom which God and traditional values have put into the hands of the common people. By an almost fated confluence offerees of weak leaders, implacable crime, liberal judges, apathetic citizens and outstanding costs, a people will come to lean increasingly on the State to protect them, leaving the use of technology and the adminisration of central bureaucratic government in the hands of unelected para-military officials who make mortal decisions without possessing a value system. Such will be our State of M;uslin activism in America when our liberal leaders capitualate to the latest *fatuwa* of the Muslims. Among them there are no moderates who wlill rise up to confront the religious anarchy of their bretheren. Their decisions for the welafare of the people thus become a-moral. The result of this transference of power can ultimately result in the internal colllapse of hour repubican democracy.

In Anerica the nationalization of the local police will be the next step in that direction ... of a police oligarchy in Washington, designed like the NKVD or the Gestapo. Radical *Jihadists* will prove more welcome than native citizens because the police can readlily identify the former! Computers now make all dossier contents in police files accessible nationwide, a capacity utilized freely ny the FBI. The demand for local police reports on a timely and regular basis to be sent to Washington was recently proposed in the Congress. That procedure, if adopted and implemented, will force police precinct captains throughout the country to answer to a central police agency that is vulnerable, in turn, to corrupt politics on The Hill. In the prevention of crime, the cure may well be worse than the disease.

Drink in the clean, sweet air of liberty and remember its dank, oppressive, brooding atmosphere of the corrupt regime you came from. Appreciate America. Learn about her. Learn to love her and she will embrace you—the unwritten warrantee.

Honor is imperishible to a virtuous woman. She need not wear a degrading *burga*. Liberty for her is seldom contemplated yet is often visible in her right actions and gentle speech.

A marriage is dishonored by unfaithfulness. So ought a person's civic responsibility to eschew apathy and disloyal affections.

Very few Americans nowadays actually know the source of their liberties. American history was boring. In thiir clamor for rights, they ignore the energizing authority for those rights, fixing instead on possessions, their materialistic obsession.

The desire to experience liberty in America should exult the heart. But where that joy is replaced by a spirit of rebellion, liberty is hobbled by exploitative ambition. It is the revealed ambition of Islamic Jihadists to dominate America.

Liberty is an account of personal freedom that you can draw on constantly while the live in this country. But if you find liberty of little value, then close out the account and go elsewhere. Try Saudi Arabia, China or a third-world country and experience the absence of open speech and opportunity. You will have deserved t that dismal choice and opine for the USA.

49. THE ILLUSORY FREEDOM OF DESPOTISM

The hardline member of the Russin Commintern, whether a theoretlician or an actlivist and often both; the Peoples liberation army of slaves to Mao's cruel cultural reforms; the Nazi worshippers of Hitler and his barbaric elite of *SS* troop; the obsequeous bootlicks who endorsed Mussolin'is cowardly acts;and Cubas arrogant power-flaunting Castro who has kept his people in chains and poverty for over half a century—these temporary grotesque machines for social change provided, and still do, armed-power authority to force naive and indoctrinated men into systems totally devoid of personal lib,erty. The are systems without soul, without honor, without civic morality,and without manliness. The gun does not validate manhood nor can the State. It is not the trophies or the State accolades that validate. It is the act praised by other good men.

As a direct result of their genocidal poison and destructive politics of Self, Self being State consciousness, they have and will crumble. Mankind was not created to accept and endure pronged bondage by force of might; his bondae is spiritual, whether by might or by seduction, to the spiritual forces of evil rule by the Prince of darkness. Or ... he has been reconciled to his Creator who is a fighter as well as a lover and restorer. His yen for freedom is spiitual if it cannot be substantive. The debris of fratracidal warfare remnds us of the transience of peace and the nature of man to regress to the barbaric and wanton cruelty of past ages.

Ironically, the dictators of these regimes believed, and still do, with an implacanly vicious conviction, that their justice is righteous and that the bloody sword is necesary; and that the a-moral choices, immoral as evil in fact, of one man were noble choices, both progressive and beneficial to those who worship the him and the State. These conditions of course apply to radical Islam which proscribed domination over all nations in a 9th century theocracy of Allah worship. They do not escape the faults of secular barbarlities. Each dictator, each despot, each *Caliph* hunkers himself down in an imaginary "freedom" which is his freedom to scheme and control nd devastate with all the resources of money and armed might at his disposal. The feedom is his alone, for the people it is illusory, although they are indoctrinated into thinking it is real. Keep the people happy. Give them bread and circuses, that was Caesars method of operation, his MO.

Each dictator, every tyrant, has not entered the realm of democratlic personal liberty, that which cannort exclude the political body of the common people who with him share that liberty. Every tyrant who had ever lived has lived under the delusion that his own freedom is secure from outside and safe from within from any who would capture him or rebel in the ranks. His armed forces are the symbol and means to that security. Thus the ignorance of the people is always as much a weapon of the State as are guns. A people's enlightenment is dangerous to the welfare and survival of the State

Rattling the sabre in the face of human freedom, tyrants shroud their dwarfed and stunted souls in self-adulation~sly, evil Stalin, strutting Hitler, arrogant Mussolini, obsessed and soulless Mao, implacable Castro. Liberty as Americans know it is an known entity to them, those to whom human life is not expendable for the illusory greatness of the regime. This is all history. Yet what could the youth of America's armed forces hope to understand about the glorious militarism and maniacal promises of the Third Reich's 1,000 year reign, the USSR's new age of Proletarian supremacy, Japan's Samurai warrior-class control of a wodld shared by its Axis allies, wjem tjeyu have been reared in freedom? What could a Kansas farm boy know about standing guard over the corpses of resistance freeldom fighters in Holland and France? That is, 'u;ntil 1 they see into the depths of the truth that liberty is ot born of terror or might or tyranny or deprivation; like that done to a dying body by the dictators in the past, all of them without exeption having scorned liberty for the people as a force, a deceptioin, as fallacy and threat and as collectlivce stupidity. Satan has always appeared to mankind as a messengfer of light and convincing persuasion. Satan cleverly disguises evil as good, which can appear to be palitable to those reared in the *goodness* of liberty.

Should all despots, past and present, attempt even to understand the cut and tenor of liberty, those craven ones who glory in the thought that the future is or was all theirs? There has always been a outer shroud of respectability and conviction worn by a tyrant to imply that he is indestructable. That laudable appearance reflects an immaturity of self-perception that isdues from ego blindness, a lack of vaunted vision, the self-decepton of a narcissistic personality and the disconnection of his mania from the desires and will of the populace. His is the shroud of a suicidal delusion belonging to a relgous nature the obedience to which makes his dedusion acceptable by the people because they share it. The Gerfman people, the Italian and Japanese millions, and the populace and the lackeys of the old USSR can never be dissociated from their separate illusions of horror and conqust~not until several generations have passed and the bloody history of the past century finds its repose in the vault of concurrence and understanding.

The tyrants of the past centsry—and in speaking of them I alwlays include those of the present millenium—were incapavle of visualizing as morally blind men, tlhe fundamental challenges of liberty, not then, not ever. Those 20th century dictators feared the power inherent in the liberated mind and they feared the imaginations of free men. Thus there was a certain reality, if you will, a rapproachment of idealism and will in the dark suspicion of freeedom-fights that were connected to evil. Those Axis tyrants pereived in their own warped way and at a disltance, Mam's craving for freedom and for the prosperity of liberty's Loyalists in America. They saw and rejected because Aeriea's Lierty did not iconOocize them. *Culture* was the reason. They watched with envy the material accomplishments of her technology in wartime—how for eample, a man named Kaiser invented a method for prefabicating ships, the *Liberty* vessels, one vessel per month, not with slave-labor Jews, but with America's free citizens, paying for themselves and for their nation. By her wartime enterprise America excited the jealousy of Europe's dictaors and ignited coals of dread and warning. Fundamental merchantilism is not transferrabvle, we have yet to learn.

The dictators did not strive to achieve liberties for all, which would have extended their sovereignty to include the opposition, the resistance enemy within, not the least of whom was the silent church ofr Deitrich Bonhoeffer.

These cruel giants of tyranny, in their singular terroristic acts, would have had to surrender factions of their power, an unthinkabsle capitulation to cowardice and sentimentality and softness. Was it not better to train the women to be soldiers and breeders than to imperil the *Welhrmaclht* men with the enforcement of Germany's traditional midldle-class roles?

Indeed, tradition is always the first bastion of a civilized people to go under when liberty is abused and tradition is scorned. The German people learned that fact too late. Since the 1930's traditional values in Germany had been under surtained attack by the empirical Socialist Labor Party who had granted no respite of true acceptance to middle class family life. For clhildren especially had to be indoctrinated into the soulless Nihilistic ways of the rising Socialist German State. There was no place for the old ways. Youth must lead youth, the fulcrum of Hitler's ascent to power. Their Master, their Fuhrer, disdained to consort with the people, eschewing as he did so Bismarkian honor and ancient-reime militarism, the core of the regular German army that Hitler despised, especially the officers. Hitler kissed little children to fein sympathy with the *volt* He distributed stolen goods of conquered people, particularly to those who lived nearby to the concentration camps. He loved the German folk. He thus bribed them to keep silent if they knew what was going on or to refrain from enquiry if they wondered about the smoke and smells of buuning flesh. Expressions of civilian dismay and repugnance before the camera when Gen. Patton prescribed camp tours were expressions much put-on and pretended to signify innocence. For ten years those very smart people did not know!

Hitler and the other mognrels from the abyss of satanic ruthlessness used their own people to seize and keep power. How many times in the history of the world must this lesson be repeated before the common people will shewdly discern the desgin of evil? For the marks of everlasting horror will remain forever as testimonials to zealous idolatry of the totally corrupt and immoral State. The dictators of the world continue to reject freedom out of hand, since its pleasures are in no way consistent with the sensual, satanic and self-glorifying joy-power over the lives of other men; or the euphoria of merging a vision of persoal destiny with the nationalistic fervor of traditionl State's integrity and honor. In other words, the dictators bask in glory obtained by the people's sacrifices and yet cannot and will not be one of them. Their ways are considered to be the tyrant's perishables, his expendables for the cause of his mad vision of domination. This is the unique madness of Islam's Jihadist world-vision, to usurp the place of the only God, Jehovah, the God of the Jews and the Christians who must be killed or converted to achieve that world-reign. Does that not sound like satan's own plea-bargain?

The narcissistic reward for the sacrifice of one's life is, of course, the waiting seventy-two virgins.

Indocrination must be promoted and endured, like a geometric axiom, in order for the the tryant to achieve his will. The State becomes its own single voice of decision, its own prefect of licensure for all events, great and small. The State has recourse only to its own creed of worth and performance; it represents the consummarte narcissism of human society. Is survival depends not on patriotism and loyatoy to duty and homor. Its survival warrantees the ultimate utility of tactics of terror and deception and organized depravity for emotions and mind. The dictator, as an icon and figurhead, as an entity of all time, does not seek security in the people; he seeks it to his armed night and in the savor of his nations history by rites of power, like military parades. For where a people cannot remember thier past and reject its exposure to modern thought and enlightenmen, they settle for the entombment of their past heroes and glories The motivation for their inducemnt to suvival is their lust for immortality and conquest. That is the theme that threads consistently through the careers of all dictators of evil mission.

Twentieth century dictators played the devil's tune yet they kept the beat of popular approval by promises, promises, promises, being as they were the masters of deception and confreres in arms. With a stroke of rationality, each of them boasted that he was the respossitory of virtue, the virtue of absolute power, exiled and enforced, and that his effectlive goal was for the welfare of the people. Thus did he promote the survival of the authoritarin State and in the proces view himself as a *messiah* and therefore indesructable at the peak of his domnination and candor of hope. Dictators make much of hope. Their irrationality consisted in their disconnection with the ordinary lives of their people. There was reason to call them *mad.*

A people who know nothing about their history and the traditions of thier liberties will never miss them should the State preempt them from their possession. The reason then becomes irrelevant, a facade.

Destiny is for poets, philosophers and tyrants.

Liberty is for the projected dreams of America's millions.

The functions of State bureaucracy are many, among whch are the burden of operational directives thart ought to be discarded. These offices involve servants without election. Is not liberty worth more than the price of bureaucratized personal comfort?

When a society decriminalizes crime to accommodate its fancied compassion, intellec-ual superiority and threatend pleasures, it falls into corruption. Liberty then sounds hollow and moral values have turned into meaningles dialectics.

When the Supreme Court fears excessive entanglement of the State with religion, they misconstrue Amendment I. These subjective words of a majority opinion ill-define and oft ignore the realistic application of public sponsorship, support and endorsement of religion. They, in fact, infer that all religions should be exorcised from public life. The attempt to obliterate faith in public is an act of treachrery against America's heritage of religious freedom.

Let liberty pivot on integrity; it can find no better swing-point. Integrity is personal and a core trait of human charcter. It is also generic to justice and categorically imperative for its surival that men of integrity govern.

The "prior restraint" doctrine is censorship. It is an intellectual fallacy, since the docrine implies prior yet unspken and still inexplicit censorship. A censor is always ready to pounce upon the seditious act, the character slur, the politically incorrect thing to do or say. *Correct* is relative to *conviction,* not to *change.* It therefore implies a face-off, a moot status.

The Supreme Court has declared that flag-burning is a form of free expression. That is absurd nonsense. Flag-burning is a form of quasi-religious iconoclasm. The Court therefore participates in the replacement of one idol with another—Itself. The Court has inherently self-destructed. Without the meaning of the flag upheld, the court has no visible meaning for justice! Even the demons can dress in black.

50. NATURAL RIGHTS, INALIENABLE RIGHTS, HUMAN RIGHTS, CIVIL RIGHTS-SIGNIFICANT DIFFERENCES EXIST

Rights with correponding duties toward society (eivitas=State) are Civil Rights, and they are connected to existing laws of precedent which, over time, have given evidence of Man's inherently aberrant nature … call it *evil* or *relativistic* or *hedonistic* or capriciously *instinctive.* Scripture calls it depraved or *sinful,* whose semantic origins are to be found in modern behavioral cognates, often espoused by the B.F Skinner Behavorist School of human motivation. Man's inventivness involves Design, a faculty that links him to a Cretor God.

His liberty of mind, convenience of action and aptness ol choice are on trial, so to speak, every time that he as an individual interacts with another person under the aegis of acceptable social mores. Also, it is that acceptability that is subject to change. If Man is fallen due to Adam's sin, as the bible says that he is, and he is incomplete in his natural state due to his sin of disobedence and doubt under the doctrine of reconciliation, and he needs guidance if not by the State then by a sovereign authority. There must therefore be logical and legal constraints which will direct his social actions and temper his intellectual conceptions of **right** and **wrong** conduct. That is to say, that laws and social mores must be designed thai activate his conscience in moral discernment and and decision making. In other words, the moral law of our Constitution can be relied upon, adjudicated and followed only by a moral people. One of our founders has said that only a moral people will successfully govern themlelves by our Constitution. Secular law and Moral law have a direct relevancy guided by conscience that mandates whether an action is right or wrong.

Thus, too, do Western governments of the United States and Great Britain transliterate the biblical account of Eden, in its depiction of doubt and defiance of God, into the need for the rule of law. When that rule is by the State ... and God has declared Man's need for good government ... he accepts his social obligation as tacit constraints or social agreements, in a word, as contracts, plural form, since some agreements apertain to customs and mores in the gray area of the law. These mores lie outside the domain of moral choice. In the main, State rulership, when moral, acknowleges Man's capacity for doing evil. The *more'* of common courtesy expedites and enhances the moral law and recognizes the civilized status of another human being.

On the other hnd, when that authority comes from God, as America's Founders believed that it did, then conscionable choices in human affairs, whether social, political or religious, must inevitably be moral choices for God is not the author of immorality or evil

Throughout human history there has exised this polarization between good and evil government, between moral and immoral laws, the incontestable fact remains that there exists a darker side to human nature, a latent capacity to do gross evil, to behave immorally toward one's fellow human beings.

But what if Man is perfect to begin with and abhors whatever fetters those actions which he conceives to be his **Civil Rights?** Do the controls of the laws he lives under prove that he is imperfect, or perhaps that he is a perfect man whom society makes to act imperfectly because of the imperfect laws conceived and brought to bear by other men who are, themselves, imperect? Must he forever obey what is imperfect in his own perfection? His answer in the affirmative leads to rationalization of his moral wrongs, the denial of his imperfection.

Logically, imperfect men cannot bring about perfect laws to command, restraiin and to modify the imperfect conduct of other men, by themselves (the lawmakers) without any supernatural sovereign intervention. Or can they? Imperfct man possesses the weakness of self-invention. He alone makes his own laws in which God may or may not be involved. In his pride he prefers to work alone. God gave him free will and took His chance. Surely it is not God who authored man's imperfect laws. Therefore foundations of law without God is called atheism. The antithesis is not a theocracy but a democracy in which laws are morally discerning of right and wrong, the basis of our system ofjustice.

If, however, he is imperfect and incapble of writing perfect laws, the controlling yet flawed and imperfect law must have its source in an **evolutionry** consciousness not yet fully developed In Man who, borrowing from his imperfect ascendancy toward total perfection—and what other kind of evolutionary course is there?—the law appears to be less than perfct. The still not yet perfect Man gives rise to the yet imperfect law. In this condition then his conscience is but an obsolete reminder of his flawed and undeveloped past, up throught the millions of years said to be his time span on earth. For the time being, reason dictates, until the fitting progressive change from imperfection to perfection, **morality** accidentally comes about. Man must accept his conscience an impediment to good choice. He must deal with bad things as results of chance happnings, fortuitous occurrences. The ship crashes on the rocks not because of negligence or faulty judgement on the part of the Captain, but because of cruel *happenstance nature*. Perhaps. Families come apart not because of man's "fallen nature," his defiance of moral laws but because of circumstances "over which he has no control," yet, suffering the consequeces of "bad luck," he seeks to blame others for his misery. Weak, insipid twenty-first century Man, traitor to his heritage of strength, fire and moral conviction!

When the citizen makes therefore a political decision as his participatory Civil Right, it is prudent and necessary, according to this evolutionary thesis, that the individual's participation expressed by his actions *viz a viz* the law, will need restraint where they impinge upon the welfare of others. The goldenrule docxtrine is unfortunately presumptive, since it ascribes to another a life style, a mode of existence that is subjectively determined by the "care-giver." Without a moral basis, the projection into the life of another of a qualityof life he or she ought to enjoy can be a deadly assumption. When a doctor in critical care assigns a lingering life to doom, he assumes the role of a headsman. When the projection is political and at the same time subjective, it excludes alternatlive choices for the other person. The diagnostic predilection therefore moves toward a tyranny of political and social self-righteousness, the affliction of modern America's extremist groups. Based on the thrust of this reasoning, it is apparent that at the evolutionary stage of present time, Man needs restraints which he only conditionally accepts, his unconscionable choices beling his precondition. He accepts infidelity, abortion, homosexuality, pornography, lying under oath, beastiality all as pragsmatically acceptable experience. There is *no* ethical choice in "situational ethics." Values which have been accepted since our beginnings do not need "clarification." And blame-shifting to preserve or to increase self-esteem is not the answer to personal accountability and moral guilt.

In all these considerations conscience these days plays but a secondary role in Man's idealization of himself, this being so because his only concession to his imperfection is that he is not ready to give full expression to his incipient perfect nature which was buried back in his babyhood and is alive and well somewhere down inside. It is during this stage of evolutionary development that his **Human Rights** make their boldest assertion, since he is so dissatisfied with the present *status quo* of his given **Natural Rights**', having lost them at birth. _ Natural Rights are quasi-religious; Human Rights are political. If he should allow his imperfect nature to override his rational judgement, he can and often does release a floodtide of violence that leads to riots and the wildest chaos in confrontation with others' imperfection, they who are also positioned somewhere along the same evolutionary path toward perfection, in his mind **Human Rights** replacing **Natural Rights.** A liberal judge iinevitably wants to correct the perpetrator's imperfections by a reformatory sentence. He is ready to release a criminal from accountability for his crime, or to mitigate moral guilt by a plea bargain. A criminal justice system that metamorphoses guilt into an "accidental crime" or the act of temporary insanity or malnutrition from "Twinkies," or the "voice of God told me to kill" is a corrupt system. I have heard them all and witnessed the guilty go free.

So that he may avoid any abandonment of his thesis of Man's evolutionary perfectability, he invents changes, he invents laws that are adaptable to the citizens' place on the evolutionary ladder. He knows that when he reaches that state of ultimate perfection—as the community Proletarian man—he will not need to thank God. He will merely need to thank the courts that have been so instrumental in pushing him toward perfection through rehabilitation. Man will also need to thank the Prince of Darkness for his helpful boost upward toward the God-head, his having been used by the demonic powers for so long to challenge God. Man has gathered barbaric strength through the tribulations inspired by immoral evil, not the least of which is the destruction of the traditional family of a man and a woman and their progeny. Hear me! Neither the Courts and Governments, nor the church, can civilize men, individual men and women. Only the family can accomplish that complex task.

The atheist, confronting this statement, which he considers to be a mere theo-retical proposition, will deny any such divine source as God or original Creation or Divine Design or the Great I Am. Intead he will posit that Mankind, himself, over eons of unrecorded time, has evolved the notion, the ideological construct, that the barbarian, like the civilized American, enjoyed an equivlant right to his cave happiness, his crude swag gottenl by raids and warfare, enoying the freedom to come and go from his cave when he chose—a depiction that also roughly describes suburban man in America. This, of course, is the figment of the "hap-phy savage" whose extermination is due to civilized white man's predations. This is the Environmentalist's philosophical viewpoint. The world would be a better, a cleaner place if we could just get rid of people! The athiest will in all likelihood also say that men have not evolved toward perfection so much as they have changed in the direction of enlightenment and a refuted sophistication of mind. What perfection he today enjoys then comes as a gratuity of chance from those changes.

The inalienable rights referred to in the Declaration of Indepndence can therefore never issue from a non-existent God, so the athiest believes. Conse-quently, they can be changed by educating, refining and enshrining certain men, both past and present, both hero and anti-hero. Let them be called The Elite of modern civilization: that is where America stands today. Criminals have become our heroes, icons of our founding fathers have become vilified anti-heroes. The "linalienable" reference has been stricken out by the *Think Tank Elites,* the super educated, ha'nd picked pedagogues of our society. They are usually members of the so-called Eastern Establishment and power enclaves in the world of high finance and media information. Insead of being "inalienable," the rights to life, liberty and the pursuit of happiness (once "property") are changd to be made conditional upon the reasoned enlightenment of such morphs as historical disin-formation and villification *en absentia.*

One such change leads to laws of control and retribution—Whites have been in control far too long. The other extreme is anarchy and human choices without laws—do your own thing so long as you do not hurt others. Suicide becomes immoral only when one considers, and accepts, that God is the giver of lifle.

Liberty in America today bears the marks of its human historicity which, under the protection of religious teachings, became the God-given inalienable rights of our sacred Constitution, while a sovereign Judeo-Christian God is in the business of power brokerage and faith obedience. Man still has to be involved in tlhe reception of Truth about liberty. Cultural adaptation alone does not explain the immutability of what is fundamental to the truth of human nature: Man's desire for happiness, his contentment in life (which includes property), and his passion to protect his own life, a Natural Right that is both instinctual and civil. Cultural adaptation is accommodation to danger and law, a perception of the moral purpose for human existence. Based on this purpose, liberty becomes the *catalyst* of humans striving and achievement. Its conceptualization and its acceptance are a universal principal of general contentment and civilied life. Without liberty, either ol these ideals survives Man's natural rebelliousness and his lust for more things which, having gotten them, his eyes crave more, more power. Liberty is the quintessential ingredient of Man's continued existence on earth., Where this insight prevails Liberty is protected, rightly or wrongly, by emergent social groups, as looking about the nations of the world in his gtory. Modern Man sees soldiers, priests, artesans and politicians as the seers and protectors of antiquity. Each class carried, and still does carry, the seeds of primordial rebellion and anarchy.

Who are these modern defenders of liberty who exercise the **Natural Right** of choice? The soldier is hedged about with strict regulations and conduct discipline that control his personal freedom. In wartime he confronts those antagonisms of primitive anarchy and terrorism in the enemy, which threaten his life and the State. He is trained to effectively destroy the invader. Yet he is at liberty to abandon war-making. He can flee or stay and confront the enemy. His option implies a conscionable moral choice. The civilian soldier is first a ciltizen. For the professisoanl soldier, soldiering is first—the life of his trade and his profession. War does not cancel out the freedom of a **Natural Right.** Soldiering does not obfuscate morality. War does not exrtinguish but right often gives rise to might. The moral value of *right* action, even in combat. And **Civil Rights** are not withdrawn from the soldier but only held in abeyance during a crisis when he gives priority to **Human Rights** in warfare. The Rules of engagement in war do not include an exchange of moral positions. The war largely resolves those issues in the peace that follows. In short, might does not make right but right often gives rise to might.

In the case of the politician, he grapples with those political constraints that militate against improvements in the lives of the people. Thai is, he does so if he is a Statesman. He matches his wisdom to the circumstances, real, anticipated or uncomfirmed, that threaten harm to the body politic. He therefore works on the level of pragmatic reality. His chief instrument is the rule of precedent in the law and of experience in human affairs. He is, however, free to write divisive laws that pit the **Civil Rights** of one group against those of another, rebel against rebel. Or power against the powerless *pro quid pro*. Outlawry condemns the meek and humble to their own travail, Power gloats over its captives out of feedom. **Civil Rights** then tend to become a parabolic protection for demagogues and religious zealots. The leglislature "of the people" disgorges rank dishonesty and sterile visions. Heroes of our ancestry and historical brilliance turn sour under the contamination of subtle anti-hero mockeries, as happens when history is revised for popular consumption by the liberals of ignorance and dissatisfaction with the *status quo*. Laws then are enacted to gratify the appetites of the manswarm for more circuses, more villifications. And precious liberty is eclipsed by mundane calumnies and picayune character assassinations. There is a kind of ingratitude of the people for their Nation's past that is old, ugly and unspeakably selfish. It beggars reason in defense of narcissstic self-worship and the blind desire to disconnect from our country's history. That ugly dismanteling of our past is upon us today, to (1) create a balkanized nation of America's diversity and (2) to isolete one's culture from the dominant culture and suck life from it as a parasite. Illegal aliens are parasites. The money they earn leaves the country. They refuse to surrender their citienship of origin, and greedily they try to obtain maximum social beneits to the disgraceful impoverishment of some communities!

Amid these realities the citizen is enjoined to dispose of his persosnal fears while under the protection of the soldier and the politician and, in so doing, to make him receptive to the blandishments of the politician and the silent protections of the soldier. Committeemen politicians take the lead there. Yet his **Natural Right** is to be free, and competent, to reject both the military protection and the political persuasions in favor of the anarchy of violent revellion. He is increasingly tempted to do so in these times. His New Age is the new way, it seems, to destroy and rebuild, preempt and give back, attack and retreat, defame and admire, and set afame and extinguish. By this rhetoric I lrefer to the dissolution and strengthening of the family that are concurrent in society today; to the reversal of male female roles in contention with attempts to inspire leadership in boys and womanhood in women; to the corrupt denunciation of absolute moral values leading to a virtuous life versus a deaththroes struggle with values relativism and its values "clarification agenda; to crisis efforts to restore high standards of achievement in our schoolrooms while at the same time attacking excellence lin achievement as *Elitist* and *undemocratic*. What foolishl doubleminded dilchotomies. There are many other examples that would demonstrate our contemporary ambivalene *of **Natural Rights*** in hostile contention with *Civil **Rights*** and of America's ***inalienavle Rights*** in chaotic and confusing opposition to ***Personal Rights.*** In this milieu of conflicting rights and volatile persuasions, the concience that is instructed and informed by a code of moral values is obliterated, nay, is scorned and trashed as "old falshioned and "unusueable." Out of the ensuing chaos rises a government that declares what is ***safe*** for the people. That is the trigger word for incremental tyranny, And so it has become down through the centuries: the people would be yoked bya tyrant king or a dictator in order to enjoy safety, security in their personal lives and contentment in bondage. Yet they are the most exposed to change and to terror when they least expect it. Be vigilant!

The aforementioned conflicting strategies, real agendls for the control of men, are strategies sprulng from Man's natural rebelliousness. He who wills himself to power intends them as deceptions of his true motives, which are to attack the *status quo* where it offends him. On a personal scale, the individual citizen works his will, as his "light," in those circumstances that are offensive to his pride and to his yearning for a chimerial happiness, and he does so nowadays with scarcely a hinderance. All tokens, symbols and realities of violence are today tearling apart the moral fabric of our society. Liberalism in government, entertainment, the media and in religion is on a rampage to extinguish moral values in America. Moral values are said by the liberals to restrlict, hinder, depress. Not just the chilcren but adults as well are being ***dumbed down*** to wear the yoke of tranny, to accomodate power brokers, beginning with an untrustworthy media that lies and manipulates the news for a poiint of view, and politicians that play upon that public ignorance that derives from media censorlship by elimination. A bureaucratic State of poisonous benignity washes over America todlay, making the world safe for the citizens in exchange for the surrender of their self-dertermination and their nation's sovereignty.

Thel inalienable right of a safe happiness has become a measure of the State's effecliveness in the promotion of the most salutary sorts of civil enterprise. This transition is accomplished by the State's conversion of private interprises into public ventures. Private by-laws, as those of the Boy Scourts, for example, are elevated to the status of public mandates. The socio-religious control of marriage and its rites of covenant commitment are rendered nugatory by the State in its arrogant attempt to communize marriage as a biological structure of consensual sex-mating of adults under State mandate, blessing and totally secular authority. Liberalism in the churches of America will eventually bring downs the sacred edifice of Christs church in order to accommodate New Age life styles and corrupt theology, all at the behest of and compulsion by the State. "Safe happiness" in education is today the business of liberal Educators who find multlculturalism the apt religion for the uneducated masses, and what once passed for "classlical learning" is expunged lin favor of mediocrity in literature., mediocrity in thought—the trivialization of virtue-and mediocrity in ambition. No greatness of soul, of thought, only the return to a Medieval society that is fascinated solely by its technology and no more. That is the true *provincialism of America* today—and Its endangerment. For where a people, we the citizens, have either forgotten or disregarded our heritage of rights as "God given," we become vulnerable to those ambitions men and women who would will themselves to power over us.

Liberty can be said to be changeless only when a new law premises the option of free choice, for when a law negates or cancels out this free option, it is a command, an order by the State of the magnitude of despotism. A free citizen has a right to be wrong, a right to make a mistake but not a right to commit an act of willful negligence that defames or injures another person. That is his *Natural Right*. Yet the State's accommodation to the clamor of Civil Rights activists whether those of the homosexuals, the extreme feminists, the pro-abortionists, is not the accommodation of those rights as necessary and good for general society, but, instead, is th eradication of the rights of the rest of society to reject or to alienate or to outlaw such clamor and the State's enforcement of its sympathetilc indulgence of such activism goalx. Thereby does the State subvert the rest of society and eventually, as a one-time paradigm of democracy, self-destruct. Such an indulgence might more aptly resemble another example. When a piece of legislation, for example, says that man may not shoot off a firearm at his neighbor's house because by its very nature a statute then operates in the absence of enforcement authority to restrain him (hopefully) that silent statute works on the citizen's conscience by virtue of his knowledge of right and wrong. Thus does the silent law promote and enorce a compliant obedience based on the the concept that all life has inherent value—the ideal—and his neighbor's foremost. The natulral law and the moral law were one in this instance. Thus not all clamor for certain Civil Rights deserves the stature of law an the permissive practice lin a society made blind or caloused to the consequences of social accommodation.

Toward this end the State becomes the "Alitprop" engine of persuasion and destruction by State propaganda.

Life and law are inseparables, and for the reason that union will not continue to exist for many years once society becomes totallyl lawless, that is, anarchistic. In fact, laws could never have been conceived except for the protection of life primarily, property only secondarily. For what other chief end? If therefore law and life are inseparable and certain inalienable laws come from God~and right is a consummate law, thele beling no Right without a corresponding law to support it—so then must the lives come from God that the "inalienable right" laws are designed and implemented to protect. An inalienable Right cannot be severed from an inalienable and God given life. For if God be God, He does not invent laws for the pleasure of amusing himsell and then give them to mankind. Nor can Man conceive of a God who detaches his Commandments from the Inalienable life He has given to mortal human beings, only to sit back—as the Deists thought—and just watch how man will misuse both his life and a "foolish" law or a foolsh life and an absolute law, a Commanlment, as the Deistic watch ticks away. God and not Mister Jefferson is the author of our ***inalienable rights*** in the Declaration. Their discovery, furthemsore, does not operate in so frivolous manner. He expects that His creatsure Man will countenance His laws with a sober and respectful attitude, laws found in the Scripture, to insure his continuation of a good life endowed witl happiness as he lives out his liberty in a society of free choices.

Human rebellion against God works to disestablish liberty. Onll the enforcement of existing laws intercepts the a-morality of anarchy and lawlessness, synonymous actions. For although men who have the evil and immoral option, the law of socielty and of God forbid murder. Muder is the consequence of rebellion against God. itl It is anti-God and when effectrive the law against homicide is not amenable to "culture changes." It is not a milestone in evolution. Therefore the State cnnot mandate its abolition, the State beilng secular and a-morallin this age. Nor ca'n doctor-assilsted suicide be legalied, for the same reason. The Court stands in error in the matter, a law that is anti-law, anarchistic. The State is not the giver of life and therefore cannot be the taker of life by proxy or directly except for the protection of society. That is the chief and only aim of capital punishmen, its examplary nature secondary, its revenge nature a surrogate attitude, its finality a retribution, its history *a* cleansing. Dotor assisted siuli4e to save money is a disgrace tol the me4ical profession, equally so when the suicide is requested for confort, convenience, or disposal of the unwanted dlying patient. Those immoral options are irrational options that elevate to the status of acceptable choice the homicidal *snuff-out* of mercy killing, like putting down a horse with a broken leg. So long as rebellious Mankind continues to think of his equity

Human Rights as *Natural Rights* and his changing codified *Civil Rights* as "inalienable," he willl have to confront God's changless absolutes … eventually.

No right can be assumed on the premise of a felt inequality. There are deficits in conduct and achievement for which the individual is responsible.

A right is like a stolen property for which loud clamor will insure its return.

A special interest right involves an obligation which, if neither voiced nor understood, nullifies the clamor for the Right. Were this not so, then cries for rights becocme mere strident anarchy.

A right is inseparable from la specific and applicable la'w. A *generic* asertion of "right" is invalid and of propaganda use only.

A right lacks coherence when it is undergird with rage and sell-rlighteousness of radicalism. A right cannot be radicalized. It cannot be presumed to exist by a vociferous consensus. It is rarely understood by experience alone.

The intellectual Elite of America are not the makers of inalianable rights … nor is the United Sates Supreme Court, not the Administration nqr the liberal advantaged Media.

A Right without a serious consideation of the consequences of its exercise is a lamentable presumption.

A Right willfully distorted is not a Rght but a mere caprice or an act of violence to which "right" is attached.

The morality of a people is directly related to their approval of honest leaders in Government. Such we do have, yet they far too often conciliate in the dishonesty of Federal extravagance and the corruption of the electoral process.

Therelis no excuse for the exoneration of dishonesty in the Congress.

A Right cannot be conjured up from class hatred. A Right is not deducable from the political consensus of the majority of the people. To say of a political opinion that it is "politically correct is an mexcuseable form of social conformity. To conform to hearsay is mindless. To agree to lies is wicked and destructive.

A Right exists independent of and apart from numbers. Conviction by numbers is Medieval. Exesssilve use of poll figures is regresssive politically

The freedoms guaranteed and protected by the Constitution of the United States are not without limitations in intepretation, performance.

A right is not to be conf used with a privilege. The former is stated in the law, the latter is inferred from citizenship. For example, you do you should answer the call as a privileged duty of citizenship.

A right is not a shield for the violation of the law. for example one cannot hide behind it while he commits mahem, arson, pillage or murder.

The emotive value of the word "Right" galvanizes insecure men, disloyal aliens and ambitions individuals to attack the base of civilied society—*liberty with responsibility.*

Not all free men will apprecilate their liberty. As to the Rights cried out for by vocal minori ties, those minorities will scorn and cast aside the rights of others that stand in their way.

A Right is the last refuge for scoundrels with out mercy and radicals without a plan.

Rights are to the tricksters and the dishonest what duties are to the disloyal—to be trashed when their use is finished.

A right that begs to be heard has often over looked its predecessor obligation.

Honor the Riights sof others ilf you would have them do likewise to yours.

The reluctance of the majority to concede a Right to the radical minority is often due not to the invalidity of the claim but to the use of force or threats of fore to secure that right.

A Right bears the authority of proscription, whether by man, by God or bv the Central Government, that is, the State. Look to its genesis in the mind of a zealot, the mind of a politician or the mind of God—found in His holy book.

A Right is not a Right because some angry and impetuous human agency so declares it to be. A Right is a Right because it existed prior to its inception on the Boston Commons or in the pulpit or the classroom. It existed ultimately in the mind of God fmd then in the halls of government

A man has a Right to defend himself, with deadly force if necessary. That is a self-evident right and is inalienable,being but a right to happines and to life.

The evidence and assumed rihts usually converge into the triune of "Life, liberty and the pursuit of happiness."Our Founders understood poverty when they exchanged happiness for property.

Liberty for all, Government by all, God above for all.

◆   ◆   ◆

WASHINGTON'S PRAYER FOR THE UNITED STATES OF AMERICA

Almighty God: We make our earnest prayer that Thou wilt keep the United States in "Thy holy protection; that Thou wilt incline the hearts of the citizens to cultivate a-spirit of subordination, obedience to government; and entertain a brotherly affection and love for one another and for their fellow citizens of the United States at large.

And finally that Thou wilt most graciously be pleased to dispose us all to do justice, to love mercy, and to demean ourselveves with that charity, humility, and paciic temper of mind which were the characteristics of the Divine Author of our blessed religion, and without a humble imlitation of whose example in these things (we) can never hope to be a happy nation. Grant our supplication, we beseech Thee, through Jesus Christ our Lord. Amen.

Parchment Note: "The original source of the prayer is the concluding paragraph in Washsington's farewell circular letter sent to the Governors of the thirteen States from his headquarters in Newburgh, New York, June 8,1783. This altered version appears on a plaque in st. Paul's Chapel in New York City and is used at Patrick Church, Fairfax County, Virginia, where Washington was Vestryman from 1762 to 1784

978-0-595-46470-8
0-595-46470-X